THE LAST STOP

A MEMOIR

by
PATRICIA STREET

FROM THE TINY ACORN…
GROWS THE MIGHTY OAK

The Last Stop
Copyright © 2021 Patricia Street. All rights reserved.

Printed in the United States of America.

For information, address Acorn Publishing, LLC, 3943 Irvine Blvd. Ste. 218, Irvine, CA 92602
www.acornpublishingllc.com

Cover design by Damonza

Interior design and digital formatting by Debra Cranfield Kennedy

ISBN—978-1-952112-56-0 (hardcover)
ISBN—978-1-952112-55-3 (paperback)
Library of Congress Control Number: 2021906080

DISCLAIMER

This memoir tells the true story of my son's heroin addiction based on real events, written documentation, and dialogue. Where I have been unable to remember fully or where I lack complete documentation, I have allowed my insights and experiences to fill in, using my best judgment. Sometimes I have taken poetic license with the order of events, related writings, and stories for the sake of the narrative. I have changed or abbreviated most of the names and, in a few cases, disguised details to protect those who may not want to be recognized.

This memoir is not a teaching or instruction book. It is designed to help the reader better understand addiction's realities through the experience of both the addict and the parent.

If you or a loved one is caught in the throes of addiction, please seek support and treatment, or it will suck the life out of you.

THE UNEXAMINED LIFE IS NOT WORTH LIVING.

~ SOCRATES

TABLE OF CONTENTS

PART ONE

THE

LAST

STOP

**A MEMOIR AS TOLD FROM
TWO PERSPECTIVES:
MOTHER AND SON**

PROLOGUE

I NOW KNOW THINGS I NEVER WANTED TO KNOW.

I am writing this memoir to share my son's addiction[1] story, as well as to give support and recognition to all of the families of addicts, who continue to struggle daily with a loved one's addiction. This memoir is dedicated to all of the mothers who get up each day, often after a sleepless night, only to wait, worry, and wonder if their son or daughter has lived through the night.

After one such night, I wrote in my journal:

> "Nighttime worries are the worst. I lay there and think and think . . . and accomplish nothing because there's nothing I can do and no one to talk to, not the one who matters, anyway. And even if he were here, he wouldn't listen to me and wouldn't want to talk unless I could give him what he wants . . . what he needs. Chances are, he isn't sleeping either, unless the last hit is still calming, but it will wear off and he will be miserably awake soon, but not worried about me. He will only be worried about his next fix, where it will come from, when, and how. He loves the process of getting and using heroin almost as much as the drug itself. I know I sound harsh. I feel harsh. I am angry. I am sad. I want the hurt to end but I don't think it ever will . . . maybe I deserve this."

My son's name was David. His drug of choice was heroin, but that's not where he started. His first taste of an opiate came from morphine, which was administered in a hospital when he was 15, to relieve pain caused by an injury. David started using heroin regularly when he was in his mid-20s. During those years, he drank alcohol and tried a variety of drugs, but heroin was the love of his life.

Addiction is cyclical. For 15 years, David rotated through active heroin use, recovery, and relapse many times over. When he was an active user, he would assure me that he could stop whenever he wanted to. He just didn't want to. When his heroin use caused him to go to jail or treatment, he would stop using for a while, transition into recovery, and promise never to use the drug again. Then, he would relapse back into what he called "full blown heroin addiction." Most of the time, all it would take to relapse would be one hit of morphine or heroin. Sometimes, he started with alcohol and prescription drugs. Either way, he always relapsed.

David's was not a fate anyone would have anticipated had they known him or our family in the early years. We were an average suburban family of four: mother, father, David, and Bill, an older brother by three-and-a-half years. David's father was a police officer, and I worked as a secretary at the boys' elementary school. Our lives centered on our community and the boys' activities. After 21 years of marriage, my husband and I separated. Bill had already moved out and on to college; David was 17 and about to enter his senior year in high school.

As a young man, David became a licensed barber, studied philosophy, excelled at chess, loved sports, and wanted to become a published author. He would have been leading a "normal" life had his drug use not led to numerous arrests, mostly for traffic violations and drug possession, which led to multiple jails and treatment programs. Still, he managed to fall in love, and at the age of 32, David married. Unfortunately, his marriage didn't correct his path or save his life. Nothing did. This memoir begins with a vivid memory of David in his highchair. It ends with his death at 39.

After David passed away, I had access to his laptop, iPad, cell phone, papers, email, and Facebook account. To present his perspective on addiction in this memoir, I use David's writings—letters, written messages, stories, essays, poetry—and conversations he had with me and others. David's letters, in particular, offer an intimate and first-hand account of what he experienced while in jail and during treatment. For about two years, I compiled and cataloged his writings, creating a timeline of his life. At the time, I didn't know what I would do with it all.

David was my child, but by the time addiction took hold of him, he was a man living his own tortured life. This memoir comes mostly from a journal I've kept since my sons were very young, letters written to David, conversations with friends and family members, and memory. What I learned and experienced, and the mistakes I made during the 15 years of his heroin addiction, comprise the foundation for my perspective on addiction.

Four years after David's death, the opioid "crisis" dominated the news. I put "crisis" in quotes, because families affected by addiction know that opioid[2] and opiate addiction are not new. Families across the nation have been in crisis dealing with drug addiction for many decades; they just don't talk about it much. In her bestselling book, *Dopesick: Dealers, Doctors, and the Drug Company that Addicted America,* Beth Macy[3] lays out the more than one-hundred-year history of opiates that led to the "massive wave of iatrogenic opiate addiction" fueled by prescription opioids like OxyContin in the late 1990s. Macy writes, "In 2012, I began reporting on the heroin epidemic as it landed in the suburbs of Roanoke, Virginia, when I had covered marginalized families for the *Roanoke Times* for two decades, predominantly those based in the inner city. When I first wrote about heroin in the suburbs, most families I interviewed were too ashamed to go on the record."[4]

The rapid rise in overdose deaths opened up a renewed discussion and brought national attention to the epidemic of drug addiction and its devastation to families across the United States. I realized after David's death that it was time to open up and add David's story to the overwhelming and confusing puzzle of the opioid crisis.

When my son's addiction to heroin became a reality in late 1999, the Internet was just coming to life. Finding information wasn't just a click away. I knew nothing about drugs or addiction. I didn't want to know. Knowing made it real. Like many parents of addicts, I was afraid of what I would find. I lived in denial that this could be happening to my son. I felt ashamed and wanted to hide the nasty truth of what David was doing to himself and the reflection on me as his parent.

Thankfully, today, information, resources, and support related to drug addiction are widely available online, and though there is still a stigma associated with having an addicted son or daughter, there is more understanding and compassion. Beverly Conyers[5] put it best in her excellent book, *Addict in the Family*:

> Despite their suffering, families of addicts seldom receive the kind of support commonly extended to families of, say, cancer patients or stroke victims. Instead, they conceal their pain in the face of the all-too-common beliefs that addicts have only themselves to blame for their troubles, that addicts could cure themselves if they really wanted to, and that addicts' families probably did something 'wrong' to cause the problem in the first place. Many families of addicts share these views, which only adds to their unhappiness.

Writing my son's story of addiction also provides an avenue to publish his unfinished collection of fictional short stories, poetry, and essays. David titled his collection of writings, "Constructs of a Feeble Human Intellect." I discovered the initial draft on his laptop after he passed away. Excerpts follow the memoir. Real life events reflected in David's writings are footnoted.

David was a self-taught student of philosophy and liked to quote Socrates, the classical Greek philosopher credited as one of the founders of Western philosophy and ethics. His favorite quote, "I cannot teach you anything, I can only make you think," was inscribed on his funeral card, and it is also the goal of this memoir. I want to help the reader see through the window of addict behavior and into the soul and mind of a young man struggling to make others understand the thoughts and ideas that made his head spin. This memoir combines David's view of himself and his addiction with the bewildering and heartbreaking journey I took with him as he traveled down the dark and dangerous road of heroin addiction.

Addiction changes a person both on the inside and the outside. There were times when I would look at and listen to my son and wonder, who is this person? Where did that little boy go who once stood before me at the front door with a friend who had a big hole in the middle of his shirt? With his arm slung across his friend's shoulder, David proudly announced, "My mom can fix it. She can fix anything!" I can still see his sweet little five-year-old face beaming up at me. Depending on me. Yes, I could fix the hole in his friend's shirt, but I could not fix Dave's addiction. A hard lesson for a parent but an essential lesson if both are to survive.

I was out with my dog last night for his last walk of the day and spotted a man standing at the bus stop. He cast a thin, slanted shadow, his hands stuffed deep into his pockets, head bent to his chest. He froze in place as we walked by. No eye contact. No acknowledgement that we co-existed. After I got to the other side of the block, I stood and watched his lonely figure in the dark. I saw a reflection of my son. Tears quickly formed as I looked down at the little terrier who rescued me two years ago. His bright black eyes shone back at me before he turned and pulled on his leash to lead me home.

WHO IS DAVID?

David was born on a warm and sunny Memorial Day Monday morning in May 1974. He immediately began to thrive as he quickly pushed himself into life and stuck his thumb into his mouth to soothe his cries. When he was just big enough to sit in his high chair, he began to assert himself. One day, he looked straight at me and loudly banged his hand on the high chair's tray. I looked back at him and said, "David, stop banging on your tray." He continued to look me straight in the eye as his little hand banged on the tray.

"Daaavid, stop banging on your tray."

Still keeping his eyes on me, David continued to hit the tray, though not quite as forcefully.

"Stop hitting the tray!" I screamed at him.

David didn't flinch and kept hitting the tray lightly, never taking his eyes off me.

Without another word, I gave him my best "do as I say" Mom look. David took his tiny index finger and very lightly tapped the tray without making a sound. We stared eye-to-eye as he scrunched up his little nose, squinted his eyes, and turned bright red—a distinct facial expression that accompanied him into adulthood. He silently dared me to tell him to stop again. I didn't say a word.

Testing the limits of his behavior became one of David's hallmarks. He was determined not to be told what to do or how to follow some designated system of rules. When he was seven or eight, he informed me that punishing him was a waste of time and would never work to make him change or correct his behavior. Overall, he was right. When punishments mounted up and it looked like he was going to have to spend the rest of his life in his room, I had to think up reasons to "recalculate" past punishments to avoid ridiculously long stretches of punishment that lacked any effectiveness. It wasn't that David was a "bad child" or mean or wanting to cause harm to others; he just didn't want to be limited to a prescriptive way of doing things. When drug addiction took over his life and punishments came from the government, he was insulted that the government labeled him a drug addict. He defended himself by writing, "I am only a man. The labels they want to put on me are their labels. I refuse to allow them to tell me who I am."

To get his way, David became an excellent manipulator long before he started using drugs. The ability to manipulate is a trait often identified with drug addiction, along with denial. As David readily admits, he manipulated others to get what he wanted, and he denied his bad behavior over and over, regardless of the consequence. In May 2009, David was required to attend a "show cause hearing"* and to write a "show cause" letter to a judge in the District of Columbia court. He later titled this letter, "The Final Refuge of a Scoundrel." His motivation: To prove his argument that people are bound by their perspectives. In an excerpt from the letter, David wrote: ". . . this letter is in no way sincere. It is the final refuge of a well-spoken, manipulative person who doesn't want to go to jail. The reason I have put it with my writings is to study my manipulations, to understand what I believe my drug-addled mind was trying to do . . ."

Despite his manipulative skills, David was an adorable and inquisitive child. He grew into a handsome man, a kind, funny, and very likeable man, which made it even more difficult not to give in when he deserved reprimand.

A CHILDHOOD FRIEND REMEMBERS

On February 3, 2015, a year after David's death, I received an email from one of David's childhood friends, who graciously shared her "David" story of growing

---

*A "show cause hearing" is meant to force someone to present themselves before a judge to explain why they should not be held in contempt of court. They have to provide a reason, or show cause, for why they ignored a court order. The full text of David's "show cause letter" is included with David's collection of writings.

up one street over from us. Our neighborhood was brand new when we all moved in, and most of the new homeowners were in their thirties with young families, which set the stage for close knit friendships and tight bonds among the parents and the children that continue to this day. Her older brother and Bill were best friends growing up and remain best friends today. When David died, we were blessed to have many old friends and former neighbors come to give support and to help us say good-bye.

Her emailed story, which she referred to as a "rugged diary of despair," provides years of memories of her friendship with David, which began when she and David were six years old. She wrote that her friendship with David was one of trust and respect. She describes childhood antics of sailing through open windows on stacked mattresses, car-tag games, and what the neighborhood looked like from every rooftop. Her willingness to share her grief and her memories helped to ease the pain of losing my son. Here's her email:

"David is sleeping in my parents' basement. David is sleeping in my college dorm room. David is sleeping in my Woodbridge Apartment. David is sleeping in my Arlington Apartment. I recognize his gait in the dark. I am so relieved to see my friend as I am weary. I need his advice and inevitable ribbing. His tattoos manifest one after the other; I visually trace his binary tattoos over and over until I dizzy myself. I am riding in David's blue Camry. He's in the hospital, he's smiling although he has just suffered severe trauma. David implores us to help him clean before his Mom gets home. Prairie Day in fifth grade is rained out—we all solemnly roll our homemade Conestoga Wagons inside around the pod. We got all dressed up for prom and can't wait to leave so our group can be alone again. When we are, at last, we are at ease and laugh freely. Everyone shouts his name in unison when he arrives at the party. He shoulders his way to the center of the group and raises his arms for a photo. He teases the teachers; they find him endearing. I wait for the phone to ring; no call means court did not go in his favor. He has an excuse; it's not his fault. I tell him he's full of shit. He concedes. He cocks his head before he volleys a riposte as the boys insult each other for amusement. He lifts me up when he hugs me. He's happy to see me. He's in a hurry. He pays me the finest compliment I have received since returning to NOVA. He's late for work so he borrows my T-Shirt. I have a belt that I am sure will fit him; it looks better on him. He postulates driver etiquette to the 'joker' in front of us, and I laugh. He peevishly asks again, 'Can I move yet?' I admonish him to stay perfectly still as I only have two more nails to polish; he scoffs but he's not really annoyed. As I come back from the restroom he smiles and raises his drink. He beams with pride when I photograph him cutting hair. He snips my bangs before we head out. He tells me secrets over drinks. He asks me about college and expresses regrets about his jailhouse education. He brings me philosophy books with the pages earmarked. He slipped five dollars into this young boy's backpack on the school bus in eighth grade because the boy lived in a small, dilapidated house. We do not laugh when driving to school; it's too early. We laugh when we slip out of school unnoticed.

"The first time my dad steered our station wagon into our new neighborhood, our family had just completed a 10-hour drive from Massachusetts. I could see my dad's patience waning as he waited for an assembly of kids to laggardly move their bikes, bike ramps, skate boards, balls, etc., so he could park at our new house. My interest in the new bedroom waiting for me dissipated as I zipped around in my seat to survey the impediment; I was overcome with relief. KIDS! KIDS! There were so many kids in this Virginia place! They were all boys but I didn't care there wasn't a girl among them; I merely thought, I need a bigger bike.

"I could never unlearn all David taught me or credit anyone else for propping me up when I fell from grace. When I was pained by friends not thinking of me what I thought they should, David would bring me a book to emotionally fortify me because "Life will never be as easy as the fourth of July when you're sixteen." He said that often—few understood it."

THE BEGINNING OF THE END?

On a Saturday afternoon in November, 1989, when David was 15, I received a telephone call from his good buddy, Geoff, who said, "David has hurt his foot and might need a few stitches."

David and Geoff had begun working a couple afternoons after school and on Saturdays at a plant nursery near our house. On this particular Saturday, they were moving a small tree using a Bobcat; Geoff was driving. David dropped a tree into the shovel and hopped up onto the Bobcat. At the same time, and before David got settled, Geoff began raising the shovel. That simple innocent action pulled David's right foot into the shovel's hydraulics.

When David's dad and I arrived at the nursery, he was in excruciating pain, pain so bad we didn't even take time to look at his foot, which was still covered by his bloody sock. We rushed David to the hospital where he remained for six days. Emergency room personnel immediately started working on David, giving him an IV of morphine. Blood instantly splattered from the IV, and a red rash rose up David's neck. The nurse had difficulty getting the IV right, but David recovered quickly, calmed down, and the rash disappeared.

At around 3:00 a.m. the next morning, the attending orthopedic surgeon updated us on David's condition. His recommendation was to amputate as soon as possible all but the big toe on his injured foot. David loved to be outside, riding his skateboard and bike. He was a beautiful athlete, who played football and baseball at his high school. The doctor assured us that because David's big toe was not hurt, amputating his smaller toes would not impede future physical activity. He also assured us that a clean amputation would prevent infection and future complications, making recovery easier and quicker.

While the doctor's recommendation slowly filtered through my brain, all I could think about was counting David's little toes after he was born. After making one of the most difficult decisions of our lives—perhaps the worst decision—his father and I did not allow the doctor to amputate. As the doctor predicted, David's recovery was painful and slow, and several surgeries followed. For the six days he remained in the hospital, David used a morphine "button" to ease his pain. David eventually lost his third toe after it turned black and shriveled up. His other toes survived but he was left with a mangled foot and refused to go barefoot, always wearing a sock. Never again did he wear flip-flops.

Almost 20 years later, on February 19, 2010, David appeared in Fairfax County court. He had been arrested for drug possession, unauthorized distribution and control of drug paraphernalia, and driving while intoxicated and without a drivers' license. The following scenario, written in the Notes app of David's iPad, shows the impact of memories from that long-ago day in 1989, when he first felt morphine run through his veins to alleviate the severe pain of having his toes crushed in the hydraulics of a Bobcat.

I JUST CAN'T DO IT!

"It was the 19th of February 2010, and I woke up early to the loud reminder of what today was to bring. As I opened my eyes, I felt the pain settling in my body and the fear overwhelming my mind. I reached over to the drawer of my bedside table, already knowing the dope was all gone. I sifted through the pile of empty baggies in the hope to find salvation. Nothing was to be found. I sat up and felt the cold floor on my feet and put my head into my hands. It's gonna get way worse before it gets better, I thought.

"My wife was running around, picking out my dress clothes and laying them out. 'Get in the shower, honey. That will make you feel better. You have to be in court in an hour, so you don't have any time to play around.'

"I stood on the cold, faux hardwood floor and went to the bathroom. I got in the shower with only one thought on my mind—heroin. I had a little money to get some, but I just didn't have the time. I started to plan for the possibility that I might not go to prison on that day and how I'd ease this pain when I left the courtroom. This thought was replaced by the realization that I had exhausted all of my continuances.[6] The truth started to settle into my consciousness that I was going away today and there was nothing I could do about it.

"I looked down to my deformed 4-toed foot, and I started to reflect on how I had gotten to this place. I thought about that first shot of morphine I received when I injured my foot. I never, ever forgot that feeling. All the pain—my toes had just been crushed in the hydraulics of a Bobcat, and they were completely mangled. It hurt so bad, and I was just a kid. I hadn't deserved an injury like that. But when they shot that morphine into me, everything just went away. I remembered that feeling in such a profound way as I stood under the warm water of the shower. I thought about my simple life and mind from that time and wondered, how did I get here?

"I started to go through my life in my mind. I knew today was going to be a day I wouldn't forget, and I started to go through other days I could not forget. I thought of joy, and I thought of pain. I purposely navigated my memories to elicit responses from myself. I was trying to find something inside of myself to give me the strength to face this day. But alas, I could muster very little. I got out of the warm shower and dried myself off. I walked out of the bathroom and started to put on the clothes my loving wife had laid out for me. I thought about how she bought clothes for me. I dressed, then went to the bathroom to brush my teeth.

"I brushed my teeth, put a little gel in my hair, and started to have visions of the jail I was headed to. This was not my first time going to jail, and I knew exactly what was in store for me. I started to envision the receiving area of the county jail and the bologna sandwiches. I thought about how I would once again have to establish myself. I thought about my last probation, which I had already violated. I thought about how, once I was established and comfortable in the county jail, they would snatch me up and transfer me back to the city jail. I thought about the receiving area in the city jail and the animal house that is the cell blocks. I thought about how I would be the only white boy and how I would have to be so strong. I looked in the mirror at my face and searched for the strength I was gonna need. It was not there. I looked at the track marks I had on my neck and the old tattoos on my shoulders. I looked at my pale skinny weathered face and said to myself, 'I can't do it. I just can't do it.' I looked down at the sink and saw the dried up blood drops that were spread across the sink and I wished I had just one more shot of dope. Just enough to get me through this.

"Then my wife came to me and said, 'Come on, honey, we have to go.'

"I looked at her with desperation in my eyes and said, 'I can't do it, honey, I just can't do it.'

"'Can't do what?' she asked."

In January 2012, David sent a Facebook message to a friend about receiving morphine for the first time when he injured his foot:

> "I got morphine when I injured my foot and loved it. Then I tried heroin. I have battled that addiction for most of my adult life. I don't want to be seen as that, but it's the truth. But now I am free, and I feel that what I have learned from that experience has enabled me to find a level of peace and acceptance of myself that has changed me for the better forever."

After David passed away, I saw a therapist to help me cope with his death, which I knew couldn't be dealt with until I found a way to close the door on the 15 years of unsuccessfully grappling with his addiction. After all those years, it had never occurred to me, until the therapist pointed it out, that November 4, 1989, could have been the beginning of David's addiction. How could I have missed that?

FAMILY SEPARATION

In February 1991, we received a notice in the mail that David had gotten a traffic ticket in Washington, D.C., which convinced his police officer father that he was using and selling drugs. I refused to believe it. His father went ballistic, and they had a huge argument. David left home, and we didn't know where he was for three days. Our marriage, which was already on shaky ground, rapidly deteriorated.

By spring, David's father and I had separated. David was in his junior year of high school. I rented a townhouse across the street from his high school, which I thought was a grand idea. Our family home had been quite a distance from David's school and, most mornings, he had to be at the bus stop before dawn, which was difficult for my night owl son. At our new location, he could sleep in and just walk across the street. Also solved was the problem of transportation to and from after school practices and activities.

We stayed in that rental until our family home sold, which took most of David's senior year in high school. Unfortunately, living across the street from school didn't work out quite like I had intended. David now had more freedom than he was used to, as I worked long hours at a new and demanding job in Washington, D.C. I had to leave in the mornings before he got up, so he was often late to school. I also had not given thought to our rental being the place to hang out during the school day, but how convenient for him and his buddies!

I cannot say for sure what drugs David took while in high school, but drinking alcohol and smoking pot became a problem. During David's senior year, I arrived home one evening to find him depressed and crying, balled up in a corner of the couch. He gave no reason. By the next day, he seemed fine. He always seemed to bounce back with a happy and mischievous grin.

That first year of family separation was difficult for David and me, but it also engendered a closer bond between us. When Christmas rolled around and I could not afford a Christmas tree, David brought home a "Charlie Brown" tree for us to decorate. And we especially liked to sit together and watch storms roll in. Even when he was older and conversations between us became difficult and angry, one would call the other to ask, "Are you watching?" when a storm appeared on the horizon.

DISORDERLY CONDUCT

A senior in high school, in 1991, David was asked to write the following letter to describe an incident during which he was arrested for disorderly conduct:

"I went to a party on Monday night, December 30. I was there with all of my friends, and we were drinking and having a good time. There were about 100 people at the party. I would say the majority of people there were intoxicated or at least drinking socially. I was intoxicated, but I wasn't that bad. I was walking around, talking to people.

"Around 12:30, the police showed up on a complaint of too much noise and to break up the party. So, I left the party. I was one of the first people to leave. I began walking up to my car, which was about a quarter mile away. I got to a corner and stood there, waiting for my designated driver and my friends. I was having trouble trying to light a cigarette because the wind kept blowing out my matches. I could not cover the flame from the wind because of my broken wrist. Officer V approached me and asked me how old I was. I told him I was 18. He asked me for an I.D. and I said I didn't have any. Then he reached in my back pocket and proceeded to take my wallet out of my pocket. He didn't like the fact that I lied to him, so he said he was going to arrest me and take me down to the station and call my guardian.

"I, and my friends, pleaded with him in a very civil manner, but he wanted to take me down anyway. My friends started getting mad and were yelling at the other officers. I told them not to do that because they were making it worse. I had not gotten upset yet. The officer proceeded to handcuff me and put me in his car. My brother, who was 21, tried to get him to release me to him, but they wouldn't do it. While driving to the station, I asked the officer to please let me go. I pleaded with him, knowing that I would get in a lot of trouble. He said he wasn't going to let a little loser go and he hoped I got in trouble. I asked him why, when there were about 50 drunk people walking up and down the street, he picked me to arrest. He said I looked like I was the worst, when about 50 feet away from me there was a guy puking all over himself because he was so drunk. I told him that if they arrest one person for committing a crime, they should arrest everyone committing the same crime. He said if there were a whole bunch of murderers somewhere they couldn't arrest all of them, so they'd arrest the one they didn't like.

"I don't understand why they would tell one person he better leave and arrest another person when they did the same thing. So, I told him what I thought of him and he told me what he thought of me. The name calling went on into the station. When I got there, other officers started laughing at me. I retaliated with words, and they did too. I asked Officer V to please come in the room so we could talk civilly, but he refused. So I started yelling and they started yelling back.

"My mom showed up and she asked the same question I did. Why did they pick me? Then the officers began to badger my mother, saying she's a no good mother and she didn't raise me right. One officer got in my mom's face and very abusively told her she better sign the summons. I got between them and told him, no one gets in my mom's face. They finally let us leave and while we were walking out, I made a mistake—a very big mistake. My mom asked me why they picked me. I yelled, 'Because they're motherfuckers.'

"In the officer's report, he claimed that after I said that, he came to get me and said I was under arrest, and I tried to push him. This is not true. He didn't say anything to me. Four officers came running down the hallway and beat me up. One officer was pushing my head against the brick wall and squeezing my neck. I could not breathe, and I almost passed out. The other three officers were hitting me and kicking me, leaving cuts and bruises all over my body.

"Later that night, my brother talked to one of the officers who was there and the officer said that beating me up made his night. Then, Officer V took me to his car to transport me to the detention center. During this ride he told me he wished we had met on other circumstances because he would kick my fuckin' ass. So I said, 'Let's do it, stop the car, you take off your badge, gun, and stick, and we'll see what happens.' He said he'd love to but he can't do that. So, the name calling started again.

"I'm not saying my actions were right, but I was intoxicated and I was only 17. He was a sober police officer and all he did was make things worse. The police are supposed to protect people, and I was not doing harm to anyone. If you give some people a little power and authority, it goes straight to their head. I guess some people just cannot handle certain authority positions. A mountain was made out of a molehill, resulting in much unneeded pain and trouble. N.W.A."[7]

I was notified of David's arrest and told to come pick him up. It was the middle of the night when I arrived. I was not initially allowed to speak with him, and the officers would not give me a copy of the arrest warrant.[8] David's letter accurately describes what a terrible and humiliating scene it was. Granted, David was obnoxious, but I had *never* been talked to in the insulting and abusive manner that the police officers used with me. Their demeanor and harsh words effectively frightened and intimidated me.

David did screw up, and he made the situation much worse when we were almost out the door. It was my first opportunity to ask him what had happened and why they'd picked him up. Instead of giving me an answer, he yelled back at the police officers, calling them "motherfuckers." Then all hell broke loose before we could get out the door. I watched as four police officers barreled toward us, grabbing him and slamming him against the brick wall before dragging him back down the hallway. I blamed David because we could have been on our way home if he had held his temper and kept his mouth shut. I blamed myself, too. I should have waited to ask him about the arrest. The police officers' intimidation tactics worked beautifully— I felt like a no-good mother.

I hired an attorney, and David was sentenced to 40 hours of community service, which he completed without complaint. This was a very trying time. For the first time in my life, I was living on my own with a very troubled young son. After working on this memoir, I now realize that he was more troubled than I ever imagined.

David sent me a note a few days after the disorderly conduct incident:

"Mom, I'm sorry about doubting you. I know that I'm trying to get easy ways out. It's just that I don't see any light at the end of the tunnel. I'm terribly unhappy with my situation, and I guess I'm just desperate to get out of it. Alcohol is a crutch. A vicious cycle. It offers temporary relief but really just makes things worse. What does one do? I will climb the mountain. I will go to school and do well. This will help me achieve a good future. I'm sorry I'm so selfish. Someday I will not be so self-consumed. It's just hard, Mom."

In February 2012, twenty years later, David sent a Facebook message and apologized to the guy who had the party in 1991:

"Hey, man, it's good to hear from you and I am glad to hear that you are doing well. I truly mean that! I know that you are a good man cuz everyone has told me you are and I believe it. You and I were just caught up in some foolishness that really wasn't about us. Childish shit. But we are grown-ups now, and it is important to allow the past to be the past. When we do that we free ourselves to have a future without bounds. I think you and I would have been friends under different circumstances, and I hope that we can be now. I am going to send you a friend request although it is perfectly understandable if you don't accept it. One thing I always wanted to tell you about that night—in the pitch black dark when so many of your friends came through those trees to defend your party, almost all of your friends ran away.

"You didn't. You stood your ground, and I always respected you for that. Ultimately, though, it was me who was in the wrong. What I did that night has always haunted me, so I want you to know that I am truly sorry for what I did. Take care. Maybe you will let me buy you a beer sometime. David"

Party Guy messaged David back:

"David, wow, man . . . what can I say? I think you are exactly right about us being friends if under different circumstances. The reality of that night is that ultimately I was to blame. I beat up --- that night, and I too have been regretting that for years. Most of the friends I had that went to my high school were pussys, and it didn't surprise me that they ran away. At any rate, David, I want to extend a long overdue hand to shake and look forward to having a beer with you. Call me anytime, bro. Seriously, call me when you can."*

---

* I don't know if David and Party Guy ever physically connected, but the incident obviously stayed with them both, and it was important enough for David to base his fictional story, "The Certain Eventuality: A Memory Yet to Come" on this event and arrest many years later.

CHAPTER 2: 1992

ADDICTION REALITY

After graduating from high school in June 1992, David was a lost soul. He did not want to go away to college. He attended the local community college and worked at Jiffy Lube. He was unsettled and always ready to party. Alcohol abuse had been a problem for a couple of years. Then he was arrested for possession of marijuana, and court dates for traffic infractions began to pile up.

In early February 1994, while his brother was away on vacation, David borrowed Bill's truck and received a traffic ticket for driving under the influence (DUI) of alcohol, resulting in a suspended driver's license and loss of vehicle insurance. Nothing was going right for David. He always seemed to get caught doing something wrong, whether he was at a party or on the road. He was a magnet for the police. In April, he left for Florida and worked on a boat for a few months. While in Florida, he used ecstasy and LSD, and only he knows how many other drugs. Before heroin, he wasn't too picky.

After he returned from Florida, he lived with Bill through the summer, but by November, David had to leave Bill's house, because he never got steady work and just lay around the house most days. I allowed David to live at my house but with the understanding that he would return to work, avoid the police, and attend college in January. David got his job back at Jiffy Lube, and for a while, everything was all right. I asked David to prepare that year's Thanksgiving offering:

> *"On this day many years ago, pilgrims and Indians came together and had a huge feast. They put their differences aside and celebrated life. I think this is what Thanksgiving is about. The celebration of life. The coming together of people, who otherwise may not, to reflect back on all that your life is—to hope*

for all your life will become. It is a celebration of acceptance, of love, and of forgiveness.

"I think it is important to remember what Thanksgiving stands for in everyday life. To accept others, despite your differences, not to judge, as no one is in the position to criticize, and to spread love, instead of hate. Just as the pilgrims and Indians, we all must learn to live together.

"There are two things in which I am most thankful for today. I am thankful for all that I have experienced, big and small, as there is no teacher like experience. I am also thankful for all those who care about me in a world of so many who do not. There are many people on this holiday who have very little to be thankful for. For these people, myself, and everyone else, I would like to express hope for the future, because hope for many people is all there is."

In December 1994, David was pulled over on another traffic stop while he was driving his girlfriend's car. There was no moving violation or other cause. He was pulled over because his girlfriend's drivers' license had expired. Without probable cause, the officer did a complete search of the car and charged David with possession of marijuana, not wearing a seatbelt, and driving on a suspended license.

The police notified me of David's arrest around 10:00 p.m. He was being held at the Fairfax County Adult Detention Center (Fairfax Jail), and someone had to go get him. When I arrived at the detention center, the building was mostly deserted and dark. I entered on the lower level and saw a shadowy figure walking on the upper level. I immediately recognized Bill's gait.

David had already called Bill because he needed to post $1,000 for bail to guarantee he would show up in court. Bill had just completed the paperwork for David's bail but didn't have the $1,000, so he put his house up as collateral. Even so, the police would not release David. We also weren't allowed to see David. Bill and I talked to the sheriff and the magistrate, assuring them that, if they released David into our custody, he would appear in court as directed. They didn't budge, so we left. Less than an hour later, David was on the phone asking me to come back and get him. We were never exactly sure why the magistrate changed his mind, but he told David that he re-reviewed his case and decided to let him go on his signature and Bill's house as collateral.

In January 1995, David appeared in court for the suspended license charge and, in March, on the marijuana charge. For both appearances, an attorney friend of mine agreed to represent David. He was not convicted on either of the charges because there were no grounds for pulling him over in the first place. David scraped by, and he knew it. After this, he assured his father and me that all he really wanted to do was get back on track and, if we would help him, go away to college.

COLLEGE VIA THE HEROIN HIGHWAY

As promised, in January 1995, David began classes at Potomac State Junior College in Keyser, West Virginia, an affiliate of West Virginia University, about 60 miles west of Route 81. Potomac State was chosen because it was one of the few colleges that would take him, it was not too far away from home, he could live on campus, and tuition was within our budget. It was dismal, cold, and threatening snow on January 5, when Bill and I dropped David off at Potomac State's small campus. In retrospect, the weather and the dingy-looking campus seemed like an omen of what the next few months and years would bring to Potomac State's surrounding areas, as described by Beth Macy in her book, *Dopesick*.

> The story of how the opioid epidemic came to change this country begins in the mid to late 1990s in Virginia's westernmost point, in the pie-shaped country sandwiched between Tennessee and Kentucky … by way of the heroin highway, camouflaged inside Pringle's cans and plastic Walmart bags … by the mid-2000s, there was a noticeable rise in overdose deaths north along I-81 from Roanoke.

David returned home from Potomac State to attend court in February and March. In late February, I received a letter from Potomac State, stating they were sealing David's records because he hadn't paid the money he owed to be in a room by himself. I was not aware that David had switched rooms. When I called and asked him about the extra charge, he said he would pay the fees when he was working during the summer. Doubtful, because he owed the courts well over $2,000, and that was before his February court date. Even if I wanted to pay, I didn't have the funds for the room or his court fees. Consequently, he did not receive his grades, he was not able to register for classes the next Fall, and what we paid to send him to Potomac State was totally wasted.

David's only achievements during his short stay at Potomac State were to run up a large tab and, as he told me many years later, to use heroin for the first time.

Around the time of David's twenty-first birthday in May 1995, he left for Virginia Beach to stay with a friend and work for the summer. He promised to work hard, make some money to pay his fines, and to "clean up his past." He learned about parasailing by working on a rental boat, and he had fun in the sunshine. At the end of the summer, he returned home. For the next couple of years, he alternated staying with his father and me, and sleeping on friends' couches. He stayed out of trouble while he attended classes at Northern Virginia Community College and started working as a carpenter apprentice. David became handy with tools and was able to fix just about anything.*

Aside from an arrest for possession of drug paraphernalia and marijuana in July 1996, David seemed fine. His life had calmed down. Over the next couple of years, when he attended family events like weddings, funerals, holiday events, dinners, movies, or family trips, there was no indication that he was using drugs. However, he continued to have a problem controlling his alcohol use.

---

* David's essay, "Aging," tells a true story about helping his grandparents fix a countertop.

In January 1998, David, Bill, and I took a long weekend trip to Canaan Valley, a small ski resort in West Virginia where we first skied as a family when the boys were young. After we organized the cabin—firewood for the fireplace and supplies put away in the tiny kitchen—we set out for dinner at the lodge. There were four girls at the table next to us, and it wasn't long before we blended and had a small party going. They were doing karaoke, and we couldn't keep David off the stage! I had no idea how much he liked to sing or that he was such a ham. We danced and talked and had a lot of fun.

The next morning, deer were grazing right next to the cabin. David and Bill fed them Pop Tarts and potato chips directly from their hands. After waffles for breakfast, I put a roast in the Crock Pot for dinner. Then, we took a hike up the mountain to check out the slopes. Back at the cabin, we played cards and a game of Monopoly until dinner. We skied most of the next day. With no TV at the cabin, we went over to the lodge to watch the NFL playoffs.

Our last day before leaving, we drove over to Blackwater Falls and had our picture taken in front of the falls, at the very same spot we'd posed during our first ski trip together when Bill was eleven and David was seven. We had a beautiful view of the mountains while we ate lunch and reminisced about earlier times. The cheerful sunny day ended with dinner at the cabin, after which the guys went over to the lodge for more karaoke and probably to see if the girls were still there. It was great spending time together with no arguments or problems.

FALLING IN LOVE

In the spring of 1998, David met Circe while playing volleyball. They soon fell in love, and they married in 2006. In the beginning of their relationship, David and Circe were a fairytale couple buzzing around in her convertible BMW Z. Circe appeared to be a successful professional from a somewhat wealthy family. In December, David gave her a diamond ring and announced their engagement at a family Christmas Eve dinner. I hadn't seen or heard from David much during this time, which didn't surprise me, because he was in love. Things with David seemed to be going well.

After our fun and successful ski trip in 1998, we decided to go again in February 1999. I reserved a cabin and Bill, David, Circe, and I set out for our "annual" ski trip to Canaan Valley. David and Circe drove together because they didn't feel well and thought they might have the flu. When we stopped for gas, I checked them for fevers, but they seemed fine. It snowed on the way, causing our late arrival at the cabin. Although we took plenty of food, it was late so I suggested going to the lodge for dinner. It was a beautiful winter's night, and fresh snow covered the ground; getting out and taking a walk would feel good. Bill was hungry and ready to go. David and Circe declined, saying they still didn't feel well and needed to stay in. The next day, Bill and I skied and again hung out at the lodge. Dave and Circe never left the cabin. They rarely left the couch.

We made the best of it but my gut was screaming at me that something was wrong. I didn't want to come across as some overbearing mother when all they wanted to do was cuddle on the couch. Maybe, I thought to myself, it's too early to impose "family time" on them. But I also knew that for the last few months, David's speech was often slurred when we talked on the phone. He would sound like he was trying to talk with mashed potatoes in his mouth. He blamed it on the phone connection.

David and Circe had supposedly started a home-based freight forwarding business, which meant they were both home all day. Circe explained that she went out and made sales calls while David stayed in to manage the phone and take orders. Meanwhile, he dropped his classes, which was disappointing. He had made good progress the last couple of semesters. I selfishly missed having him send an email or call me to talk about what he was reading or working on. But I told myself to let it go and to give them time to adjust to each other and the challenges of being self-employed.

In March, I had two wisdom teeth pulled. David drove me to and from the oral surgeon's office. I noticed once again that he didn't look right. His eyes were bleary, his skin sweaty. Rather than settling in and hanging out after we got back to my house like he usually would, he left and returned multiple times throughout the afternoon. His behavior was weird. However, other than instinct, I had no reason to question him, and I didn't want an argument.

In July, David and Circe dropped by unannounced and had dinner with me. David had the same glassy-eyed look and was sweating profusely even though it was not a hot evening and the air conditioner cooled the house. It also struck me as strange that David was wearing a long sleeved shirt and jeans in July. This was the guy who liked to ski in shorts! Again, I kept my mouth shut.

David and Circe had started living together first at her townhouse, but then they rented a house with a pool not far from where I lived. The few times I visited, the place was littered with huge piles of dirty clothes that were dotted with cigarette burns and holes. Dirty dishes crusted with food and ashes were scattered throughout the house, on the counters, and in the sink. I was embarrassed for them but reminded myself that they were adults. This was their home. It was not my business how they ran their household even though this was out of character for both David and his girlfriend, who had been personable, clean, organized, and well-dressed. Something was up, but I kept quiet.

In October, they were evicted from their rental, although they didn't tell me, and they began to look for another place to live. They asked if they could stay with me until they found a new place. I agreed, provided they would not smoke in the house. During the week, I was working full time, leaving early in the morning before they were up. When I arrived home in the evening, they were usually sequestered in their room watching TV. As far as I could tell, neither worked even though they claimed to still be running the home-based freight forwarding business.

During the weekends when I was home, David would leave early in the morning, supposedly to pick up something for their business and return about two hours later. Then, they would both immediately go into the bathroom for an hour or so. Silly me didn't want to be nosy, so I gave them their privacy until one Saturday morning after they had been at my house for about a month. David returned from his morning excursion. As usual, he and Circe went into the bathroom. This time, I listened. I waited. Nothing. Quiet. When David finally came out of the bathroom, I confronted him, "What's going on, Dave? What are you two doing in there?"

David became furious. "It's none of your damn business what I do in the bathroom! Jesus Christ, can't I go to the bathroom in peace!"

I told him I didn't believe him and then screamed, "Why does Circe go in there with you? I don't hear the shower. Where do you go in the mornings, Dave? What is so important that you have to go every morning, but you don't bring anything back? Something is going on. Something's not right. Dave, is it drugs? I think you are going out to buy drugs. Please tell me what is going on!"

A horrible scene ensued, and for the first time, David physically scared me. I became so afraid, I told David and Circe that they needed to leave. They immediately packed up and left to stay with David's dad. I felt terrible, wanting an instant replay, during which I would handle the situation better, but it was too late.

FINDING THE TOOL KIT

David's dad, now retired, allowed David and Circe to stay in his basement where they had a bedroom and full bath. Not long after they moved in, he entered the basement bathroom for a tissue. The tissue box had been replaced with another box he didn't recognize. He didn't give it a second thought when he opened the box to see what was in it. He couldn't believe his eyes. He discovered David and Circe's "tool kit"* of drug paraphernalia. Unlike me, David's dad didn't waste his time asking questions. He immediately began to search their things and Circe's car. He found hundreds of used syringes in a large plastic trash bag in the car's trunk. I couldn't understand why they hadn't disposed of the used needles. I learned later that keeping used needles is typical addict behavior.

---

* A drug addict's "tool kit" is vividly described in David's fictional story, "Through the Void Travels a Momentary Exchange of Perspective."

I could no longer deny what had been under my nose. I could not hide from the fact that my son was using heroin. Dirty, nasty, scummy heroin. It took me months to be able to even say the word "heroin." I still don't like saying it. I was numb with fear for both of them. I was also very angry. Angry that the David I raised could put this poison in his body. Angry that I allowed denial and shame to guide me away from being strong and seeking out the truth. Angry that right in front of my eyes, he was destroying the sturdy body and inquisitive brain I had nurtured. Angry that I made excuses to myself about his slovenly lifestyle. Angry that I allowed David and Circe to lie to me. Angry that I didn't have the courage to confront him sooner. Angry that I was a failure as his parent.

By now, David and Circe had lost just about everything. They drained Circe's bank account, pilfered money from her family's account, and pawned everything they had of value, except for Circe's car. According to what Circe told me later, they blew through about $80,000. Their whole situation was disgusting and sick. Avoiding dope sickness[9] was now their major concern. With their funds running out, they were forced to cut back after a year of free flowing heroin. The addict's dark side of using heroin hit home. Party time was over. They were desperate and needed to use the drugs to avoid the pain of dope sickness.

FIRST DETOX[10]

Everyone was excited about the approaching new millennium. The turn of the century. A once-in-a-lifetime kind of New Year's Eve. But not us. In December 1999, our top goal was to get David into a bed at the Fairfax County detox facility. We finally did, and he stayed for a week. He resisted going, but we told him if he refused, he would be living on the street. Heroin hadn't let him know yet that living on the street was part of the deal if he was going to be an addict.

David wouldn't let us take him to detox. He insisted that he and Circe would meet us at the detox facility and promised to be there at a prescribed time. His father, brother, and I got there on time and waited. And waited. It got dark. We continued to wait. We worried that he would lose the bed. Finally, Circe's BMW Z swung into the parking lot. David and Circe emerged from the car, looking more like they were going to a fancy party than to a treatment center to be detoxed from heroin. They were both "floatin' high on the cloud." This is when I first learned that when addicts think that they are going to have to give up using for a while, they go for one "last" fix. This is classic addict behavior, which David repeated time and time again before going to other detoxes, jail, or rehab.

While David was in detox, Circe stayed with a friend and then with David's father for a few days. Soon after Dave left detox, Circe departed for an extended overseas visit with her family. During her absence, David made a point of telling me how much he loved and missed her, and was anxious for her return. In February 2000, he and I took a day trip to ski locally. David suggested the trip because, as he put it, "We won't get many chances to do something all by ourselves much more because Circe will be here."

When Circe returned to the U.S. later in February, she and David resumed living together, promising they were done using heroin. As David predicted, I didn't see much of him during 2000. In July, he briefly worked as a bartender. By November, traffic violations and arrests were piling up again. He was in court on a variety of counts, including speeding, reckless driving, seatbelt violation, and possession of drug paraphernalia, marijuana, and forged vehicle plates and stickers.

In early March 2001, David and Circe lived with a male friend of Circe's. He called and told me that David and Circe were still on drugs, weren't paying their rent, and had trashed his house. When I told David about the call, he made all sorts of excuses. He said the friend was a liar, had gambled all his money away, and was trying to get money from him. I didn't believe either of them.

I contacted Circe's father, who lived overseas, and told him what was going on. A month or so later, Circe's father came to the U.S. David's father and I met with him, David, and Circe to discuss our concerns that Circe and David had become addicted to heroin. Of course, they both denied it.

Our meeting was a disaster. Before the discussion could even get started, Circe and her father began loudly arguing in their native language while the three of us sat there with no idea of what was being said. Circe explained to us that she and her father weren't arguing—that was how they communicated. It was a bizarre exchange, but Circe's father must have understood what was going on because he took her back home with him. I did not have contact with Circe while she was gone for several months. As far as I know, when she returned, she had stopped her heroin use.

David was serving six days in Fairfax Jail for traffic violations when Circe left the U.S. with her father. New arrests mounted up for driving on a suspended license, speeding, breaking and entering, theft, and an attempt to elude police after being given the signal to stop. David also had court dates for previous infractions and bench warrants.[11] It was difficult to keep up with what court dates correlated with what violations and which jail terms resulted from what court dates. I was also given an education on how to deal with the corrections system, including setting up a telephone connection, the visiting process and hours, contributing to David's commissary account, and the humiliation of talking on the phone to my son through a pane of plexiglass when I visited him.

DOGGY DOOR BREAK-IN

In late April 2001, I noticed that my CD rack was empty. The wooden cubby-holed CD rack was tucked into an eight-inch gap between the wall of the stairs going up and the pickets of the chair rail going down. I probably passed by that spot several times before I stopped and stared at the empty rack. *What the hell*?! An eerie feeling of being watched came over me as I stood mid-way down the steps and looked around. Nothing else seemed disturbed. Then I checked the basement. There, I found the doggy door ripped apart. I spotted an envelope marked with "Mom Only." It contained the following long note, written on several small yellow-lined Post-It notes after the culprit got caught in the doggy door as he tried to enter my home.

"April 24, 2001. Mom, I am very sorry! I did not mean for these things to happen, but I promise that everything will be returned by Friday. I know these things mean a lot to you, but I would never take your stuff if I didn't know for sure I could get them back. Of course, I have rationalized my actions (you can live without this stuff for a week or two, but I may not). I will not be back again. I am very sorry, and I promise I will make it up to you someday. Or I will die. I don't want to die so I have a lot of work ahead of me. I feel I have been one step away from this position I'm in since I was 17. I have always just fallen back on a family member. Well, this is what I need to do. I have to stand up and take care of myself. I have had a very difficult time, but I'm not crying about it. I am not going to cry anymore. I need to learn to be a man and take care of myself. I will go away, and when I come back I will be a man that you can be proud of. Please don't call the police, I know I deserve it, but I will get you your stuff by Friday. Let everyone know this and that I love you guys. Next time you see me, I will be a Man!!! Love, David

"PS: About the basement doggy door. I would not have damaged it like that on purpose, but the first time I crawled through I was actually able to squeeze through that door, but it didn't occur to me that I hadn't eaten in two days. That's why I came in the first place. I got in and pigged out. Well, the next time I tried to squeeze through, I got stuck. I mean I was stuck bad. I couldn't go in or get out. I was like that for half an hour and I started to freak out. Picture it—awful and pathetic. I remembered that I keep a utility knife (Leatherman) on my belt. I took the door apart and freed myself. It was a horrible ordeal. I don't think I have ever found myself in a worse position than I was then. I didn't want you to think that I was just coming over and destroying anything that got in my way. It truly was unintentional . . . Sorry!"

Just imagine my six-foot, 170-pound son resorting to crawling through a 10" x 12" doggy door that was meant for a 15-pound dog to get something to eat and to steal from his mother to feed a habit that was killing him. On top of that, Patches was jumping around and nudging him, thinking he had come to play with her. She was so excited to see him as he tried to free himself. David told me later that being stuck in the doggy door with his dog licking his face was one of the most humiliating events in his life. He had had a key. Guess it got lost.

David also started pilfering items to pawn—mostly tools—from his father and brother. Until the doggy door break-in, we hadn't considered that he would steal from us and didn't keep an eye out for that red flag of addiction. This is an important lesson to learn early when dealing with an addicted loved one. Until he cleaned out the CD rack, Dave was clever to take things that wouldn't be noticed. He was also careful about whom he stole from. When I confessed to a dear friend about David's drug use, she immediately accused him of stealing jewelry from her when we were there for dinner a few months before. I was ashamed and embarrassed beyond explanation. David denied taking the jewelry. I didn't know what to believe. Just having him accused was humiliating. I learned later that the jewelry was found. But the experience was an eye-opener for how people, even good friends, now viewed us.

I had to do something. Something drastic. I had to respond forcibly. David was completely out of control, and I was terrified that he would kill himself or someone else. After a discussion with his father and brother, I agreed that having him arrested for the break-in to my house was the only way to rein him in and get him off the street. Our ultimate goal was to get David into long-term treatment. David had aged out of our health insurance policies long ago, and neither his father nor I had the funds to pay the high price of drug treatment. We needed help.

Bobby Newman's[12] book, *Secrets to Successful Recovery Solutions: What They Don't Want You to Know about Addiction and Treatment,* gives practical guidance for when addiction turns your loved one into a thief:

> Don't allow your valuables to 'wander off.' Take an inventory and keep them under lock and key if you think your loved one is addicted. If things come up missing, call the authorities and

make a report. You have to make it known that this is not OK and will not be tolerated. Yes, they might get into trouble, but they should if they are stealing from you. Remember you might be saving their life in more ways than one. What if they steal from someone else and get caught. They could get killed not to mention the chance of overdose.[*]

I called the police and had David arrested for breaking and entering my house. David needed to understand that it wasn't the items we cared about. Because of his drug use, his strong young body had become emaciated and sick, and the mind he so cherished was becoming severely damaged. Having my son arrested was one of the hardest things I've ever had to do. After his arrest, the police provided me with a statement of items that he and Circe had pawned in Arlington, Fairfax, and Loudon counties since October 2000. I recognized many of the items David pawned. He received a mere $50 for my wedding rings, and they were returned. None of the CDs or the tools were returned. Circe pawned an expensive watch and diamond cocktail ring I could not identify.

WRITE-UP IN *THE WASHINGTON POST*

At the time of our decision to have David arrested, he was busy trying to get into another house in Reston. According to David, it was a friend's house and he was only trying to enter the house to get Circe's checkbook back.

On May 1, 2001, my mother read about David's arrest in *The Washington Post* newspaper:

David [full name], 26, of no fixed address, was being held last night in Fairfax County Adult Detention after county police arrested him in Reston. Police said a neighbor saw someone attempting to break into a rear window of a residence in Reston but fled in a car when the neighbor approached him. The

---

[*] Newman, *Secrets*, 2020, Kindle, p. 45.

> neighbor called the police. On their way to the scene, police
> officers spotted David's car on Reston Parkway at Fox Mill
> Road, stopped him and put him under arrest about 6:00 p.m.
> Saturday. He has been charged with burglary, possessing drug
> paraphernalia, and driving while his operator's license is
> suspended.

My mother, who lived just a few miles from me, immediately called me. I was mortified. She knew David was struggling but didn't know the details or the extent of his drug use. She was upset but handled the news remarkably well. She told me that a family member had "warned" her about David some time ago and advised her not to let David in her house. Rather than being embarrassed and demeaning David, she was antagonistic and dared anyone to tell her who she could let into her house, let alone her grandson. Although my mother was difficult in many ways, and I couldn't always trust her version of conversations, in that moment I was relieved. I didn't care whether she was telling me the truth or not. Keeping David's addiction "secret" was hugely stressful. I still wasn't ready to share the gruesome details of his addiction with her, which I don't think she cared about knowing, anyway. At least now I could stop with the pretense of everything being fine. It wasn't.

On May 8, 2001, a warrant was issued for David's arrest for the doggy door break-in. It was an awkward and desperate attempt to get help for David, but the court officials knew what was going on, and they worked with me as we moved through the hearing process. All we could do at this point was give David tough love and our full support for recovery. We stressed over and over that we didn't take this step to punish him but to get him off the street, away from drugs, and hopefully into long-term treatment. David was sentenced to 12 months in jail (10 months suspended) and probation for one year, which was added to other convictions and the Reston house break-in. David also was required to attend an evaluation of his drug use and to follow all recommendations of the court. Our hopes were high that these actions would lead him to recovery from using heroin.

CHAPTER 3: 2001

INCARCERATION / LETTERS FROM JAIL

In May 2001, David was incarcerated in Fairfax. His June 1 letter highlights the realities of jail life and the people he was forced to live with. David expresses confidence that he can stay off drugs and suggests a plea bargain with me.

"June 1, 2001. I'm sorry I haven't written to you earlier. I have enjoyed your letters though. I just spoke to you last night. We had a very unpleasant conversation. I want you to know that I fully intend to do the right thing here. I am going to take care of my drug problem. I need to take some time to really concentrate on where I went wrong. What happened to me? Hindsight is 20-20 so I need to take advantage of it. It is very hard to do here in jail.

"For the most part, I spend most of my time just keeping myself together. That's what I don't think you realize. There are a lot of hard headed people in here. People don't get better in here. They get worse. There are fights about every other day. Say the wrong thing to somebody, and you will have to defend yourself. Then they will put you in the hole for 30 days. Believe me, these are not the things I am interested in writing about, but it is the reality of where I am. Just like the visiting glass and phones, it is just like the movies. There is a big Spanish gang called M.S. They hate the blacks, so fortunately I seem to be the right color. They are too busy with each other. Anyway, I'm sure you are admiring my lovely handwriting—everyone does. I am writing with a rubber pen, which doesn't help.

"A guy just got the call to go home. We all cheer when that happens. It makes me very sad, though. Only thing is, this guy is really messed up. He is a

Muslim Indian, who claims to be from France. He is here on a stalking charge. He had court yesterday and they said that he could go home and charges would be dropped if he will just stay away from Joyce (the girl). He has been here three months but is very unhappy with the verdict. He says he is going to file a motion to get the restraining order lifted. No matter how much we tell him that Joyce doesn't love him and all he has to do is move on, he just won't hear it.

"Commissary just came around the corner. Everyone gets all excited when it happens. Everyone yells COMMISSARY all day long, trying to make people look. Then when it really shows up, no one believes it. It is the only thing we have to look forward to, other than gym and meals. Due to a lack of paper, I have to use the paragraph sign to save space on paper.

"This is my plea bargain with you: Petition the judge to withhold adjudication for a period of time equal to the statute of limitations. Order mandatory drug tests and drug rehab (New Beginnings). The case is Null Processed if these conditions are met. If not, I can be re-indicted on the two felony charges. I will agree to waive my right to counsel and accept the maximum penalty under the state law.

"This works good for everyone. The judge and prosecutor get a good statistical chance of getting two felony convictions on a person who deserves it, and I get the opportunity to do the right thing without having to live the rest of my life with a felony conviction. It won't be easy, but I am confident in my intention to stay off drugs."

After discussing his plea bargain idea with the attorney who previously represented David in court, I wrote two letters back to David about his legal options. I wanted him to understand my worry that he was more concerned about manipulating the situation and getting out of jail as quickly as possible, rather than addressing the problem that got him there. I had to somehow make David understand the seriousness of his situation, not only legally, but also mentally and physically.

During a visit with me, David tried to assure me that he was going to stop using heroin. He was emphatic that he could not continue to use heroin and lead a decent life. He said that even with an endless supply of money, which he no longer had, he knew he had to stop using heroin. What he didn't mention was that he wasn't ready to give up trying.

David's June 16 letter to Circe while in Fairfax Jail had a very different tone than his letters to me or to his brother:

"June 16, 2001. My Dear Sweet Circe, Honey, I LOVE YOU SO MUCH! And I miss the hell out of you. I think this may be the first letter I ever sent you. Pardon my handwriting—I'm writing with a rubber pen. I have told everyone in my cell block about you, but when I close my eyes and I see your face and hear your beautiful voice, I feel like crying. I love you so much and I can't believe I have gone so long without talking to you. YOUR BEAUTIFUL VOICE!!! I want to cry now thinking of you. I don't know why. If it's the combination of the tragic events that have transpired or if I'm contemplating the possibility that I would never see you again. Regardless of what it is, there is no doubt that my love for you pumps through my veins as strong as ever.

"OK, listen, first of all, I understand that people have been telling you that I had some kind of party while you were gone. That is complete bullshit—you know this. We talked every day. If you believe what your father and M say, then you would have to be crazy. Watch out for my family, too. They are trying to tear us apart. I remember you were worried that [family] would work on me, but it seems to be working on you.

"I have been locked up now for two months, and I have heard nothing from you. I just got your address today. I wrote a letter and got an international stamp a month ago. The mail comes every night and I keep thinking I will get a letter from you. BUT NOTHING. It seems to me, you must believe what these lunatics have told you, because you could have found out where I am and written to me by now. I need you honey, but I need to know, where do you stand? Are you coming back to me or not? I hope you are, but I will understand if you don't. PLEASE COME TO ME! I get out in five weeks. July 20, 12:01 a.m. I have had dreams that you would be out front waiting for me. I want you soooo bad. I think of your naked body. I want to feel you and kiss you all over. I am very fired up!

"I hope you don't think I was with someone else. I just remembered that M told you that. That is ridiculous. Like he would know what I do anyway. No, honey, I have been celibate since you left. AND IT'S PUTTING A HURTIN' ON ME TOO!!! Also, I hope you don't think I was trying to steal from those people. That is ridiculous, too. That fat piece of shit was taking your checks, so I decided to go and get them. The window was wide open. I didn't break in like they said. I saw it and decided to go in and get what belonged to us. The thing is, I didn't look around to see the neighbor sitting in his backyard looking right at me. He called the police. I didn't steal anything. That's why I didn't get charged with larceny. They pulled me over right down the road. They took an inventory of everything in the car. Nothing belonged to them. They dropped the charge to a misdemeanor and are letting me go. They know I'm innocent. Even though 'fat fuck' was trying his damnedest to set me up. FUCK HIM! The cops aren't stupid. He tried to say he was missing a camera and some other shit, but they didn't buy it. I would have had it if I stole it.

"I wish I could talk to you. I want you to come and pick me up on the 20th, have a great time together, and then get us another place. I am going to be on probation for a little while. This means regular drug tests. I also have to pay my fines and keep a job. My family is telling you that I'm going to rehab for a few months. This is NOT true. I may be doing an outpatient thing where I go once or twice a week, but that's it. I need to get a place and a job.

"We should move to West Virginia and get a little place, a couple of dirt bikes, and a couple of dogs. I have a way for us to make some good money if we do this. It would be wonderful. Right now, I have nothing though. If you can't come, then I will have to figure something out. My family has made it quite clear that I can't stay with them. I have a backup plan.

"I don't know if your father still has you on lock down, but even if he does, that's all the more reason to get the fuck out. Please COME TO ME! Whatever you have to do. I need you here, and I don't want to lose you like this. I don't expect you to support me. I will take care of you. If you can come, maybe with a little bit of money, we can start up something good. I will work my ass off to make sure you don't ever have to work again. I will take care of my baby. But you will have to make sacrifices. I know your father will be against it. You have to make some difficult decisions. I hope you have made some moves by now and have some money and are ready to go. You have a little more time, but not much.

"This time we are really going to do it, though. Marriage and kids. ASAP. We can go to the court right when I get out and get married. You just need enough to get you here and enough to get a place. I am sitting in jail. It is very difficult to make plans in here. You are on my visiting list. I always hope that some way I will get a call for a visit and you'll be sitting there. I would be soooo happy. Your beautiful face. Your beautiful voice. I miss you soooo much.

"Honey, if you are the same person I've loved for three years, then you know that we need to put this together. It won't be easy. But I'm willing to do what I have to do to be with you. Sacrifices will have to be made. People may get upset. But I just can't live without you. You're my best friend in the world and the most beautiful woman I have ever known.

"Make some moves, honey. Put something together. LET'S DO THIS!!! COME TO ME AND BE WITH ME FOREVER I love you, honey.

"PS: I can get us some E-doggies[13] for when you come. Don't worry, nothing else. But E-doggies will be great for our reunion!!"

Circe wrote back to David and said she would be with him if his family hadn't told her she was no longer welcome. She had gotten a divorce and would marry him ASAP if he still wanted to. In the letter, Circe expresses her love for him, and how hurt she was when a friend notified her that Dave left detox with a woman, and that she needed his promise that would never happen again. She said she no longer talks to her parents or M, and cautions David not to send mail to her at her parents' house because she would not get it.

David was in Fairfax Jail when he wrote the following long letter to his brother Bill over the period of a week in late June 2001. In the letter, David is losing his perspective, intellectual spirit, and capacity for deep thought. Jail life sucks with its filthy, disgusting food, cellmates, living conditions, and loneliness. David asks his brother to keep his letters, which are purposefully written in the form of a journal so that someday later he can read them and find himself.

"Dear Bill, It's about 2:00 a.m. Friday morning. I am writing this in the dark. There is a huge rainstorm tonight. It's practically a hurricane. I was reading when the lightning started, so I decided to sit on my desk and watch the storm. I used to like doing that. I decided I was going to indulge in a nice depression and watch a storm. It isn't working, though. I just don't get depressed like I used to. I used to find comfort in it. Nowadays, it seems like I don't feel anything at all.

"I feel as if I have lost my intellectual spirit. My capacity for deep thought is all but gone. I would rather read. I have read five books now. I just received *The Catcher in the Rye*. It's the book that John Hinkley and the guy who killed John Lennon were obsessed with. I'm already about half way through it. I'm not that impressed yet. Even though I found myself thinking about how I would just go and stand in the rain if I could get out, like Holden Caulfield, the main character, would do. He does stupid things, wishes he hadn't done them, and then justifies them to himself. I can't decide if I like the story or not.

"I have no definite understanding of anything. I can't even remember my songs to sing to myself. I don't know who I am or where I'm coming from anymore. I have spent so many hours in deep thought in the past. It's all gone now. I only remember doing, not what I thought about. Maybe I'm going through another phase in life. If so, why can't I remember my other phases? How am I supposed to learn if I cannot use my perspective?

"These are just thoughts I'm writing down. If you don't mind, I could keep somewhat of a journal of my thoughts in the form of letters to you. You could hold them for me. Maybe someday I will find myself within them. It has stopped raining. The only thing left is that same old view, add a puddle.

"It's Friday morning. It's nasty outside. They turned half the lights out so everyone is sleeping. It's very quiet for a change. I've been reading. I found out what the catcher in the rye means—the guy keeps picturing a thousand little kids playing in a field of rye. There is a cliff in the field. He pictures himself standing at the bottom of the cliff and catching the kids as they fall. He said he would do it all day. I'm not quite sure what it means yet. I took a break to try to soak it all in. I think this guy is going to freak out and start shooting someone. Either that or absolutely nothing will happen, and the book will have been a total bore.

"I'm trying not to think about the new charges. I've got M in a blatant lie. I don't think a cop is going to want to help someone who lies. M obviously has something to hide. It's hard to think about the future when you don't know what's gonna happen. I was looking forward to my release date. Now, I sit in limbo. The only advantage is that time goes a little faster when you're not counting it down. The filthy disgusting lunch is here.

"It's just after dinner, and they opened the door to my cell. I'm lying in bed, still reading The Catcher in the Rye. It's turning out to be pretty shitty and eventless. I don't know why anyone would be obsessed with it.

"Time is getting tough. I'm lonely, and it has become boring. There are only 12 people in my block now. The two guys I liked the most got sent to Trusty on the same day. They made life a lot better in here. One of the guys was my cellmate and the other guy would come in our cell—all night we would bullshit about everything. Now I have this cell to myself. I have more space but I'm lonely. One guy got immediately fired from PRC [Pre-Release Center] when he went over. He had a co-defendant there, and they have to be kept separate. He got re-classified and sent to a different block on the B floor. The B floor is the worst. They have 10 people living in a room the size of your bedroom. Now he's sending me letters every day, crying about where he's at. The first letter I got, he was at the PRC, bragging about the Mountain Dew he was drinking; the next letter he was singing a different tune. Anyway, they were both good guys. It won't be the same in here without them.

"I have nothing good to read. I don't have any envelopes to send this letter. This sitting in jail shit sucks. I wish they would send the guy back. He was kind of burnt, but a good guy.

"GOOD NEWS today!!! A guy came by and called my name. It scared the shit out of me. I thought he was going to serve me with papers. He offered me the opportunity to go to the PRC for the rest of my time. I said yes, of course! I am going to be a Trusty. This is very rare. Trustys are everywhere in this jail, but very few are in the PRC. I didn't even put in for it. They just offered it to me. They have vending and soda machines, people wear street clothes, and the food is supposed to be a lot better. Steak and cheese subs, pizza. I was just thinking today how I would like to get moved to Trusty. This will make my time go a lot better. Only problem, if I get hit with those other charges, I'll get sent back here right away. You can't have pending charges and be in the PRC. PRAY FOR ME!!!"

In late July, David wrote a shorter letter to Bill, giving an update on how court went and getting moved to a new place in the jail with new work duties.

"July 31, 2001. Hey, Bill, I just got done with court, and I thought I'd drop you a note. It doesn't look good. I pled guilty with no agreement. My lawyer thinks that is the best way for me to get a program in a reasonable amount of time. As of now, my sentencing date is November 1. If I were to go to trial, it would probably be January or February. Then, if I'm found guilty, I would have to wait another three months to get sentenced, putting that around April or May. Since they probably would convict me, I bypassed all of that by pleading guilty and will go straight to sentencing.

"They will be doing a PSI [Pre-Sentencing Investigation] report on me. Someone will come to interview me. I'll have to write a letter to the judge and everyone involved reads it. Then they do an interview with everyone there to support me. My family—you, mom, dad, and anyone else who would be willing to help me. They make a point system out of my previous record. It allows them to know who I am, instead of just sentencing me based on the charges.

It's a good thing. It will be very important at that point to emphasize my need for treatment as well as my desire to get into it.

"I just got moved to the work block. My job is serving trays and cleaning up. It's not very demanding so I still have plenty of time to work out. Most of the people work in the kitchen, so it is very quiet during the day. I had a couple of guys I worked out with in the other block. Today, I worked out alone. I have a walkman so I can rock out while I work out. I'm just gonna have to make the best of this. Take care, Bud! I hope you are well. Your Brother"

Toward summer's end, David was released from Fairfax Jail. However, he quickly relapsed back into using heroin. It's unclear where he was living. He was arrested in Washington, D.C., for possession of heroin (case dismissed) on September 30. An October 15 letter from his probation officer indicated he was expected in Prince William County District Court on October 23, 2001.

HOMELESS / BACK IN JAIL / IN THE HOLE

If Only...

Over the years, David had numerous "if only" moments that would be the ticket to make his life better: "If only I had a scooter... if only I had the money to go to bartending school... if only I had a truck... if only I didn't go to that party... if only I didn't lose my license... if only that cop didn't pull me over"... on and on.

After David exhausted his options for where to live in early 2002, he said to me, "If only I had my own place." So, in early February 2002, a friend, who owned a rental condo, allowed David to live in the condo between rentals on a trial basis. If it worked out and David took care of the condo, he could stay. David was elated and full of promises to stay clean of drugs when he moved his few possessions into the condo.

The condo was conveniently located on a bus route to town. I loaned David my bike for short excursions. Within a month, my friend was receiving complaints from neighbors about parties and people coming and going from his condo at all hours of the day and night. When we checked on the condo, I was once again ashamed at the disgusting manner in which David was living. It was obvious that he was allowing "squatters" to sleep there. The condo, like other places David lived while he used heroin, was trashed.

By mid-March, my friend evicted David from the condo. Now, he was homeless. He had no idea where the bike was.

David began rotating among homeless shelters and living on the street. The middle-of-the-night calls for help were exhausting. It was excruciatingly painful to answer his calls and to find a filthy David, who hadn't eaten in days, shaking so badly that he could barely feed himself. Sometimes I would take him for a meal but he would have to eat in the car because he wouldn't be fit to enter a restaurant. After he ate, it would break my heart to drop him off at the nearest shelter. Other times, I would take him home with me for the night to shower and sleep on the couch. David would then set off the next morning in clean clothes, a backpack replenished with food and toiletries, and promises to never let it happen again.

Then came that first rainy and cold night when David called me around 1:00 a.m. He said his only shelter was rolling himself into a piece of carpet lying on the sidewalk—would I *pleeease* come and get him? For the first time, I said, "No." I wanted so much to go and get him, to bring him home to a warm shower, watch him enjoy a meal, and to keep him safe at least for a night. But, I knew I had to stop *enabling* David. I had fallen hook, line, and sinker into the addict enabling trap. I had to learn the difference between enabling and detaching with love[14] from David's addiction. He needed to reach his bottom,[15] and answering his calls and giving him what he wanted only made his bottom deeper.

ADDICTION IS A CHOICE?

In March 2002, a psychologist friend offered to meet with David. Due to doctor/client confidentiality, he was limited on what he could tell me about the session. He did report back that the session went well. David spent about an hour-and-a-half with him and seemed to open up. It was the psychologist's professional opinion that David was not currently using but definitely needed help to overcome whatever anxieties were causing him to choose to use heroin and numb himself. He gave David a 50-50 chance that, if he did not face his demons, he would end up back in jail and continue to use. On the bright side, he believed David was genuinely interested in giving up heroin and did not seem suicidal.

David completely fooled the psychologist. When we talked about the session some time later, he said he was using heroin heavily at the time they met. He said that the psychologist was easily fooled and only heard what he wanted to hear. Nonetheless, David enjoyed talking with him and telling his story, but probably enjoyed more how he was able to manipulate and fool him. The psychologist wasn't even a small challenge for David.

David was in total denial that his drug use had anything to do with his problems. He may have fooled the psychologist, but he must have been thinking about choices when he wrote his thoughts about human drama and the inability to "just live free":

HUMAN DRAMA

"When we free our minds, we are in completely new territory in our brain, and as we proceed through this *discovery*, we are literally rewiring to this new concept. It ultimately changes us from the inside out. If I change my mind, will I change my choices? If I change my choices, will my life change? Why can't I change? What am I addicted to? What will I lose that I am chemically dependent on? And what person, place, time, or event that I don't want to lose because I may have to experience withdrawal from that. Hence, the human drama."

THE INABILITY TO JUST LIVE FREE

"Sometimes I think I need to be in an oppressive situation in order for me to have a direct challenge. A duel for my freedom. A worthy opponent to whom I can display my abilities. A force to overcome. A fight to win. Freedom does not suit me. There is no direct challenge. The indirect challenge of becoming a successful American doesn't seem to be enough to interest me or to keep me motivated. I can overcome any force as a direct result of my inner strength, but I don't know how to just live free."

NO GET OUT OF JAIL FREE CARD

Arrests continued to mount in D.C. and Arlington for traffic violations and possession of heroin. In early April, Dave called me in the middle of the night and asked if I would come pick him up and take him to detox. I picked him up and delivered him to an Alexandria detox facility where they fortunately had a bed. He walked out the next morning.

Love us or hate us, when addicts go to jail, they lose control and become needy for their families. I've read that during active addiction, the addicted brain convinces the addict that he is in control and doesn't need anything or anyone other than his preferred drug, even when his sober rational brain tells him differently. Then he goes to jail. Because the addict has used drugs to numb his feelings and block unpleasantness for so long, he's convinced that he is indestructible and needs no one. But once the addict is thrown into the abyss of emotional discomfort and physical pain, his belief that all he needs is his beloved drug is shattered. To get what he wants and needs, classic addict traits kick in—manipulation, denial, and empty promises.

As much as I hated it when David was in jail, it provided an odd sense of relief. At least I knew where he was—he was off the streets, had food to eat, and was not using drugs. Or, so I thought. I was sorry to learn that being in jail, rehab, or residential treatment didn't necessarily mean he was safe or that he wasn't using some type of drug or alcohol. Addicts can be very creative when looking for a high or to avoid being dopesick.

By May 2002, David was rotating among jails in three different jurisdictions. He kept us informed of his life through letters and weekly visits. His letters were mostly about how to plead in court, conditions in jail, and what he was reading and thinking about. He toggled between deep sorrow and contentment. One letter would rant about chaotic jail life and the "maniacs" he had to live with. The next letter would be grateful for the time to read and ponder his thoughts. Little did I know then that his journal-like letters would become the glue for this memoir.

In the following letter to his brother, David expresses deep sorrow and regret for his behavior and for taking his family for granted. He asks Bill to visit and to help him get through being in jail.

"May 11, 2002. Bill, Hey Man, I just wanted to write a quick note. I intend to write one like this to each member of my immediate family. I think it's important to make this my first. The 4th step in AA [Alcoholics Anonymous] is 'Admit to the people you have wronged the exact nature of your wrongs, and make amends wherever possible.' Well, I have selfishly taken myself and my addiction way too far. I have taken you for granted. I have not appreciated the unconditional love you have given me, and I don't deserve it. I thank God for you guys, though, when I have gotten involved with girls and all, but deserted my family. Out on three-day drunken, drugged out binges with no cares, it seemed, in the world. I thought I could just ignore all my responsibilities and loved [ones] for these people who don't care about me at all. Neither girls nor friends have stood by me.

"I know I don't have to stand alone in this world, because I am lucky enough to have a family that loves me. Although, I truly, truly have a broken heart. I don't totally know what from. I just feel that way. I'm gonna have to find a way to fix that, find some way to stay clean and lead a good life. The thrill is gone. I would love to see you. Please help me get through this."

Also in May, David sent me a homemade Mother's Day card, complete with a poem and a little "Hallmark" crown drawn on the back. Getting notes and letters like this was heartbreaking, but it gave me hope that if David could just stay sober, the son I knew was still there and capable of coming back. I had not accepted or fully recognized the manipulation aspect of addiction. Then again, maybe he was being sincere and not just saying what he knew I would want to hear. Honestly, I didn't know. I was walking a tightrope and taking responsibility for someone I could not control. I was also convinced that what I said and did, or didn't do, could ruin any progress in a split second.

"Happy Mother's Day!!!
My dear mother,

How tolerant you have been.

You've seen me come, go, and back again,

With all the trouble and the hell,

You seem to love me just as well.

I hope you take some time to play,

And have a wonderful Mother's Day.

Wish I was there!"

What made this Mother's Day "card" a little credible was that his hand-writing was legible. This was a good sign because he scribbled wildly when using, when he was in the throes of coming down from using, or when he was desperately needing to use. He sounds optimistic in the following letters, and he talks about the complications of living in jail, getting cleared for Trusty status, and his plan for phases of his recovery.

What was disturbing and maybe not so sincere was his pride in my "accomplishments." Having him say that made me feel sad and selfish. He's referring to my returning to college and finishing my degree. It was painful to visit David in jail on the morning of my college graduation at the age of 50. It should have been David graduating that day, not his mother, and we both knew it. I hoped that he would be encouraged by my example. However, I also knew that his little buddy heroin had a tighter hold on him than anything I did, reinforcing another hard lesson one eventually learns in the school of addiction: Don't let addict madness overwhelm and stifle the goals and achievements of other family members.

"May 16, 2002. Ma, I know you're gonna get this later but I want you to know how much I appreciate your being there for me and that I don't just love you for your tolerance of me. I love you for who you are and what you have done. I'm very proud of you and your accomplishments. I just hope to someday make you proud."

The next letter:

"Mom, I just now today got some of my commissary. I didn't get everything I ordered. I got a toothbrush but didn't get the toothpaste. They are complete morons. I got envelopes, though. I had the card I've been wanting to send but things have changed since then. Today, my cell block is 'locked in.' It's punishment for a couple of guys acting stupid. They also took the phone and TV from us for two days so I can't call. The good news is that I went to medical today and got cleared for Trusty status. They should be calling me any day now!

"I've got the phases of my recovery all planned out. I've spent the first two weeks suffering severe punishment. Two weeks to cleanse my sickness. Down with the Sickness is a song. Anyway, I still haven't shaved. When I go to Trusty, I will get a free haircut and a shave. Then I will begin a month and a half of thankless labor. I will think and contemplate while I work. Give something back, and be a little more comfortable. I will work 13 hours a day, come back to the Trusty quarters, spend time using the phone or writing a letter, then go to sleep and do the whole thing again the next day.

"After my court hearing on June 25, I will go to the PRC and start the three month IAP [In-House Addiction Program] program. There I will be able to really look at who I am and what has happened to me. I will be able to get the close counseling and guidance I need (I put in for a mentor, too). I plan to make my total thought process change and become the person I want to be. Then I will go to work release. I will be able to work and stay at the jail at night. I can work seven days a week if I want. Save all the money I make minus my fines, and I would like to pay my debts, credit cards, repossessed truck, and anything else I owe so I can prepare for the future. I want to regain good credit with no one on my back.

"When I get released, I will move into an Oxford House, continue to work, participate in the House activities, pay bills, and sleep. Then I will meet a nice girl, have a kid, and live happy without drugs, or even temptation. By this time, maybe I will have my license back and enough credit to get an apartment and a cheap car.

"GOD I HOPE I can follow this plan! It is truly what I want. I hope you'll be there to help. I may need a ride from time to time. I've already taken a number of steps to set these wheels in motion. All I have to do is continue to believe that I can do it, and continue to want it. . . which may be the hardest part. Wish me luck!"

Another letter followed:

"May 21, 2002. Dear Mom, it's about 7:00 pm. I'm up in my cell, hiding from these maniacs. I'm tired of reading all of the time. I decided to write you. I still haven't gotten a letter from you. I got one from Dad last night. It was short. He said he wants me, Bill, and him to go to his place and go deep sea fishing. It sounds fun. Then I started thinking, how can I go out boating without drinking or smoking? Then I thought, as long as he has some good snacks, I'll be all right. I'm gonna get fat, though. I realize something is wrong with me. I always have to put something in my body. I feel like I can't enjoy myself without something coming in. Indulging myself in some way. I know I need to change that. But how? What do I do?

"Today I went to court for the petty larceny [charge], the people didn't show up (good news). About an hour later, I was served with a probation violation summons (bad news). I may have to do the 10 months they suspended in that case last year. Ten months misdemeanor time is actually five months, I would only have to serve half. Still that is five months on top of whatever I get.

"I just spoke to you and then Bill. You all made me feel a lot better. It's nice to have someone to talk to, Bill said something I hadn't thought of. In Arlington, I already served like 10 days, so maybe I can just get time served. Then I could go directly to the PRC. That makes a big difference. It's amazing how you can go over something in your head a thousand times and never think of something so obvious. That's why it's good to talk to other people. They may see something you don't. I'm not worried about how much time I get here, as long as I can get to the program, and then work release. I hold my plan so close to me. I will be so disappointed if it doesn't work out. I would hate to serve my time being completely unproductive. WISH ME LUCK! Hopefully, I'll get called to Trusty soon. Goodnight!!! Zzzzzzzzzzz"

Dave being in jail was a learning experience for all of us. Commissary in jail is a big deal. It's equivalent to having money in your wallet outside of jail. An inmate who has money in their commissary account has power. To get that power, the inmate needs someone to fund their commissary.

"May 29, 2002. Hey, Mom, it's about 6:45 Wednesday. I just got off work. I just got written up with a 109. Every time I leave the block, I have to move this magnet with my name on it. It's like a chart with different locations on it. He said I didn't move it when I went to work. I'm almost positive that I did. Anyway, it's no big deal. It's just a warning. When it happened everyone started crying 'conspiracy.' Everyone gossips so much and are so involved in each other's lives. You can kind of lose yourself in it. I think some people like it here. I don't. But I sure am glad to be a Trusty. Every time I look at that word—Trusty—I think of how it's spelled wrong. It's probably a made up word (not in the dictionary) but it seems to me it should be spelled TRUSTEE. Whatever, sometimes I can't help but think of dumb things.

"I finally got commissary today—a pen, pad of paper, stamped envelopes, a portfolio, socks—just about everything I need. They were out of T-shirts. I'll have to wait till next week. These polyester jumpers don't feel good against bare skin and make my chest itch. I'm not sure if it's the jumper fabric, the metal buttons, or god forbid, I've caught some fungus in here. Hopefully, it will go away when I get a T-shirt. One guy said it's the detergent.

"It was nice to get your letter and project yesterday. I plan on reading it when I have more time. I finally got the books. I'm gonna go play volleyball.

"PS: I finally got a haircut. He did a great job too."

PARENTS' SUPPORT GROUP AT JAIL

Fairfax County sponsored a support group for spouses, siblings, and parents of incarcerated family members. Initially, I felt humiliated and embarrassed to join such a group, but I desperately needed help. Someone to talk to honestly about my son without feeling shame and guilt. My initial feelings and fears swiftly flew away as I sat with other family members just like me searching for answers. We met in the evenings in a dreary room at the courthouse. Sitting around both sides of long rectangular tables pushed end-to-end, we shared our stories, fears, and disappointments. We all had the same questions: Where did we go wrong? How do we fix it? What should we do next? Most of all, why, why, why? So many questions. And no answers.

What I remember most about the support group was being surprised that our stories of how we got there were so similar. We were a diverse group in race and economic and marital status, with one common denominator: Our family member ended up in jail because of drug use. The actions and behavior of our loved ones was so similar, we could almost all have been talking about the same person. Only the faces were different. It was like a mask was passed around the table as each story was told. And, as each story was told, the room filled with sadness and feelings of despair and uselessness. No one knew what the hell to do. There was only one consolation: We weren't alone. As small as that consolation was, it did help to share our worries. At that time, the word *addiction* wasn't even muttered.

David's June 9 letter opened with an excerpt from *Queen of the Damned*.[16] His explanation of what he considers "true poetry" and the "allure of poetry" is on target. I often used poetry to communicate with David because I knew he would pay more attention. I don't think my letters or words of worry and suggestions for what to do ever had much impact. I needed to somehow make him *feel* what I felt.

This letter is full of "maybes" and also talks about his surprise that I attended the jail's support group as the parent of a 28-year old. David couldn't comprehend that just because a child grows up, parents don't stop being parents, especially when that child is in trouble and hurting himself. It became apparent over the years of his addiction that he did not understand the impact his addiction had on me and other family members. It was nice to have him write about his appreciation for his family and to admit to being wrong about his earlier belief that we only loved him under certain conditions. When David wrote this letter, he was mentally edging toward a better place. It was a good sign that he was trying to understand and putting into words why he thought about certain things. Having him say that he wanted to find out what he can "really" do if he can just stay sober was monumental. This was the David that heroin stole from us.

"June 9, 2002. Mom, this is a small excerpt from *Queen of the Damned*:

'But you see, I still don't really fully understand what happened. I don't know whether or not it was a tragedy or merely a meaningless venture. Or, whether or not something absolutely magnificent might have been born of my blundering, something that could have lifted me right out of irrelevance and nightmare and into the burning light of redemption after all.

'I may never know, either. The point is, it's over. And my world—my little private realm is smaller and darker and safer than ever. It will never again be what it was. It's a wonder that I didn't foresee the cataclysm, but then I never really envision the finish of anything that I start. It's the

risk that fascinates me, the moment of infinite possibility. It lures me
through eternity when all other charms fail.'

"I think that's great writing. I hope you can understand it the way I do. I
think that's the allure of poetry, writing, and song. It conveys a feeling, an
understanding that one could not explain simply by describing it or trying to
force an understanding. One must manipulate words to get a reader to feel it,
not just comprehend it. That is the difference between what I refer to as
'true poetry,' or just the putting into words of one's emotions. Describing the
way you feel is not poetry. Making someone else feel that way, what you feel,
or what you want them to feel, that is poetry. I am drawn to this
understanding. I don't know why, or what it means, or where I should take it,
but I am drawn to it nevertheless.

"It's Sunday evening about 10:00 pm. I feel like writing, so I'm writing to you. I
can't believe you went to that support group and there were so many other
parents there. Especially for a parent of a 28-year-old! Maybe I have
followed some sort of specific pattern . . . a natural possibility. Kind of like a
fork in the road and this is one of the possible destinations of a person who
chooses a specific road. Maybe I'm not just a crazy man drifting through time
on my own wave. Rather I'm following a specific pattern. Conforming to a way,
an understanding, and I don't even know it. Maybe there is no individuality in
my thinking. Maybe I'm just a sheep of a different shade . . . just an offbeat
thought . . . nothing important.

"It was nice to see you Saturday. It's always nice to see you. I appreciate
your support so much. It really makes me feel good to know how much my
family cares and loves me. I can remember how many conversations Circle and
I had about how my family loves me only under certain conditions, and I was
better off without them. They only want me to make them look good or have

nothing to do with me. I know that's not true, and I thank God it's not.

"It was nice to hear from Dawn, even though I'm a little embarrassed. They must think I'm crazy. They may be right. I like who I am though. I just need some time sober and productive. To find out what I can really do. Maybe I'm a dummy. Maybe I have myself fooled. I want a chance to give everything I have. See what I can really do. I really want to get back to school. Well, I better hit the sack. I feel like there's more I could include but I'll just send this like this. Talk to you soon."

David wrote to his brother about his move to another cell, and his new job in the kitchen called "Dietman."

"June 29, 2002. Bill, Hey Man, I'm writing to you from a new cell. I now have a pencil because I took a new job in the kitchen called 'Dietman.' I prepare all the special diets for the jail, although I'm wishing I hadn't taken it. There's a lot of paperwork, thinking, and work. I chose it because it's only 4-6 hours a day, and I get other perks like sodas and milkshakes.

"Right now my brain is fried. I've been filling out printouts. Things change in the jail every day. People move, leave, and come in. I have to keep track of all of that. I've decided to stick with it because I need to get my brain working again. I want to return to school, and this will be good preparation. I will have more free time now, so I will be writing more often.

"I got off the phone with you Thursday to go to an AA meeting. It turned out to be a great meeting. I really enjoyed it. The mail lady is here, and I want to get this to you. Hope you come see me this week."

Because David had court dates and jail terms in several jurisdictions, he was often moved from one jail to another without us knowing, which caused our letters to be returned unread. My July 3, 2002 letter to David in Fairfax Jail was returned as undeliverable. This letter was light and cheery (my current approach). I told him the news, sent jokes, belabored how hot it was, enclosed a picture of a friend running a marathon in San Diego, noted upcoming weddings, and said that I would see him on Sunday. I'm sorry that he didn't get this letter, because most of my letters were not so cheery.

On July 6, 2002, Dave wrote:

"Hi Mom, it's 6:30 p.m. I'm in my room. I haven't been able to reach you so I thought I would write. I should be doing paperwork for my job, but I left my blank worksheets downstairs. That is a bad thing. I need to have my paperwork done for tomorrow. Hopefully, the other Dietman will have extras.

"I hope all is well. You must be really busy. I hope Monday in court goes well. I can't wait to find out my fate. At least I know that the maximum I'll do for my violation is five months. Even though that is a long time. I will be happy when next week is over. WISH ME LUCK!!!

"I got your card. That was nice. I still haven't received anything from anyone else. I know everyone is busy. I think about how things will be when I get out. I'm very optimistic. I don't have any negative thoughts. I know I can do it. I have a plan, and I plan to stick with it. Then I think about all of the other things I want to do. Play tennis. Work out. Go down to Dad's place in the Keys. I feel like I'm being released into a different world than I came from. I feel very good about it. I could use a couple more dollars for shampoo and deodorant, and this is my last envelope. How 'bout that three-cent raise in postage! Take care, Mom

"PS: wish me luck Monday and Tuesday."

The following letter was dated July 11 but postmarked July 24, two weeks later, because David didn't have an envelope. It wasn't unusual for his letters to be long and written on multiple days, depending on writing supplies, whether he was transferred to another jail, locked down because of a fight, or if he had a stamp.

"July 11, 2002. Hey Ma, I know this is old but I just got envelopes so I thought

I'd send it anyway. I'm sitting here in this cell. Locked in 23 hours a day. My head is spinning. I've been reading and sleeping. But as far as writing goes, I can't bring myself to do it. Things have gone bad, 'yet I can still breathe.' That's from a song . . . I can't remember which or by whom. As of now, I have a release date of July 28. All I can hope for is that they don't go forward with that indictment. It's all the difference in the world.

"I went too far and now I'm paying the price. I have moments of claustrophobia, ready to freak out in this little cell, then reason kicks in. Maybe I got too comfortable and confident. Maybe I need to be broken down further. Forced to starve and to feel the pain . . . the sickness. The food is terrible here, although I haven't been hungry. That probably won't last. I don't mean to worry you with these thoughts and feelings, but I have no one else who I feel can understand. Who knows me? The key is that I don't forget. Save this letter. Let me never forget the pain and anguish I have caused myself.

"I talked to Bill tonight. I'm sorry I didn't call him much the past month. That was selfishness. Me wanting to hide from the real world. It's unfair to him. I have time to play volleyball, but I can't give my worrying brother a call. I'm still a procrastinator. That word makes me think of Dad. He's right. I am a chronic procrastinator. I never want to do anything, even mildly unpleasant. Bill said Dad just sent me a letter. Fairfax will send it back to him.

"All I do is sing to myself. I love music so much. It was a horrible thing to sell those CDs—mine and yours. When I get out, I'm going to start another CD collection. I can think of a thousand CDs I want. I know horribly sad depressing songs to sing when I want to indulge my sadness. I guess that's something they can't take away. My memory. The songs in my head. The ideas, the poetry, the thoughts. It may be scattered, but my mind will survive and overcome. The key is to never forget this pain and misery.

"3:15 a.m., Friday: I just put down my book. I find it so entertaining and thought-provoking. I must continue to read no matter what. I continue to stay up all night and sleep all day. It's not so bad. I get to avoid the terribly boring one-sided conversations with my moron of a cellmate. I wouldn't mind this so much if I had this cell to myself. I quite like this time I have to read and write. As long as I have books, pen and paper, and maybe a walkman, I would prefer solitary confinement to general population.

"I enjoy camaraderie with my fellow man and I really love to play volleyball, but I need to spend more time with myself. I tend to lose myself in the company of others. Especially when I'm well-liked and popular. I find myself basking in their approval. These people that I will never see again. I am a good leader, though. I never seek to have fun at other people's expense or to expose weaknesses. There is a lot of that in these types of situations. I believe I can thrive under any conditions. So it is not necessary to prove that to myself anymore.

"I need to continue my studying. The improving of my mind. I keep having dreams and unconscious thoughts. This just came to my conscious awareness—the Saratoga McDonalds. I have had numerous flashes in vivid dreams of late. They are like fantasies. I wonder why? Maybe it's some connection I have to innocence. Going there after little league baseball games. Or maybe a past glimpse of true happiness. My family all together after some sort of event, going out to eat. Just a thought!

"As depressing as this situation is, I feel like I have lost the understanding of real depression. I remember depression but it is something I have not truly felt for some time. Just like the feeling of time moving—fast or slow. I see it go the same no matter what. I do remember days of the past seeming to take a lifetime. *TIME MARCHES ON* (a song).

"My mind grows. I love to think. To gain a new understanding. I just must keep this going. I have a tendency to want to shut down. I am most alive when my mind is alive. I hope to live a long time. Something must come of this thought. What will become of me? Is this all part of me achieving some great understanding? If that even exists. Or is thought like that the ingredients for madness? Is there a greater understanding? Why do I seek it? I have nothing, not even clothes, yet that is not my chief concern. Finding my direction. Being what I need to be. This is of utmost importance. I know this stuff isn't making much sense. Maybe these are the random chaotic thoughts of a madman. Who knows?"

David's July 12 letter comes from Arlington County jail. He's been transferred from Fairfax where he was a Trusty with privileges. He's back in general population, where he is very much in the minority and not happy.

"July 12, 2002, 6:45 p.m. They moved me today. I got lucky to come to general population in four days. It's good, but this block is not. 100 people, and maybe eight of them are white. Out of that eight, about five of them don't realize they are white. I don't think I am going to like it. But, it's better. They have a nice gym with weights that I have access to all day. I plan to work out in the mornings. My cellmate says no one is out there then. Then, if I get a walkman, I can listen to music and work out. By the time I get out, I will look like a movie star or a world-class athlete. That would be nice.

"My cellmate is the only person I've talked to. No one else has any desire to talk to me, except for this one guy. He came to me when I was eating and told me I was sitting in his spot. The guy was half my size. I looked at him and told him I would get up when I was done eating. All my stuff was laid out in front of me and I had a mouth full of food. I didn't want to get up. Besides, there were plenty of other places to sit. So, he sat beside me, trying to look tough. All 5 foot 4 inches of him. I felt like I could have crushed him, and I wanted to because he was trying to make me look bad. I don't care, though.

"I know what I'm gonna do—read, work out, listen to music, and write. I'm going to bring my tray into my cell and eat there from now on. These people have nothing to offer me. Typical jail stuff! I met so many cool decent guys on that Trusty block in Fairfax. I guess that's the difference though, they were Trustys.

"I hope they don't indict me on those bogus charges. Everyone I've talked to says, 'Don't plead guilty.' They will have difficulty convicting me without any actual drugs. They need to be able to weigh what I had. Show how much I made. Residue is ridiculous. I'm hoping it was just a threat if I get in trouble again . . . yada yada yada. I don't want to be here with these IDIOTS!"

The following paragraph is dated July 16, but the second page of the letter was written on July 15. Obviously, David didn't realize he put a letter to "Jeff," dated July 15, in my envelope. There was no closing to my July 16 letter, so maybe Jeff got the last page of my letter. Based on the text of Jeff's letter, he was someone David met while a Trusty at Fairfax. There's been a riot at the jail, and he has been locked down for three days.

"July 16, 2002 [first page]. There was a huge riot here Sunday. We have been locked down ever since. That's why I can't call. I don't know how long it will be. I hope you put money in [my commissary account], then I can send this out, get word to you. My cellmate went home today. He was a good guy (not the one from before, a different guy). I hated to see him go, because who knows who I'll get next. It's nice to have the cell to myself, though, while we are locked down. I don't know when this will end.

"July 15, 2002 [second page]. Jeff, Hey man. I'm sittin' here in Unit 4B of

Arlington County Jail. We have been locked down for the last three days. There was a mini riot in here. Get this, man. Arlington is fuckin crazy. The charges that brought me here were unlawful entry and possession of drug paraphernalia. I get to court, thinking I'm gonna get to go home for a little while. Then, my lawyer came back to talk to me. She said this is the deal. 12 months, 10 suspended for unlawful entry and they will drop the paraphernalia, but they did a test on the pipe (which was a brass pot bowl) and it came back positive for pot, cocaine, and heroin!! They are going to indict me on possession of cocaine and heroin (both felonies), and as part of the deal they won't go forward with the marijuana. THESE MFERS ARE CRAZY! Residue in a pipe. The pipe wasn't even mine. It was this chick's, but of course that doesn't matter.

"Anyway, as of right now, I have a release date of 7/28/02. If they don't come through with the indictment by then, I will get a little time out there. They are definitely going to hit me hard, though. My lawyer says at least a year. And, I still have my violation in Fairfax, which was supposed to be on 7/11/02 but Arlington didn't send me to it. That should be continued since there is no bond or anything holding me to it. I will be released here on the 28th and just have a court date pending for it. The good news is that my mother is sick of the bullshit they are putting me through, and she is gonna get a real lawyer. One who can take on both Fairfax and Arlington with the goal being, to quote my mother, 'Get your ass out of jail and into a program as soon as possible.' That sounds good to me! Plus, like I said, if that indictment on the coke and dope doesn't come through by the 28th, I will get a week or two OUT THERE! I hope so!

"So, what's jumpin' off over there. I didn't know I was leaving. I left so fast I didn't say bye to anyone. I definitely miss it compared to here. It's better than the regular blocks, but it's got nothing on the trusty blocks there. It's a *definite possibility that I'll be back though. I know Tattoo Joe should be here by now, but I haven't seen him. Tell everyone I say Hi and not to commit any crimes in Arlington. Everyone here is gettin' massive time. Some of the numbers I've heard are crazy. Let me know what's goin' on with you and the latest gossip."*

Jeff's letter shows that David had formed a "community" of friends at the various jails, and they kept up with each other. While incarcerated in Arlington in 2002, David formed a close relationship with a woman serving time on the woman's side of the jail.

By July 2002, I estimated that David had been hooked on heroin for close to four years—almost half his adult life. He was constantly in and out of jail. His self-study of philosophy was in full swing and had begun to dominate our visits and telephone calls. We would argue about the irony of his situation and the philosophical beliefs he espoused. Especially his theories about motivations versus actions and, ironically, TRUTH, since what I got from him most of the time was lies. David's interest in reading and writing about philosophy continued whether he was actively addicted, sober, or crisscrossing jails.

According to David's record, he was arrested on July 18, 2002, in Arlington, charged with possession of heroin and cocaine, and sentenced to 42 months confinement, 39 months suspended, and four years supervised probation. On July 22, he had a probation violation on a misdemeanor offense and was sentenced to 10 months, to begin immediately. I was traveling for work on those dates and cannot verify whether or not he had been released from jail and then sent back to Arlington jail.

In August, David sent me a birthday card to "gift" me a smile for my birthday. His words are sweet and caring, and they exemplify what a schmoozer he could be. However, my guess is that he was feeling sorry for himself. He knew full well that nothing I did eclipsed my worries over him and his situation.

"August 17, 2002. Mom, thank you for being there for me. I hope you have a good

birthday and that you can reflect on your past 51 years and smile. Smiling is an amazing thing. It's just the movement of facial muscles but it really can change your state of mind. So, right now smile a bit for me. That is my gift to you. You should feel better, if only for a minute. I know a birthday doesn't mean much to you, but I hope you do something special. Even if it's just renting a movie and relaxing. You don't seem to do much of that lately. I'm glad you're looking for a new job that you will enjoy. I think you work too hard. Then you will have a complete life. Good home, relationship, and job. I just hope you don't worry about me too much. I do need your support but I don't want you to waste your valuable time worrying about me. With the help I will get and the support I have, I will be fine.

"Anyway, I hope you're not working and I hope you have a nice relaxing day. Happy B-Day Mom."

Dave got along well with just about everyone, unless it was a cop locking him up or someone who wanted to mess with his perspectives. He especially adored people who gave him something interesting to think about. It didn't matter what color they were or where they came from. He loved learning from people. Just one of the many things I miss about him. "Stinky" Dave writes from Arlington Jail about his commissary order and prospects for where to go for treatment when he gets out of jail, and he tells a story about meeting a "very wise" little African guy.

"August 30, 2002. Hi Mom, I'm watching tennis—Kuerten and Safin. It's a pretty good match. I wanted to write you and get you that information. Good news! The money went into my account in time for me to get commissary yesterday. I got everything except deodorant. I was 10 cents short. Can you believe they would give me popcorn but not the deodorant? I think that's crazy. In Fairfax, if you were short money on your order, cosmetics came first. I will have enough to get one of the cheaper deodorants for Tuesday. I'll just have to be stinky till then!

"I've talked to a few people 'who know' since I talked to you. They say that the Phoenix House is the best bet for my situation. They will accept me prior to me getting sentenced (unlike Second Genesis, who requires a court to sentence a person to the program). That would be a big chance to take. From what I understand this judge is the head judge of the four. Meaning he does administrative things with the jail. He also works directly with the sheriff to come up with 'alternative sentencing.' He is a program judge. That is good and bad. It means I'm almost guaranteed to get a program, but he is a big proponent for the ACT [Assertive Community Treatment] program. I have spoken to a guy who had a very similar situation as me a few years ago, and he went before the judge with an acceptance letter to the Phoenix Program. The Judge went with that since he could see the guy had done some footwork to get help on his own; it looked like he really wanted it.

"I know what you're thinking—he's back! I know that concerns you but he did stop using. He got a probation violation for driving on a suspended license. He said that I need someone on the outside to do some footwork. I will write a letter and it shouldn't be a problem. I will need a social security card and TB (tuberculosis) shot. Both of which I can do here. They give TB shots to everyone. I just need proof. I have put in to my case manager to get a SS [social security] card. This jail is so much better than Fairfax. We have case managers. No request forms. That's nice! Even though the case manager is mean. It's still better.

"I am enclosing a commissary slip so you can see the prices and what I'm dealing with. I could live comfortably on $20 every two weeks. $15 works for cosmetics and batteries but I can't get anything extra. I plan on using many stamped envelopes in the near future. Anyway, whatever you think is best. I will endure. There was this little African guy in here for about two weeks. He was on hold for immigration. He's a student at Loyola. I said something, complaining about jail. He said in a thick accent, 'You must endure. It will make you a man.' I thought that was very wise. I must endure! Thank you for helping, Mom. I don't know what I'd do without your help."

David loved to have deep, thoughtful, and ideological discussions. When I would add a dose of practicality and reason, he would fire back at me that I wasn't listening, that I didn't "hear" him, and that I wasn't even trying to understand his perspectives. I would blast back that I heard him and understood perfectly but that his actions and behavior spoke louder than his words. He didn't like it when I added reality to our discussions.

After one such discussion and to show David how much I was trying to hear and understand him, I wrote him a poem and titled it "Listen Smart."

LISTEN SMART

A good ear
An open heart
From those you love
You'll never need part.
I want to listen and
I want to hear
What you have to say.
To close my heart
And listen smart.

Just because I gave you life
I feel I have this certain right
To know who you are.
To open my mind
And listen smart.

I want to understand
How, with you, young man
I fit in the plan.
To give you space
And listen smart.

Some things I cannot bear
If those you chose again . . .
But let's not dwell there
And listen smart.

This message I send to you
Is full of love and
Meant to show sincere intent,
But practical too.
So it's up to me to open up
And listen smart.

Listen . . . means don't be fooled!
Hear your needs . . . our needs

And hum along.
But always, always be true
And listen smart.

You're not alone,
Which can be good . . .
Can be bad
And can be a burden for all.
But well worth the weight
When we open up
And listen smart.

Listening smart isn't always the same
And not the other should you blame
When worries warp and trouble the mind,
It's up to us to open our hearts
And listen smart.

Dave writes in his September 2 letter that he agreed with the context of the poem and it did get him thinking. What I hadn't expected the poem to do was to bring to mind a problem he's had with his extended family, who he felt had not taken the time to really know him. It was true. I know exactly what he's talking about. David was the youngest child and grandchild, he was adorably cute, and his extended family never really got to know him or to view him as an adult.

"September 2, 2002. Mom, I just got your poem. I thought it was great! It's good to see that you would be willing to open up like that. We do need to listen smart. Hear the words and not try to decipher some alternate meaning, but hear them for what they are (sometimes). You know, it kind of illustrates a problem I've had with my entire family. None of them have ever taken the time to really know me. It's nice to be loved, but I would almost prefer respect and understanding. What is love without knowledge anyway? If you don't understand me or my perspective then how can any of us ever get past the initial, new baby, cute kid, make me proud adult. If that's all people want then they will probably avoid me anyway. Good, they don't deserve to know me. I feel I have more to offer than just being cute. For example, interesting conversation. I can also be quite funny. I have much to offer that I sometimes think some people couldn't care less about. I don't want to dwell on this point, though. Reality is what I want.

"I think about the future. I am so eager to start. So much I want to do.

"I realize after re-reading this that listen smart also means sometimes deciphering alternative means. I don't mean for my reaction to seem so negative. I have read your poem several times, and I think I understand what you're saying. It makes me happy that you actually want to hear what I have to say! Now that you're listening though, I hope I don't let you down!!!"

David was still locked down in his cell on September 11, 2002—one year after the twin towers fell to the ground. What a day September 11, 2001 was . . . I was sitting at my desk a block away from the White House. People kept rushing past my desk, headed to the lunch room. I had no idea what was going on. When I got up from my desk, I glanced out the window and saw a wave of what looked like hundreds of people flooding down the street next to the Executive Office Building moving toward Pennsylvania Avenue, which was also congested with people. I ran to the lunch room. We all stood and watched TV as the planes flew into the towers. Except for gasps of disbelief, the room was silent. We couldn't believe our eyes or the tragic words of the commentator. Chaos and confusion overcame everyone as we scattered back to our workstations and waited for instructions, which came swiftly.

Go home and stay safe! My car was blocked in the garage but it didn't matter because the streets were jammed tight with cars and people. Nothing was moving. I'll never forget the guy who had a TV on the roof of his car in the middle of the street, broadcasting the news. I guess he had it plugged into his cigarette lighter for power. I met up with some of my colleagues and we started walking down Pennsylvania Avenue, and across Key Bridge to Rosslyn, where we were able to catch the Metro to the burbs. I don't remember being afraid on that walk—seems strange now.

"September 11, 2002. Hi Mom, I just got your letter with the commissary budget in it. Thank you. That stuff is really gonna help. Well, it's 9/11. It really is powerful. It makes me feel sad and patriotic. I'm sure a lot is going on out there. We are locked down. Another whole day in a cell. I won't think of my pain today though. I will think of those poor people who lost their loved ones. WHAT A TRAGEDY! You didn't come visit yesterday so I'm expecting you to come today.

"I'm going to call my lawyer tomorrow with a list of questions. If she acts annoyed by me calling, I am going to discuss it with her. These are my questions: What can I expect from the Pre-Screening Interview? When can I expect it? What should I have prepared? What is the felony on my record, and what do I have to do to prove that is an error? (The fact that I am a first time felon is very important in my sentencing. It can make all of the difference.) What do I want to say in my letter to the judge? What rehabs does she think I should be contacting? And a very important one: what are my guidelines?

"The judge goes by a set of guidelines based on your record. They could be 0-6 months, 1-2 years, 2-4 years, etc. She is supposed to figure all of this out for me before I go to court. I want her to tell me if she intends to do anything to help me, or is she just going to show up in court. If that's the case, I am in big trouble. If you have any suggestions, let me know."

David's September 23 letter finds him feeling young, calm, and settled into a routine. He's getting exercise, digging deeper into things he wants to read, and looking forward to getting out of jail even if it only means getting into residential treatment—our goal—which took longer than initially thought and extended David's jail term.

It's probably correct that I wouldn't want Dave to read and be influenced by Huxley's book, *The Doors of Perception*. Published in 1954, the text elaborates on Huxley's psychedelic experience while using mescaline (a hallucinogenic drug similar to LSD) and the insights he experienced. I don't recall talking further about the book, but I suppose he read it.* Friedrich Huxley, aka Freddy, the name he gave to the protagonist in most of his stories written many years later, must have been influenced by Aldous Huxley and Friedrich Nietzsche, another philosopher's work he liked to read and quote.

"September 23, 2002. It's 11:45 p.m. Friday night. I haven't written in a little while. I felt relatively good today. I have been working out, playing basketball, and reading that Abnormal Psychology book I told you about. I really enjoy the opportunity to read anything I want. The library here is OK, but the lady who runs it goes to some big library near here twice a week. I can put in for anything I want to read, and she'll get it. I have always had a lot of different things I want to read, although I can't always remember what they are. So, as things come up, on TV or in conversation, I write them down and get a book on it. I put in the other day for (I know you would probably prefer I didn't

---

* David mentions reading Huxley in his fictional short story, "A Brief Moment of Clarity."

read this but I have always wanted to) Aldous Huxley's, *The Doors of Perception*. I am quite excited about getting it and looking forward to reading it.

"There are other things I want to read or that I have thoughts about: I would like to read about Leonardo DaVinci; he did so much, but I don't know enough about him. 'Neechy' (I don't know how to spell his name), a philosopher. Plato, and I want to read in more detail about Freud. I read about his basic principles in the book I have now. I don't agree with a few things. I know he uses the word sex in very broad terms, but I didn't agree with certain things, e.g., *Oedipus Complex*, the *Four Sexual Stages*. It's kind of fun gathering information even if it never comes up. I feel young today.

"Enclosed is part of the letter The Phoenix House sent to me. What I need is a 'funding source.' This is something I think you can help me with. I made a phone call to Fairfax ADS [Alcohol and Drug Services] but I didn't get anyone. I left a message for someone to contact me or you. It is difficult for me to make these calls. I have to go through the deputy, he has to approve it, etc. There is a list of other contacts and possible funding sources in that letter. Maybe you could call some of them. I know the rehabs don't want to talk to you but maybe the funding sources will. If we find a funding source, then I should be all right.

"Second Genesis will accept me and give me something I can give to the Judge. Then on Nov. 1st I can hopefully get sentenced to them and probation. I will just have to sit here till a bed opens up. It will be sooo nice to leave here. To get started on my new life. I intend to continue with my reading. That's the thing I guess I never realized when you would try to get me to read. I can read anything I want and learn cool stuff. There is a lot I would like to know. Life is good! Real life! Not denial, coping mechanisms, drugs, co-dependent people. Independence will be refreshing."

When the case David refers to in his November 9 letter was finally heard, he was in Arlington County Detention and had a court-appointed attorney. The court sentenced David to incarceration with the Virginia Department of Corrections (DOC) for the term of 3½ years, all suspended but three months, with the condition that he must enter and complete the Second Genesis Program and any other program fixed by the Fairfax County Court. David was ordered to remain in Arlington County Detention until he could be released directly to Second Genesis—the news we had been waiting for. In addition, his driver's license was suspended for six months, and he was placed on probation for four years, which included substance abuse counseling and/or testing. Costs included $948 for the heroin case and $898 for the cocaine case.

"November 9, 2002. Dear Mom, I'm so sorry I haven't been writing. I guess I just have a lot on my mind. This continuance in court was hard on me. I hope I still have the support of my family. It was nice to see you in the courtroom. I'm in kind of a 'purgatory' type place. I don't want to start anything new until I know my fate. I have been going to a substance abuse class. It's good, and I enjoy it. The girl who teaches it is about 35 years old, overweight, and a former drug addict. Seven or eight guys from my block attend with me. We discuss the class and look forward to going. It is a six-week class. and we have four weeks to complete it. I will get a certificate if I'm still here to finish. It's a start!

"I know it's rare for me, but I don't have much to say. I left a message today for my court appointed lawyer. I hope she does something for me. She is truly the worst counsel I have ever had.

"Nothing much changes here. People come and go. Yesterday, I finally got a single cell. I have been waiting for three months. I no longer have a new thought. I just can't seem to win. It's all right, though, at least I have no roommate. I can now stretch out and relax. I don't have to hear my idiot roommate rapping out loud like a retard! Anyway, I feel good. No extremes. Mild ups and downs. I have good people to talk to.

"I play a lot of basketball and have been playing quite good. I am always one of the first people picked. I really enjoy it. It's mostly black people who play. They stay under the illusion that only black people can play basketball well. Since I am good, they call me 'white chocolate.' I don't really like that, but at least I know it means they respect the way I play. I love sports and competition. Let me never forget that. Anyway, take care, Mom. And remember that you are always in my thoughts, even if I don't write."

On November 26, I sent a letter to David at his address at Arlington County Detention. The main purpose of the letter was to enclose copies of police records that I picked up at the Fairfax County Courthouse. This letter said how impatient I had become with David. I was tired of his complaints and his philosophical ideas that did nothing to help his reality. He needed to stop feeling sorry for himself and to accept responsibility for his actions. I wanted to make it clear that it was high time he tried to understand my perspective, instead of me always having to decipher and understand his perspective. I wanted to make him understand that he wasn't the only victim of the "unfair fairy." His family was a victim of his addiction, too.

I had found tough love. The only problem was that Dave didn't get my letter. He had been transferred back to Fairfax Jail, and my letter was returned to me sometime in December. I gave him the letter a couple of months later. The letter opened with the following quote from a poster I saw at the courthouse—good food for thought for both the parent and the addict:

Watch your THOUGHTS, they become your WORDS
Watch your WORDS, they become your ACTIONS
Watch your ACTIONS, they become your HABITS
Watch your HABITS, they become your CHARACTER
Watch your CHARACTER, it becomes your DESTINY

David was back in Fairfax Jail and not at all happy with his return when he wrote on December 1. He obviously had not received my November 26 letter with the records about concurrent parole violations or my rant about his taking responsibility.

"December 1, 2002. Mom, it is Sunday, the first of December, and I am sitting in the worst place I have ever been. Once again. I'm OK, though. I will endure. I am much better off than I was seven months ago when I was in the same place. I still feel good even though I'm here. It is amazing how horrible this place is compared to Arlington [jail], and criminal the way these poor people are treated. Everyone here looks half asleep all the time, unshaven, no haircuts, not showered. It's horrible. Like a big cage full of rats. We are fed through a hole in the door. I will be putting in request forms for Trusty every day. Hopefully, I can get there quickly.

"About my time. I just wrote a detailed letter to the court. I am confident we can get this concurrent, consecutive thing cleared up. More important than that, I must get that slackin' lawyer to do his job. Plus, I need to get the ADS [Adult Detention System] people to come here and interview me as soon as possible.

"If all were to go well and I could get in front of the judge quickly, I could be out of here quickly. So, I have to be sure I have all of my business here finished. Thank you for all the help you have given me. I know it has been a pain. It's a shame I have this lousy lawyer. Hopefully, I will hear something this week. It would be terrible if I had to remain here for several months and then go to prison. I must do everything in my power to stop that process now.

"Well, Mom, I'm sure I will speak to you before you get this. Most of all, I want to thank you for your help. I am lucky to have you guys."

In mid-December, David was back in a Fairfax County Courtroom. His brother, father, and I attended. We wrote letters to the presiding judge in both Fairfax and Arlington counties to show our support and to renew our request that David be sent directly for treatment from incarceration. Our wanting him kept in jail until he could be released directly to treatment was at the core of David's animosity toward us. He wanted out of jail ASAP, and he blamed his family when it didn't happen. I visited him regularly and most visits were good, but our February 22 visit was not good at all.

I don't think there's an ounce of sincerity in David's 2002 Christmas note. He was sad and depressed. I was, too. He sent two letters dated February 22. His description of his dismal surroundings and daily routine included overcrowded living conditions, fights, and hemorrhoids. Charged by a deputy for two counts of aiding someone committing an in-house crime, he claimed innocence. Even in his dreams he gets no peace. In the second letter, he expresses remorse for his "foolish behavior" and for "forgetting the laws of perspective" during our visit and his first letter. He begs me to get him out.

What I had to shield David from and not give in to was my extreme guilt. Reading my son's words broke my heart. I helped put him in these awful situations. I was sure that a better parent would be able to find a better solution. My brain knew that he had made the choices that got him there, but in my heart, I was convinced that my failings as a parent played a larger role. Still, I had to remain strong and on course in order to get him into treatment. Fear drove me. I was convinced that if he were released and back on the streets of Southeast D.C., he would die there.

"December 25, 2002. My Dear Mom, I am wishing you the best on Christmas, and I wish I could be there to share it with you. Still, I know that I can be happy for what I do have and that is a great, loving family. I truly do feel lucky this Christmas. Merry Christmas, Mom."

February 22, 2003, Letter #1:

"Mom, I just got back from my visit with you. I feel very guilty. I did not want to make you feel bad. I am breaking down. The situation I am dealing with is very difficult.

"Let me try to make you understand. I am in a 15' x 20' area with 20 people living in it. There are 10 cells with two people in each cell. One person has a concrete bunk, the other is on the floor. At 8:00 a.m. every morning, we have a thing called 'lock out.' We are locked out of our cells for the day until 5:00 p.m. The idea is to prevent people from sleeping all day. It's a decent idea in theory, but they did not take into consideration how that forces 20 different criminal personalities to interact all day. There are only 10 chairs, so 10 people have to sit on either steel or concrete. Hemorrhoids are very common among inmates.

"The block is made of concrete. With the TV blaring daytime TV and people talking loudly, there is a sensational echo. I cannot escape it. It is impossible to read or write. Because we are locked out of our cells, tension among inmates is multiplied. A person cannot retreat to his cell if he wants to get away from someone. There have been two fights in the last two weeks, both ending with a puddle of blood on the floor.

"All day is spent in anticipation of dinner. Lunch consists of four pieces of bread and two pieces of fake cheese. It is not edible. When dinner finally comes, it is not enough. The entire place revolves around food. People with commissary are in charge. But in direct contrast, they are also in danger of being stolen from, or worse.

"At 8:00 a.m., lock out time, we wait for morning inspection where we line up against the wall. We are searched and our rooms are 'shook down.' They go through all of our stuff and throw it all around the room. Every day at 5:00 p.m. when the doors open, we have to clean it up.

"The classification system here is completely without reason. This block has people with charges ranging from driving on a suspended license to three people convicted of murder to another accused of molesting his son. Ironically, two of the three murderers are very nice guys. Car thieves are always jerks.

"The TV broke and a guy was messing with it. When the deputy came, someone yelled to stop it. I was sitting nearby, and she accused me of warning him. She charged me with two counts of aiding someone committing an in-house crime. I am going to have three people testify for me that it wasn't me but she has already said she saw me do it. She said I was clearly this guy's lookout. I may go to the hole. Right now I am forced to listen to a white guy, who thinks he is black, rapping at the top of his lungs.

"I am very strong and believe I can endure all kinds of punishment, but the pain here is constant. Last night I had a dream about a black guy who decided he would no longer take the treatment we receive. He decided to fight the deputies. He was beat down mercilessly by them but then got back up. They beat him down again, but then he got back up for more. I wanted no part of it. I started to analyze what the dream means, but it doesn't matter. I get no peace at all.

"I am not telling you these things to make you feel bad for me. I just want you to understand what I am dealing with. I know that you are OK with me being in jail because I am safe and sober. This is not OK. It is completely inhumane and uncivilized. It is conducive to violence. I did not mean to yell at you. I did not plan it. I have seen so many people come through here with charges the same or worse than mine, and they come and go. I know that I would not be here had it not been for that letter. I can't help but have animosity for that. Plus, my family's apparent indifference to what I'm dealing with. I know that it is not your fault. You just cannot understand what this is. I don't know what I want or what you could possibly do. There is no solution. I accept responsibility for the things I have done and know that I have acted horribly.

The fundamental problem is that this punishment does not fit the crime. Over a year in jail, then 18 months of rehab. Most people work their way up to long-term rehab. I know I seem like a cry baby, but I am in much pain.

"I want you to understand that I am not the same person that got released from jail last time. I have been through so much. I have learned so much. You have said several times that I will end up in Southeast if I leave jail. The idea of that is ridiculous to me. You don't know me at all.

"Mom, you have been very supportive during all of this. I love your visits and letters. Please, help me get out of this place. I don't know what you can do but this place is bad. I am prepared to work hard. Fix my life. Make amends. Do all kinds of wonderful things. Sometimes it just isn't the way I deal with things. I actually deal with this quite well. I am the best card player around. It's what I am dealing with. I simply must get out of here. I hope you will still come see me."

February 22, 2002, Letter #2:

"Mom, It has been a few hours since I wrote that [the above] letter. I realize that I was forgetting the laws of perspective. To you, I am probably some ungrateful brat who stole from his family and was completely selfish. You have supported me despite my foolish behavior. I am truly lucky to have you. I am just having a hard time accepting the length of this waiting list. Plus, the situation I have to live in until then. It is constant pressure. Even as I sit here trying to step outside of myself and relate to your perspective, I fall right back into mine. Even someone like me, who is aware of my thoughts, trying to control them is an amazing challenge. It is amazing how pressure can cause me to yell at my mother and try to place blame. This is a common coping mechanism. Then desperation got me to beg my mother to help me get out of this position. I do believe that you overestimate my ability to make something happen from here. A person definitely needs someone on the outside to get things done.

"I want you to know that I am aware that I am being foolish, yet I am having great difficulty controlling it. Wish me luck!"

IN THE HOLE

David begins his March 2 "looney" letter from the "hole," a six-foot square cell in solitary confinement. This letter is long and written over multiple days. Life in jail has worsened as troubles with the deputies mount and David becomes more contrary. He's still waiting for his appeal to be heard. He writes about solitary confinement, his time theory,* and he explains his method for escaping pain and finding his "happy" place.

"March 2, 2003. Mom, I was trying to give you a call tonight but the deputies here are complete jerks. One just made me angry. It was cleanup time. I was to clean up my cell. He handed me the mop. You know what, forget it. It's unbelievable and completely foolish. These deputies are psychotic. It's Sunday night, and I am still in the hole. They have not heard my appeal so I have not technically been in the hole. I have been on Administrative Segregation (A/S) and not Disciplinary Segregation (D/S). It's the same except I have been getting regular food. I'm fairly sure they will hear my appeal tomorrow. Then when they reject it (and they always do), I will actually start D/S tomorrow for five days. Plus, there will be no visiting for seven days, which won't actually start till I go on D/S. You could have come this weekend but won't be able to come next weekend.

"So, I will be in solitary confinement for an extended period of time. It is what I make of it. I have several magazines and books. I read constantly. They will take all of that away when I go on D/S. Reading soothes me. It takes me

---

* David's time theory appears prominently in his fictional story, "The Certain Eventuality: A Memory of a Time Yet to Come."

away. I particularly like magazines because I can read about so many different topics, people, and places. Sometimes I enjoy magazines more than most books. Plus, the beautiful pictures. I have been reading Outside Magazine. It's great. It's all about the outdoors and the sports people do. Rock climbers, kayakers, snowboarders, and skiers. They have the most beautiful scenes, and when I read about the athletes, it's like I'm there. It's nice. I have read two of them cover to cover and then again. I can leave this foolishness. I am quite content alone, though. There are two other guys in cells right next to me. I can't see them but we can talk through the wall. They try to start up conversations, but I would prefer if they didn't.

"I have made an important realization. It definitely applies here but I think it does in life too. When I am aware of time, I feel pain. When I occupy my mind, I go away from that pain. I am free from time. When I am reading or thinking good thoughts, I am happy. Although, generally, to truly be away, I cannot be aware of this. Eventually, I leave this 'happy' place and come back to reality. The pain is there to greet me, but I still can look back on the journey I just took and see that I was happy. I think it is a possibility that true happiness occurs only when we are not aware of time. The ultimate goal, I think, would be to fill my life with things that occupy me this way.

"I must not put myself in a position where I watch the clock. There is nothing worse than having a terrible job that makes eight hours seem like an eternity. Even if that were to take place, I think I have a counter to it. I started doing it when I was a Trusty back in May. It made me go off, away from the pain. Being a dishwasher (my job at first) can be painful. I would sing sad depressing songs to myself. It was amazing how it worked. I continue to do it, naturally, not on purpose. It's as if [in] embracing the pain, I fend it off somehow. It's a valuable lesson. You see, I was a Trusty. It's a terrible job, but the alternative is even worse. So I had to cope.

"By feeling the pain, truly embracing it, I realized that the pain isn't really that bad. The pain was mostly a state of mind. A bodily defense, to get me to stop doing the unpleasant thing that I was doing. My brain is an amazing thing. It will trick me into doing things it wants. Even if it is not in my best interest. To become aware of this and to be able to deal with it is an important obstacle. I must embrace the pain.

"Tuesday, March 4. All of that I wrote is good, but this is getting old. They still have not heard my appeal. They are supposed to have only five working days to decide. Today will be the fifth. It is now 6:00 p.m., and they did not show. Maybe the charges will be dropped. If they don't dispose of the charges (when a person originally gets them) in seven days, they drop them. I'm sure I won't have luck like that. It seems that luck has not been with me lately. Losing my Trusty position, the long waiting list, this. I know that luck does not actually exist, but maybe there is a force in the universe that causes bad fortune to spawn more bad fortune."

At this point in the letter, David wrote the following paragraph about transference of energy—he was obviously deep in his thoughts—then crossed out the paragraph when the reality of his situation brought him back to the letter.

"Transference of Energy:* Let's assume that there is a transference of energy from person-to-person that we perceive subconsciously, sort of like an electric current that passes from person-to-person. Not that we can read each other's minds, but we could perceive their state of mind. Then, if that were the case, bad fortune could cause a person's energy level to be off. This could cause a negative reaction with other people."

---

* A transference of energy returns in two of David's fictional stories, "A Brief Moment of Clarity" and "Through the Void Travels a Momentary Exchange of Perspective."

The letter continues:

"That was foolishness, I know. It was a passing thought that seemed interesting and worthy of writing, but when I put it to paper I realized how foolish it sounds. Even if that were the case, it would have no effect on the waiting list, or the fact that I am here in jail. Bad luck (or luck) does exist. It is a series of similar happenings, bad or good. We call this luck.

"I'm just rambling now. I have many thoughts that seem great but by the time I get them on paper, they are gone. Perhaps seven days in this cell is getting to me. It is only 6' x 6'. A perfect square exactly from my head to my feet, with a toilet and a sink. It grows more and more difficult to occupy my mind. I have nothing left to read. I have a book by Jean Paul Sartre, a French philosopher. He goes into that realm of philosophy that deals with politics. Not too fascinating. Plus, it's way above my level. Without my dictionary (they took it), I can't understand half of it. He also refers to Kierkegaard, Marx, and several other people I have never read. It's too advanced for me. So, I am left with my thoughts.

"I will go ahead and send this. I'm sure I will write more later, but I want to be able to start over. This one got a little looney. Take care, Mom."

THE POWER OF A SMILE

Many years later, David posted on his Facebook page the following about the power of a smile and how he chose to be happy in 2003 while he was locked up and in the hole at Arlington County Detention.

"It is amazing to me the power of a smile.

"When I was locked up, I had to do 30 days in the hole, solitary confinement. When they put you in the hole, they take everything you have. Nothing to read, eat, nothing. I was sooo hungry. But after a few days I realized that this was my moment where I could break, or I could rise above. Everything I ever had had been taken from me. Everyone was against me, and I could have just become angry and resentful.

"Something happened to me in the hole. I let go of all of my attachments. I realized that the only thing I had was truly the only thing I needed. My mind. I realized that it is not what happens to me. Rather, it is how I react. I also realized I have the power to control my reactions and to choose how I want to feel. I have the choice to be free, or I could be a slave to my resentments and insecurities. I chose to be happy. No other human will ever again have the power to take happiness away from me. If they want to be miserable they will have to do it without me. I do not allow myself to wonder what others think of me; this will drive me crazy. I am OK with myself, and that is all that matters.

"I have gotten my worldly life together, but that transformation I experienced in the hole has stayed with me. They could take it all away again and chain me to a wall in a dungeon, and I will still be free. You cannot imprison a man whose mind is free. We can choose to be happy regardless of what is happening. Sometimes I may have to force a smile, but it does something to me. It's like my mind believes it when I just smile. I become happier. It's kind of like working out. Sometimes I have to force myself to work out, but I always feel good after I do it. I have never once in my life felt regret after working out or smiling. So even when I don't want to work out or smile, I know if I do, I will be glad I did. That's a pretty good one. I think I'll post it."

JAILHOUSE GRIEVANCE

A quote from Benjamin Franklin opens David's March 6 letter. He's still in the hole and his appeal has been denied. Enclosed with the letter was the grievance he wrote defending himself against the Deputy's accusation that he committed an in-house crime, which resulted in him being sent to the hole. His grievance is long and detailed. He defends himself by quoting a rule from the inmate handbook, makes the case for why he should be given Trusty status, and describes being forced to eat the "loaf." When it came time, he decided not to file the grievance due to repercussions, and he didn't want more time in the hole.

"March 6, 2003.

'Dost thou love life? Then do not squander time, for that is the stuff life is made of.' ~ Benjamin Franklin

"Mom, do you like the Franklin quote? It was in one of my new books. I liked it. Another day in the hole. I got the letter about my appeal yesterday. Denied, of course. I keep coming across these moral dilemmas. I knew I should not appeal, but I felt that I was right. I just can't believe such corruption exists all the way up. What I learned is that it's not always about being right. Sometimes you have to just 'take one for the team.' I wrote up this whole grievance that I was going to file, but I'm not going to. I can't use their system to fight them. They will not let you win. No matter how right you may be. A person must wait to get out, and then maybe he can do something. By then, no one cares anymore. I just know not to ever come back.

"I sat up all last night thinking about my future. So much I want to do. I know that by going to this program [rehab], I will be able to get myself set up. I will have plenty of time to find the right job and the exact things I want to accomplish in school. Plus, I will have help from many different people and a new network of friends. Hopefully, positive people who are into cool things. I know I'll do well. Within an institution, I have always been successful. I fail when I'm out there all alone. I need to have a method, a system to work within. Under those conditions, I will excel. Bye for now, Mom. I will write again soon."

MOTIVATIONS VS. ACTIONS

David's March 8 letter explains why the deputy came and took him away in the middle of a visit with me. He finishes our conversation in this letter. He's troubled by my "apprehension" about his study of philosophy. I did get frustrated with all of his philosophical talk, which had nothing to do with being a parent with a "baby complex" as he accused me of in his letter. I also didn't give a damn what Nietzsche, Huxley, or Freud had to say. The least of my worries was that David would find religion. It just annoyed the hell out of him that I always brought the discussion back to his addiction to heroin. When he thought I didn't understand his motivations and I would respond with something like, "What's going to motivate you to stop using heroin?" He would get upset and agitated. He couldn't understand that all I wanted was for my son to stop destroying his brain and body with heroin. I admired his desire to be the "purest thinker" and a writer, or I wouldn't be writing this memoir to preserve his thoughts. I just wish he was here so that we could argue a little more.

"March 8, 2003. Mom, I just got back from your visit. They decided to put me on D/S the precise moment I was having a visit. I'm sorry about that.

"What I really want to discuss is your apprehension toward me studying philosophy. This troubles me. It seems that you are under the impression that I am, in some way, searching for a religion. You must understand that I am just trying to collect information. I told you about Nietzsche, because I was excited to get it. Today, I also read a thing about the life of Sacajawea, the teenage Indian girl who helped Lewis and Clark explore the Northwest. Another article, about the formation of galaxies, was very interesting.

"I find it amazing that, after all of the conversations we have had, all of the letters, you still cannot seem to understand my motivations. This is a key part where philosophy plays a role. We as humans seem to put way too much emphasis on the act a person has made. All the while neglecting to examine that person's motivations. For example, the husband has a wife who cheated.

He becomes consumed with the act, the fact that she did it, but he doesn't consider why. Has he treated her poorly? Perhaps it was a form of revenge, or perhaps she is just a tramp. All of these possibilities should be taken into consideration before he makes any decision on a reaction. But, he often fails to do that because he is consumed with the act. It is the motivation that holds the pure essence of an act.

"My motivations are to gain a better understanding of the world around me in its purest form. Not of common understandings that are based on some propaganda forced on society years ago and now accepted as a truth.

"You seem to perceive me as a perennial follower. That I am looking for a star in which to hitch my wagon. That is, in a major way, my fault. So often, since I was a kid, I let you believe that I was led into situations in order to spare myself the responsibility of the action I took. It was selfish but a natural defense mechanism for me. You were more than willing to accept it because you did not want to believe that your son was a vicious person. If we were all being honest, you would have seen that I was neither vicious nor virtuous. I was young and being selfish and foolish. Then I would use it to try and weasel my way out of it.

"You also seem to hold on to this age-old notion so common of parents about their children. You see, it seems that parents become stuck in a 'baby complex.' They knew their child when it knew absolutely nothing. They taught it how to read, speak, etc. Then, when the child becomes an adult, the parent doesn't believe that child could have gathered more knowledge, or specifically, different knowledge than the parent. The parent refuses to learn anything from the child and just nods proudly as the child attempts to express himself.

"If you truly knew me, Mom, you would be truly proud. Not just because I am your son, but because I am and intend to be a virtuous person.

"In conclusion, you don't have to worry that I will become some kind of Nietzsche follower. There was a time when I was very interested in getting to know everything I could about Freud. I read all about him and his ideas and came to the conclusion that he, in many ways, was a psychotic. I did retrieve valuable information from it that I use as part of my ultimate understanding. I am not going to become a member of any cult or follow some extremist into some nonsense. I also think you are concerned that I am looking to be some kind of preacher of the unorthodox, and I am going to go around embarrassing myself quoting fools and making outlandish claims. Ultimately, I just want to gain a pure understanding [that is] free from perspective and truly objective. I would like to be the purest thinker I can be.

"This may sound like foolishness but it is only a small part of the person I would like to build. You will not hear these things come out of my mouth in basic conversation. I mainly tell you these things because I believe you are capable of understanding them. Plus, I would like to put some of my ideas on paper, so I put them in the form of a letter to you. But your disapproving glares make me think that you haven't heard a word I've said. Let me know what you think."

OUT OF THE HOLE

David finally got out of the hole! His March 17 letter focuses on getting into a local treatment center.

"March 17, 2003. Mom, thank you for the letter and info you sent me. That is the kind of stuff I love to get. I'm just sorry that our visit had to be wasted on such a topic. I just hope I can get into [a treatment center] as soon as possible. Then I will be able to show you my true intentions. I hope you can send me more info, Mom. I know you don't know whether you can trust me or not. I must get out of this horrible place. Then I can prove myself. I enclosed the signed form for the bank account."

I received the following get well note from Dave when I was recovering from a hysterectomy.

"April 1, 2003. Hi Mom, They sent me this card with no envelope to fit it. Anyway, I thought it was nice with the pooch sacked out on the porch. His ears flop out on the ground like Patches's ears used to do.

"Well, I wanted to let you know how much I have thought about your operation. It's strange. I have never really thought of you as fallible in any way.

"It hurts me to think that you are in so much pain. I wish I had been able to visit you in the hospital to offer you some kind of solace. I hope you feel better soon, and I hope this was the right thing to do. Take care, Mom."

CHAPTER 5: 2003

DRUG TREATMENT

It seemed like forever ago that the Court ordered Dave to be transferred bed-to-bed from jail to drug rehab. Finally, on May 2, 2003, he was released from jail and went directly to Second Genesis,[17] a drug treatment facility in Maryland, where he stayed until February 2004. David was just shy of 30 years old, optimistic, and had a positive outlook about the future. He was also nervous and curious—it had been a long time since he lived on the "outside." This new phase in his life was an opportunity and challenge to overcome the beast of heroin addiction.

Second Genesis was welcoming and had an open door policy. David's treatment was divided into phases. As he progressed through each phase, I could visit the facility, meet with him at a designated location, and pick him up for excursions or when he needed medical care. Our new normal was to celebrate holidays and birthdays at Second Genesis. His brother, friends, and I often attended family days and picnics. I attended family counseling sessions with David. We could telephone anytime, so letters did not go back and forth as often as they did while he was in jail. Most of his thoughts and ideas during this time come from the journal he started keeping when he arrived at Second Genesis.

Upon entering Second Genesis, David was asked to complete a questionnaire about his drug use. He wrote in his journal that he didn't know how to focus his answers to the questions because, for him, using heroin and drinking alcohol were two different addictions.

ALCOHOL VS. HEROIN

"Some of the questions make me see that I had different addictions when it comes to alcohol and heroin. When I started using heroin, I almost completely stopped using alcohol. My entire addiction and behavior changed. I would lose control of myself while drinking, yet I could maintain some degree of control of my life. When I started using heroin, I wouldn't lose immediate control, but I lost control of my life. I'm not sure which one is worse. I don't want to act foolishly while drunk, and I don't want to destroy my life and body while getting high. Which one should I focus my answers on? The two topics are quite different. It's almost as if I was two different people."

David's approach to court-ordered drug treatment was, "say what they want to hear, endure, and get out." Even though he knew he was hooked on heroin, he repeatedly insisted that he could stop his dependence anytime he wanted. He loved heroin and no amount of counseling or family pressure was going to change that. David's goal was to learn how to live with heroin, not without it.

During David's first phase of treatment, contact with the outside world was limited. He could write and receive mail with no restrictions, but incoming mail had to be opened in front of a staff member to ensure that no contraband entered the facility. I was able to visit on May 9 to take him clothes and toiletries. On June 9, we received David's invitation to attend Second Genesis's family and friends gathering on June 14:

"Hi, Mom, I want you guys to come! Whoever wants to come can come. Bring some seafood. Can't wait to see you guys again!"

His brother, a couple of his friends, and I attended. It was a beautiful day for a picnic. We took food and sat out under the trees—just like "normal" people. Dave looked great. He was back to his normal weight, full of smiles, and happy to see us. I got big hugs. We took pictures. The only physical reminder of his drug use was the backs of his hands. His hands were big to begin with, but injecting heroin into them had left them permanently red and swollen.

David seemed to have adjusted well and had already made friends with everyone. Even now, when I say the word "but," I think of that summer day. Sitting around and talking with sober addicts was kind of tricky. I was talking to an older guy in his early forties, and every time I said the word "but," he corrected me. He said that in treatment they weren't allowed to say "but." The word "but" is a connector and indicates contrast. The program was to stay positive with no "ifs, ands, or buts."

Before long, it was wild and crazy at Second Genesis. David's July 14 letter describes a "guilt session" and the repercussions of having the "house" closed.

"July 14, 2003. Hi, Mom, Well, things are pretty wild in this place. Staff is really shaking things up. They set up this thing they call a guilt session. Everyone was told to write all of the guilt they had (guilt is any information you know about any rule infractions). Some people told all kinds of things. The staff already knew about many of the things. Then they put everyone in a huge circle in the kitchen—mind you there's 120 people here—put people in the middle and interrogated them. It was very tense the whole week and interesting how they got people to spill their guts. All kinds of things came out.

"We found out that one of the counselors had had sex with three different clients. He was fired. Another girl had sex with about seven different people. Some people were drinking. Almost every girl in here was having some sort of relationship with someone. The pressure on these people was so intense that about 11 people left. Everyone is in an uproar. People are nervous and fearful of being exposed.

"Right now we are in 'clinicals' or a 'closed house.' All of the regular groups and job functions have been suspended. They split everyone up into three groups. The people who committed serious infractions got what are called 'contracts.' They have no privileges, they have to wear stocking caps on their heads and a sign around their neck, they can't sit on soft chairs, and they have to do work all day. The next group of people, who are suspected of bad behavior or who have committed minor infractions, receive select privileges. The third group are people who are not involved in this stuff and staff believe are here to get treatment. I am in the third group. We get the most privileges, but we still can't use the phone.

"They took all passes so I don't know when we'll get another day out. Overall, it seems to be the most effective treatment I've seen since I arrived here. I will continue to follow the rules. It's really not very difficult. People make it difficult on themselves.

"At my six-month point, I will go to an interview at the transitional house, and I can start working. At eight months, I can move there. I will try to get the most out of this place and plan for leaving. That's it for now, I just wanted you to know that I am OK! I got your package. Thanks!"

By August, David was already thinking about what he would need when he left Second Genesis. Even though it was an overwhelming list, he was upbeat and positive. It was a sign of progress that he recognized the need for a plan to repair the damage he had done to himself, rather than his usual procrastinating—a giant step. Enclosed with the letter was a "Peanuts" comic strip that reminded him of our dog, Patches. I was optimistic and hopeful that David was finally on the track to recovery.

"August 2003. Hey Mom, I talked to my vocational counselor (the real good lookin' one you met), and I am hoping she can help me with the practical things I need to address. She seems to have access to the stuff I need . . . my credit report, birth certificate, social security card, and college transcript. [She can] get my passport back from the police and a couple more things. It's time to start working on a plan to repair the damage I have done to myself. When I was talking to her about it, she was concerned that I may become overwhelmed. She said she felt overwhelmed just hearing all the stuff I need. I'm gonna take it one step at a time.

"I'm starting to see some light and things will keep getting better if I keep doing the things I've been doing. You'll be amazed. These people think I am a responsible, hardworking, punctual, together person. Sometimes I think I'm just faking it, but I just keep doing the things I'm supposed to do. I hope I can keep it up. I write everything down and take care of things as I need to, instead of procrastinating. This is great practice for real life. I know I can do it.

"I hope all is well with you guys. Tell everyone I say Hi! Take care Mom!"

By September, David entered the phase at Second Genesis, during which he attended daily AA meetings outside of the facility and could also leave with a day pass. On September 14, he and I spent the day together so he could go to the eye doctor for new glasses. We also went to a movie, clothes shopped, and had dinner at a restaurant before I returned him to Second Genesis. We had a wonderful day, and my optimism grew that he was finding a way to live his life without heroin. The next day he wrote to me.

"September 15, 2003. Hi Mom, I had a great time yesterday. Thank you so much for being there for me. I am soooo lucky. I sent off the letter for my [college] transcript this morning. I LOVE this new organizer. I am using it right now. I can't wait to start school. I have only read a little bit of that article you gave me, but I get so excited about stuff like that. It's like when I would get a brand new Maxim magazine while I was in jail. I wouldn't even want to read it because I'd be so excited to get it. Maybe I want it to be so good and I'm afraid I'll be disappointed. I'll read more tonight. What a great title: 'The Futile Pursuit of Happiness.' I hope the article can compare to the title. I would like to write things like that someday. I will! You'll see! I find philosophy and psychology so fun.

"This has been quite a sociological experiment I have done for the past few years. I hope I can look back on this and see it that way. I have learned so much about myself and others. The future that I hope to have will attribute much to these experiences. I don't believe in fate, but maybe this is the route I had to take. Well, this was supposed to be a quick note to thank you for such a great day and the help and support you are giving me. I love you so much!"

WHY SHOULD I KEEP A JOURNAL?

Dave's entry below is taken from his Second Genesis journal:

"September 27, 2003. I was told that it might be a good idea for me to start a journal. It is fairly uncomfortable to me, but I can't seem to identify exactly why that is. Maybe I don't feel worthy of a journal, meaning that my life just isn't important enough, yet. For me, the real motivation for writing is the thrill that when I write an idea, it takes life and grows as I write. My life may not be worthy enough yet, but my writing and ideas are worthy, which will be the basis of this journal—ideas and thoughts.

"If I continue to keep this journal going, I could use it as a form of 'home base,' a place of pure understanding or 'realness.' I can then go back later and decide whether my idea or thought was actually ingenious or if I was just lost in a world of fantasy. Plus, it can be a place where I study my own ideas to find out exactly what I think. I have all of these thoughts, but I have trouble remembering them. I can write something, put it away for a while and then when I read it later, remember—that justifies this journal 100%."

BATTLES WITH THE COUNSELOR

David found a worthy opponent with his Second Genesis counselor, who made him feel threatened that he was going to lose power. For what seems to be the first time, David met someone he could not manipulate. He began planning tactics to battle with this counselor. He continued to fail, causing inner turmoil. David's frustration was obvious. "Family" referenced in his October 1 journal entry translated to David's Second Genesis "family" unit. Family units or groups were formed by clients in the same stage of treatment.

"October 1, 2003. I had an interesting day. We had a family meeting, which is always a very intense endeavor. I prepare tactics to battle my counselor. I usually fare well as a debater, but I cannot ever seem to come out victorious. His power is too great. It's not that he's so bright, he just uses his position to control the debate. He is sharp, though. His ability to intimidate causes me to falter. I have appeared foolish many times in these groups. My ultimate goal has always been to gain position and get into a place where I can have an element of control in my relationship with him. Unfortunately, I have failed. I think it is because my counselor is so self-absorbed; he simply doesn't care about his client's perception of him.

"When it comes to other counselors, I can convince them of what I want them to believe. I can gain position and control the conversation. I simply cannot do it against him. So, today, I went with a different plan. I was quiet during group, which is unusual, and when the spotlight came to me, I displayed the pain I was 'supposed' to be feeling. It worked quite well. The fundamental problem with my manipulation is that I actually feel the feeling I am pretending to feel. Then I have trouble turning it off. I was depressed all night.

"Then I talked to a friend here who is very insightful. I opened up about all these things. I told him about how my manipulations manifest themselves inside me and cause a reaction that causes me to falter. I also told him how I have a desire to explain how I am destroying someone, which causes me to lose sight of my objective. I don't like to look foolish and that can cause me to lose my angle. I know I must keep my objective up front. The end is more important than how I look now. I must accept the fact that I cannot beat my counselor, and I must stay quiet and move away from him. Give him the power he demands. I can use this experience, though.

"I can't battle people like him who have power over me. It causes me inner turmoil. In a position of equality, I could beat him, but reality demands that I cannot win. I must learn to choose my battles. I guess I do know how to choose my battles, but this one was thrust upon me. So, I must learn to accept defeat, comply, and take these people down from within, or retreat.

"I must remember that my capabilities will be with me as long as I can maintain my confidence. That is my primary weakness. Without confidence, I am powerless. When deemed powerless, I must retreat, regroup, and choose a new strategy. I will not progress without my power—when it slips, when the words don't come, when I become aware of myself—succumb, comply, and retreat as quickly as possible. Regroup and choose an objective strategy. Don't allow emotion to influence me. I must maintain objectivity. I have gotten myself in a position where I have forfeited all power."

PERSONAL ATTACK

In David's October 2 journal entry, he describes a personal attack from another Second Genesis resident. He gives no outward response to the attack, but on the inside, he's fuming.

"October 2, 2003. Today in encounter group, another client made a direct personal attack on me. He was talking in general and said, 'Now if someone has a blatant attitude like David, then I understand using encounter group.' I gave no outward reaction to it. I did feel the blood rush to my head, and my heart started beating, and I was angry and confused.

"After I thought about it, I have decided that my tactics must have been effective. You see, the last time I dealt with him he was using the tactics I had seen him use on other people. He uses direct intimidation. He's not very intuitive, but his tactics are generally effective. During the encounter, I was looking another way. I turned back to him, and he had his typical mean look. I said, 'Wow.'

"He asked what that was about. I said that he had a threatening disposition. This was, in any other situation, a powerful move. You see, all he has is this tactic, and I took his 'bullets.' He was not happy about that."

By October 14, David's tolerance for Second Genesis was fading and making him feel depressed as expressed in his journal.

"My tolerance for this place is growing weary. My friends here are moving up and out while I continue to suffer the consequences for my actions. I know that it is when I am at my weakest that I must be strong, but that is also the most difficult time to be so. I think of a friend whose patience is amazing, and that gives me an element of strength.

"I have just been reminded of the tactic I used in jail. To sing songs to myself that are extremely depressing. I think I know now why that works. I feel bad, but it doesn't compare to the pain being expressed in the song. That's why the depressing song paradoxically makes me feel better.

"Metallica: 'I have lost the will to live, simply nothing more to give. Emptiness is filling me to the point of agony. Getting lost within myself, nothing matters, no one else . . . I was me but now me is gone.' (Fade to Black[18]) So beautiful!"

David's treatment at Second Genesis was focused on learning alternatives to self-destructive behaviors brought on by drug use, as well as methods to stay "clean" (stop using drugs). Second Genesis's approach included teaching methods to deal with problems and to change attitudes and behaviors. He learned about "triggers" that bring back old and destructive behaviors. Internal triggers to use drugs happen when an addict feels lonely, bored, sad, or depressed. External triggers are the people, places, and things associated with drinking or using drugs. Learning about triggers was important for me, too. David's October 16 journal entry exemplifies learning to identify emotions and reactions.

RATING ANGER

"October 16, 2003. I had a disagreement with my new roommate. He gets on my nerves with his farting and obnoxious ways. I told him how I felt and he said for me not to talk to him. I told him I'll talk to whoever I want. I was fairly angry, about a 5. My reaction was (Behavioral) (Emotional), I felt disrespected (Cognitive). I wanted to disrespect him back (Physical). My heart sped up and blood rushed to my head."

TESTING POSITIVE FOR COCAINE

David had been at Second Genesis for six months when he relapsed and tested positive for cocaine. I was furious. I felt tricked and cheated by all the sweet letters, visits, and calls. I'd thought I had my son back! My disappointment with David's relapse was painful. I realized that the past few months had given me false hope. I lost confidence that treatment was getting David where he needed to be to stop using heroin. What I didn't fully understand then was how common relapse is for addicts, especially during first attempts at treatment.

David's October 27 letter is long and thoughtful and reflects my feelings in three major ways: First, David opens up and is perplexed about his situation. He cannot understand what he has become. Neither can I, especially now that he has relapsed. Second, he reflects back on a letter I sent to him that he said, "Took me through your emotions and let me really understand what you mean." I was glad to have him admit to understanding my feelings, but sad to recognize the internal debate of using versus normal that raged inside him. Third, he describes his inability to make a fellow resident understand why he should never try heroin and rightly compares his frustration to how I must feel about my inability to effect his drug use. A lightbulb moment.

Most important in this letter is his reaction to his statement to himself: "If I could just stay off drugs." Profound to Dave. Obvious to me. Yet, drugs are "dear" to him and the one thing he would protect with all of his strength. With this letter, I believed that David and I were getting on the same wavelength about his addiction. He knows, and I fear, that he may never be able to give up heroin, not because he cannot, but because he doesn't want to, or so his brain keeps telling him.

BIGGEST MISTAKE I EVER MADE

"October 27, 2003. Mom, I have been wanting to write to you, but I have been hesitant. So, I have put it off. I must let you know how I am doing even if you don't want to know. I am having a difficult time right now. People who were my peers are now moving up and out. I guess it's for the best, though. I am where I need to be. I don't really know what to say and have no profound ideas to relate. I can't understand what I have become.

"A young guy in here gave a seminar recently (that's when you tell your story and people give you feedback). He mentioned how there are drugs he's never done but has always wanted to try. I know he's talking about heroin, because he has asked me several times what it is like. I spoke up and said that the biggest mistake I ever made was trying heroin. Once you know what heroin is about, you will always know and can never turn back time and not know the feeling that heroin gives you. I pleaded with him, 'Please, don't try it.' I would give anything to give up the 'knowledge' of that feeling. I cannot. I guess it will always be part of me. I know that what I said didn't change anything. I just wish I could shake him and curiosity would fall out of him, but I can't. He will do what he will do.

"I guess that's how you feel, too. I'm sure you wish you could just shake me, and I would become right. It's almost like we care about others more than ourselves. I can give such good advice to others, but have very little desire to apply it to myself. I guess I think I can control myself. Isn't that a funny concept? I have never been able to control myself before, so why do I think I can now?

"Well, things are getting back to normal around here. I am working in the kitchen and have been really focusing on this problem I have. I feel like I have made more progress in the past couple of weeks than I have made the whole time I've been here. My counselor and I are now communicating openly (well almost, he's kind of difficult). We have developed a pretty good relationship.

"I am working the 12 steps. I am on step two. Each step is pretty detailed and takes a while. I then talk it over with my counselor. I am required to find a sponsor at an NA [Narcotics Anonymous] meeting. My counselor did not understand why I couldn't have him help me with it. I told him I just can't be completely honest with him. If I'm gonna truly deal with my issues 100% honestly then I need to be 100% honest. I can't do that with him. He may never let me leave! I also told him that it would be like trying to be 100% honest with a parent. It's just not possible. That's the whole point of NA. It's supposed to be one addict helping another. Someone who can help but won't judge.

"I think about your letter a lot. It took me through your emotions and let me really understand what you mean. It makes me sad that I caused you so much grief. I don't want to hurt you. I just want to live with you in my life and to be a good son. I want to go on ski trips, call you and tell you how my day was on a Tuesday night. I want to talk about the classes I am taking and things that are going on.

"I was outside the other night. It was very clear, and I could see all of the stars and the moon. So beautiful. The future I would like to have flashed before my eyes. The only words that could come out were, 'If I could just stay off drugs.'

"I hadn't noticed that another guy was nearby. Given my mindset, I felt like I had just made a profound statement. I expected him to respond with elated agreement, but he did not. As a matter of fact, he just said, 'Hmmm.'

"At first, I kind of resented his 'Hmmm,' but then I thought about it—what I said wasn't profound at all. It's totally obvious! Why couldn't I see that before? I have blamed my drug use on everything but avoided admitting that I need to make a commitment to stop using drugs. I guess I did that to protect the thing that I held most dear to me. To say that to myself would mean that I would have to believe it. To make a commitment to stop would mean that I would actually have to do so. I've never made that commitment. I must make an unbending resolution to never do heroin again. I cannot disguise my desires or I will act on them. I must take that step that I have (unconsciously) avoided taking. I must expose the things that I hold dear.

"I know that referring to my reservations never to do drugs again as 'dear' to me may sound strange, but in all honesty, they are the one thing that I would protect with all of my strength. They say that insanity is 'doing the same thing over and over and expecting different results.' Then another person said that it's actually, 'doing the same thing knowing what the results will be and doing it anyway.' Do you think I am insane? Maybe. I must go to bed. Good night, Mom."

PRIORITIZING FAMILY

On November 6, 2003, I spent some time with David. I took the morning off from work for a dental appointment. I was leaving the dentist and headed to work when David called my cell. He was at a Falls Church clinic for an interview to get county-funded health insurance.

I jumped at the opportunity to see him and swung by the clinic, which turned out to be a good thing because I was able to fill out a form he needed. With me there, he didn't need a notary. We also got to talk some. Talking with David could be difficult and this morning was especially difficult. I had to decide—was this a day to be understanding and compliant or a day to be tough and resilient? Oftentimes, I would walk on eggshells as I tried to say all the right things, but on this morning, I said what I thought. It wasn't so nice.

It seemed to me that David's attitude toward treatment had turned negative and turbulent. I was worn out, and my patience was exhausted, especially with his recent relapse. I was on the edge of believing that David's addiction to heroin was not on the road to recovery when he sat before me and exclaimed, "I'm just not ready to quit, Mom! You need to understand, all the excuses I've ever given for using heroin were lies. I'm just telling you the truth! I use heroin because I love it!"

He was trying to manipulate me into accepting his heroin use! How would he ever recover from heroin addiction if he literally loved it? I could only stare at him. If what he was telling me was true and not just frustration for his recent relapse and setback in treatment, I could not continue to be there for him.

I responded, "OK, glad you told me that, but you need to understand something, too. If you are not at a place in your treatment where you're ready to stop using, then you're on your own. I cannot continue to watch you kill yourself."

David opened his mouth and started to speak but I cut him off, "Don't even try to tell me again that I'm being silly. It's not silly, and you are killing yourself! If you can get back on track to stopping your heroin use, I'm there for you. I am not going to accept that you are giving up and going back to your 'dear' heroin. Damn your dear heroin! You aren't the only member of this family who needs support and love!"

I looked into my son's big brown eyes and had absolutely no confidence that my words had any impact on him. However, walking away wasn't so easy.*

In the following two excerpts from *Addict in the Family,* Beverly Conyers captures the addict's love not only for his drug but also for the addict lifestyle:

Excerpt #1:

> While everyone will experience the physical high of the substance, the high seems special for the addict. It is more powerful, more meaningful, and more profound. Certainly, many addicts quickly develop an emotional connection to their substance of choice. They are apt to use the language of lovers when describing it: 'It was what I was waiting for my whole life.' It was what I'd always been looking for.' 'Oh my God, I was in my glory.' 'I couldn't get enough of it.'

Excerpt #2:

> A heroin addict wrote, 'I love the low-down, dirty lifestyle that goes along with being a junkie. I love sticking needles in my arms. I admire the bubbly, red blood when it trickles into the syringe.' Another addict describes using, 'You sort of get addicted to the whole drug lifestyle, the process of getting drugs, how you get high, whom you get high with, what you do for money. It's so baffling, but it's more than the drugs. It's the whole process, preparing the needle, hearing the whoosh when it sucks up the drugs, cooking coke on the stove, shooting it into your arms, all of that. I love the way the needle feels.'

---

* David's character, Ike, in his fictional story, "Through the Void Travels a Momentary Exchange of Perspective," exemplifies an addict who loves his drug.

MEETING WITH THE COUNSELOR

In early December, I called Second Genesis and set up a session with David's counselor. During my last visit when I was standing in the hallway, I overheard a fellow resident mention David's girlfriend. I couldn't believe my ears. No mention of Circe had been made in calls, letters, or during visits. Yet, Circe had been visiting David, and all his buddies knew about it. David was proud to show off his lady. I could understand that. I could also envision all his progress going down the toilet. It became evident that David was playing us both for clothes and anything else he wanted.

David's counselor knew he had a girlfriend who visited. What he didn't know was that she had a history of using cocaine and heroin. It was a *big* no-no for a resident to have a visitor who they used to do drugs with. David's counselor said they had no idea she was a former drug user and he would put a stop to her visits.

When David tested positive for cocaine in October, he told his counselor and me, "On the day I was out with my mom going to the dentist, I unexpectedly ran into a friend, and he gave me the cocaine."

This didn't make sense. David had no opportunity on that day to unexpectedly run into a friend while I was with him. He would have had to strategically plan the meeting before I picked him up or after I left him back with the Second Genesis group at the designated meeting spot in Alexandria, which could have been a possibility. However, the timing would have been difficult.

David changed his story when I visited on Family Day, November 22, when he said, "Mom, I didn't tell you right about the cocaine. I didn't get it from a friend while I was with you. A guy at Second Genesis gave it to me when I got back that day."

I told David I didn't believe him and accused Circe of being his supplier. After all, cocaine was Circe's drug of choice. David screamed in my face, "NO! I didn't want to tell you I got the cocaine at Second Genesis, because I and all the residents would get into a LOT of trouble."

David insisted he had not met up with Circe and she had not supplied him with cocaine. He also said he had already told Circe not to visit him anymore. I didn't know what to believe. I dreaded the thought that the lies were starting up again.

David had been getting day passes more often than I realized to attend AA/NA (Narcotics Anonymous) meetings and other events. It wouldn't have been difficult to meet up with Circe or to get drugs. Getting cocaine at the treatment center was way worse than getting drugs on the outside, which would have been a good reason to change his story. Because of the information I provided to David's counselor, they closed the house. I got a very angry voice message from David when he learned about the session I set up with his counselor. David wanted nothing to do with the three of us sitting down together.

CLOSING THE HOUSE

David was really pissed at me. His December 13 letter explains that it wasn't only my call to his counselor that got the house closed down. There was much turmoil at Second Genesis, and the counselor I talked to had moved David to another counselor. David's letter makes light of his relapse and tries to assure me that Circe isn't going to be back in his life.

"December 13, 2003. Hi Mom, Sorry I haven't written sooner or called but things are kind of hectic around here. A lot of things are going on. Many people have left, used drugs, had sex, etc. They shut the house down again. I don't think it will last, though. When people do things we all have to suffer. I wasn't involved with anything so it won't affect me too much, except that the passes and phone calls have been stopped. My counselor moved me out of his family so he is no longer my primary counselor. He is the head counselor and had to reduce his number of primary clients. I got put with a new female counselor. I asked my old counselor why he would move me, because people who have major problems tend to get moved into his family. He said that I seem to be doing fine, and he's not too worried about me.

"With the exception of my relapse, I haven't gotten in any trouble here. I do know that you are not as satisfied with my progress. I wish I could make you believe that I am going to do the right thing. I am, but only my actions will prove that. I'm not talking to Circle anymore. I never really was, but she has been trying to get me back. She concerns me very little, but I know she concerns you a lot. I know you are worried she will wave some money and easy living in my face, and I won't be able to resist. I can, and I will. I know what she wants from me, and she won't get it.

"You must understand that I am lonely over here, and it is nice to have someone out there who thinks about and wants me, even if it is her. I don't need her, though. I should start going out looking for work in early January. That is what I've been waiting for. This place has not been easy. I'm in my eighth month and ready to roll.

"You have to understand, Mom, this is a behavior modification program. It is designed to expose my negative behavior so I can change it. That's the part I think you don't see. Often times by telling or having the truth revealed to you, it seems that I am no different or worse than I used to be. I am changing these behaviors, but it isn't easy. My plans remain the same, and I hope that I will have your support. It means so much to me. I am going to be honest with you and myself. I will finish this and move forward.

"They say this is a behavior modification program designed to get on your nerves. It certainly does. I think I will be better off having done this but it is soooo annoying. I am being patient but it is sometimes difficult. I'll call you as soon as I can. I hope to see you soon!!"

David's December 16 letter states that he wants to forgive and forget the call I made to his counselor. On the other hand, it's clear he needs help more than he needs to stay pissed at me. He's about to enter the conclusion phase of his treatment and is in dire need of an ID.

I had made the mistake of giving David his birth certificate and other documents when he and Circe appeared at my house unexpectedly one Saturday afternoon. In particular, he wanted to see the paperwork from when he was 15 and his foot was crushed. He angrily told me that I should have gotten more money for him. I explained that because his injury happened while he was on the job, the settlement was paid under workmen's compensation and I had little recourse for how much they paid. Because he only worked a couple afternoons a week and Saturdays, they paid very little. Maybe he thought he got some big settlement and I kept it from him. It was a nasty scene.

When David and Circe realized that there was no money to be made off his old injury, they left. Little did I know then that they were in the throes of withdrawal and desperately needed money to keep from being dopesick. Like everything else he owned, he later had no idea what happened to his birth certificate or any of the papers I gave him that day. It took some time and lots of paperwork, but I finally got him a new birth certificate without having to drive to Richmond, which was a small step considering all the other pieces David had to put together to resume building his life back.

"December 16, 2003. Hi Mom, First of all, I would prefer to not make a big issue out of this phone call you had with my counselor. Things took place the way they did, and I will deal with it here. I am going to be in the Conclusion Phase soon. That's when I go out to look for work. I need a birth certificate to get an ID and will definitely need an ID to get a job.

"I think they are gonna be sending me to DRS (Department of Resource Services); they help with people like me. For job training, they will buy me whatever I may need to start a new job; tools, boots, clothes—whatever I need. I'll be able to get bus and Metro passes also.

"A guy in here, who is also from Fairfax, just got a job at a law firm downtown doing office services. That's what I put down as my primary job prospect. I would love to work in that environment. Plus, I like being downtown. Putting myself in that environment will be helpful . . . positive career oriented people. Plus, I'm sure a place like that offers benefits, and he says he makes decent money. I need to put a resume together and to get a NOVA catalogue.

"I have so much to do. It's overwhelming and nothing seems to be working out. I need to make a plan and to get my credit report, college transcript, birth certificate, ID, and drivers' license, and I need to go and take that eight hour driving class. This stuff is frustrating, but it's about living life on life's terms. I just have to keep plugging away.

"Well, the house is still closed. It's tough when it's like this, but I have to keep my focus on the future. Sometimes it's easy to 'lose myself' in here and forget about the reality that awaits me. I am excited about the future but a little nervous. I hope it's a healthy nervous. I will make it work!! :)

"I hope all is well and everyone is happy. I'm sure you'll have a good time at the lake. I hope to see you guys soon."

As the holidays approached, David remained at Second Genesis. We stayed in close contact as he became more anxious to leave. In this last phase of his treatment, he had a lot of free time away from the treatment center. An indicator that David was using was his handwriting. If he was not using, his handwriting was relatively neat and readable. If he was using, his handwriting was hardly legible. David's December 16 letter was neat and controlled. His holiday greeting on December 24 was written large and scrawled across the page when he wrote:

"Hi, I just want to wish you guys a Happy Holiday Season!!! I am doing just fine, and I hope to see you guys soon. Sorry, I didn't have a card to send. Love, Dave"

CHAPTER 6: 2004

RECOVERY / RELAPSE

During January 2004, David called often when he was out for an AA/NA meeting or other activity. He was very frustrated that he wasn't being allowed to read the plan he wrote for leaving. He repeated over and over, "I am just so ready to leave!" Even so, he sounded good and was upbeat about getting on with life.

LEAVING SECOND GENESIS

After nine months, on February 12, 2004, David left Second Genesis and moved to a residential "sober" house in Merrifield, VA. He looked good—physically and mentally much better—like a strong and healthy young man eager to get on with his life. It had been a long time since he'd faced the outside world. His primary focus was getting a job in the next two weeks. His idea of a job at a D.C. law firm was not a good one given the proximity to where he bought his drugs. In late February, he started a temporary job working in office services at a lobbying firm in Rosslyn, VA.

One afternoon a few months later, David was with me and my future husband, Greg, running errands at the mall. When we got back to the car, David said he noticed a sign in the mall's barber shop window about apprenticeships. I said, "What a great idea! Why don't you go back in and apply?"

I could see that he wanted to but he was hesitant. Greg started teasing him about being a "stylist." He and Dave bantered back and forth good naturedly about the difference between a stylist and a barber. It took a lot of prodding and encouragement, but he finally went back in and applied while we waited in the car. He was thrilled when he was accepted and easily completed the apprenticeship program. A year later, David became a licensed barber, launching a career he would enjoy and practice on and off until he died.*

During the rest of 2004, it was wonderful to have David free to visit and attend family events, including a family picnic at his brother's house to celebrate David's 30th birthday. He helped me around my house with repairs and projects, and often stopped by for meals. The change in him was remarkable. Both of us steered clear of any conversation about his "dear" heroin. It wasn't long before he transitioned from the sober house to an apartment.

Getting out of jail or treatment is difficult. The mental and physical hurdles are stressful and scary for both the addict and their loved ones. Not only is the addict fighting urges to relapse back into using drugs, but continued court dates, fines, and outstanding warrants come rumbling back along with old debt. Those who love the addict live in constant fear of the beast's return.

David was making regular payments for the court fines, but he still had to deal with looming continued court dates and collection agencies. Prince William County issued a warrant in debt, trying to collect on $1,140 owed to a hospital from when he overdosed. It's not clear when this overdose happened, but his brother's address was on the warrant so it was probably before he went to jail in 2002. I sadly learned after David's death that he overdosed multiple times.

ARGUMENTS OF TRUTH & REALITY

Truth was a hot topic for Dave. He wrote in his journal that he wanted to "develop a test that measures a person's ability to perceive the truth." We no longer exchanged letters but emailed often. In the following email, David responded to an article I emailed to him about truth and reality:

"December 24, 2004. Hi Mom, Some fairly interesting stuff. Especially at first. The arguments of truth and reality have always been two of my favorites.

---

* In 2011, David's experience as a barber must have inspired him to write the fictional story, "The Man Who Played by the Rules," about a wimpy guy with an overbearing wife and kids.

"Nietzsche said that truth was to lie according to fixed convention. Which I take to be sarcasm, but it reminds me of the conversation we had in your kitchen, where I said men were required to lie about their true desires in order to be accepted by women.

"The other good one is reality. Kant said that we cannot ever experience true reality because we are bound by our perspective. I tend to agree w/ that rather than Hegel. But I do believe that certain enlightened individuals can achieve a more pure understanding of reality than others."

In January 2005, David resumed classes at NOVA. He was openly excited and optimistic about the future. So was I. Life was good . . . very good. In hindsight, it was during this time that David may have had a real chance to make recovery his last stop on the crazy addiction train. He continued to communicate regularly and was repaying his father monthly for loaning him money to buy a truck. David and I met weekly to play tennis, and we often had dinner together.

Although I didn't know it at the time, at the end of January, Circe was emailing David information about apartments to rent. On February 11, 2005, David became a licensed barber.

RAISING THE SHED AND HOPE

Mother's Day in 2005 is especially memorable. The shed at my mother's house had become dilapidated. After my dad passed away in 1998, my mom hired a lawn service so she didn't really need the shed anymore. But when the shed became an eye sore, it was time to replace it. My sister and I got our families together and made a plan to build a new shed for our mother on Mother's Day. The evening before, we demolished and carted off the old shed. Bright and early the next morning, new sweet smelling wood arrived and we all got to work. It was a beautiful and warm day as we measured, sawed, nailed, laughed, painted, and "raised" the shed. The new shed was a perfect place for my mother to pot plants and stow her gardening tools. My niece blessed the shed with the final touch of a hand-painted plaque that read "Nanny's Shed."

One of my favorite family pictures of all time is everyone scattered together in front of the completed shed as the afternoon turned to evening. My two strong and beautiful sons stretched out on the grass in front of the shed. Everyone wore big smiles after a day of hard work and a job well done. Burgers sizzled on the grill, waiting for hungry mouths to complete the day. After all we had been through, having a sober David with us, laughing and having fun was absolutely priceless. I was so very hopeful that David had forever beaten away the beast.

GOOD ADVICE

Although barbering was his primary job, during the summer of 2005, David started an eBay business selling various items such as razors, CDs, iPods, and clothing. He resumed classes at NOVA for the fall semester and joined "AdultFriendFinder" online. Circe was not happy about it. In David's September 27 email to Circe, he is upset with her for redirecting his email address on the site to her email address. What's most interesting about David's email is his advice to her about how to change her behavior.

"September 27, 2005. Email subject: Sneaky. Hi Honey, they sent me an email for you redirecting my email. That's fine with me. The last thing I'm concerned about is some stupid shit like that website. I haven't gone there since the first day I went there. Now that you have taken control of the account, you should be able to check my usage. So do that and stop being an accusing little jerk. Your routine of sneaking around in the morning so that you can check my email and phone is disgusting to me. I was hoping you would change, but that little psychotic glint has returned to your eye. The way you behaved Friday night was disgusting. You literally begged those people to be your friend and then went to the bar to try and find another friend. I put up with that shit, but don't think I don't notice. It is not appealing at all. Please just hear what I am saying and don't take it personally. If you can accept what it is that you're doing, then you will be able to change it; if you continue to deny it, you will continue to do it."

Circe emailed David back, saying that his words and actions were hurtful. Within a couple days, they were emailing fun stuff back and forth and had made up. I wonder if David ever looked back on that email and questioned why he couldn't follow his own advice.

RECONNECTING WITH OLD FRIENDS

When David was using heroin, he isolated. When he wasn't using heroin, he was good about keeping up with old friends. The following emails are from David to the childhood friend who wrote "A Childhood Friend Remembers" in the beginning of this memoir. She was now living in New York. David's October 20 email gives her his perspective of his past couple years, drugs, and being in jail. Not seeing this email until after David passed, I was surprised and disappointed to learn that he had distributed marijuana and cocaine. There was so much I didn't know.

> "October 20, 2005. Hi, isn't the internet cool? I don't know what to say in terms of catching up. I am just livin' and tryin' to make a dolla. My brother is in Florida with the hurricane coming. He says he's just gonna stock up and have a hurricane party. I guess I'd do the same. My father thinks he's crazy. I think it would be crazy to leave. You only live once!!! Plus, it's not like he's in some ghetto right next to a levy. He'll be fine.

> "I guess you've heard a similar message as others that I was in dire straits and some melodramatic cliché of a drug-addled deviant who was on death's doorstep. This is some people's interpretation of my behavior. I was in jail during our 10-year [high school] reunion, which would definitely give credence to these ideas. I won't deny that I may have lost my way, but it was in a different context. I will explain: In my relentless pursuit to avoid having a job or doing any kind of work that forced me to get up every morning or do some menial job that made me hate

my life, I took to some illegal endeavors. I began distributing marijuana to finance my intended carefree lifestyle. This was not very profitable, and I soon discovered the profitability of cocaine. Of course my self-control has never been strong, and I became my own best customer.

"Things evolved from there but not to the extent of this sad, sad picture that has been painted. I did have to go to jail for 2 years, though. That was simultaneously the best and worst thing to ever happen to me. Funny how life works that way, huh. I didn't have some realization to turn my life around, though. You see, this is the reason I believe people so commonly fail. I just grew up a little and decided that if I wanted to move forward, I would need to accept some responsibility. That was my real problem.

"I saw TC last Christmas Eve at Fast Eddies in Springfield. We had a couple of beers and started bullshitin'. Next thing I knew, we were both drunk as shit. I mean real drunk. I felt like shit Christmas morning. It's different for me now. When you spend so much time in a jail cell, you really think about your life and the people who have affected it. That's the sum of my ideas for now. Rock & Roll, David"

Dave writes to her again on November 3, sharing his thoughts about living in New York and relationships. In late December, David and several friends from the old neighborhood meet up for a reunion of sorts.

"November 3, 2005. You have painted a great picture of NY. You have balls and that is what it takes. So many are driven by their fears but you are taking the hero's path. That is good! NY represents freedom in my mind. It seems to be the place people go to embrace this real life without being bound by family and others like them who want to guide my life. It is a place to take total control, or maybe even sacrifice the need for total control, which is somewhat of an illusion anyway. You can fail or succeed—it all depends on you. The fact that I have had my mother nearby to fall back on has been almost crippling to me. I don't allow my mother to help me anymore. I pay for school myself, even though she would do it, I don't consult her about things when I am scared and want her to tell me that everything will be OK.

"I envision NY as the place where freedom and self-reliance converge. Really, NY is just a state of mind for me. It's not that I specifically intend to move there (I have no reason to); it's that I am now making happen what happens to people who move to NY. If that makes sense to you. Anyway I am proud of you and hope I have the courage to do what you are doing.

"I will respond to your relationships with this, which I have concluded from my own experience. For a healthy relationship to work, I must first have a true knowledge of myself. Then I have to remember that I do not own the person I am with. This is what starts the intense jealousy that causes relationships to become more about control than love. People are going to be self-absorbed and use the people close to them to get what they want. That's just the way it is. Unless you want someone who worships you, but then you will not respect that person, which is just as bad. I think it is best to just live my life and hope people are honest with me, but I must be able to stand alone. I think people are drawn to that, which causes me to not have to stand alone. That's the duality of life. To get what we want we have to honestly be able and willing to do the opposite. We have to be able to stand alone before we can stand with others.

"That's enough philosophical talk. Anyway I am probably not the best source of ideas on how one should live his life. Do you still talk to SC? I put his name in the search too but he wasn't in there. I would love to hear from him. I have thought a lot about him, DS, PM, BH, KT, not so much SB (he was a nasty little fucker), but I still love 'em all.

"Anyway, I have to go to class, I have two classes up at NOVA, which are two hours apart. I did that so I could study in between classes. It's helpful sometimes but most of the time I sit around with nothing to do for two hours, thinking how I'm such a dumbass for scheduling my classes like that. Anyway, this helped pass the time. In the immortal words of Paul McCartney, as interpreted by the great Axl Rose, 'LIVE & LET DIE.'"

32ND BIRTHDAY

In January 2006, David began a Spanish class at NOVA. His eBay business was rolling along, but he began to experience trouble with distributors, especially out of China, and he was getting complaints about his products. Circe was out of the country visiting family when she learned David was not being faithful to her. In March, she emailed him and said she wanted out of the relationship. However, it wasn't long before their roller coaster relationship resumed, although clandestine from both her family and ours.

It was a beautiful warm afternoon in June 2006, when friends and family gathered at Top Golf to celebrate David's 32nd birthday. We started our golf games and ordered food and drinks. The only one missing for the first two hours was the guest of honor. The first games finished, and we ordered another round of food and drinks. I avoided looking at David's brother, because I was sure he was thinking what I was thinking, and neither of us wanted to think it. I kept an eye on the parking lot and waited . . . and waited. Time inched along as an overwhelming sadness took the place of a happy celebration. The atmosphere of the gathering stayed jovial. Aside from a few comments on proposed reasons why David might be delayed, everyone appeared to ignore the fact that he hadn't shown up. I pretended to be unconcerned. But I knew. I didn't have to see David or hear what he had to say. Being late or needing a $20 bill are two of the many trademarks of drug use. If he showed up, I knew there would be no point in asking why he was late or in ruining the day with accusations.

David finally appeared in his shiny new convertible Mustang with the top down. He was full of energy and had a cheery smile. As he made his way through his guests, everyone slapped him on the back, wishing him a happy birthday and telling him how great he looked. David looked better than great . . . he sparkled. I gave him my best Mom smile and a hug as I looked into his bright brown eyes and he grinned back at me with a hearty, "Hey, Ma!!"

DIVORCE THE FAMILY

I didn't see or hear from David much after the Top Golf event. After a difficult conversation later in the summer, David sent me the following email in September:

> "September 8, 2006. Hi, I just want to send a short and sweet email to you. I want you to know that I have been a happy guy for the past couple years. I have been productive and well-rounded. I have felt that my family instills in me a great deal of shame and guilt because of my past mistakes. This is the reason I have tended to avoid you guys. I am not angry at all until you accuse me of being angry. Then I say all the wrong things. I have searched for the life I want to live and come to the conclusion that I want a family. Circe and I bought a condo in Reston, and I couldn't be happier with it. The only thing that has plagued me was my feeling that I had to lie to you guys. I will not live like that anymore. I am going to be successful and well-rounded, and I hope that I will have my family with me to share it."

As disappointed as I was with David's news, at least we were communicating and I knew what was going on with him. The best I could think to do was to remind him of good times and that my love was unconditional. I emailed Dave back and tried to stay positive:

> "It's good to hear from you, and I am glad that you are doing well. I will not continue to defend myself or others in the family who have given you unyielding support. Even if we aren't the family I had hoped we would be or the family you think we should be, you are stuck with us. No matter who you are with or where you are, I will always love you, try to do what's best for you, and care about what happens to you, even if you tell me that it's better for you to avoid us. Thank goodness we had about a year when things were good between us. I will especially remember those tennis evenings and telephone calls when you rattled on about what you were studying and reading and writing. I hope you haven't given up on completing your education.

"Then, of course, as a young boy so eager to grow up and live life, smart and quick as a whip, a talented athlete, kicking the dirt the few times you struck out or missed a high fly, sometimes giving me a hug so tight . . . That's what I think about when I miss you. I do not carry thoughts of shame or guilt regarding you, so there's no reason for you to do so. The important thing is that you avoid drug use, stay healthy, and are leading a productive and rewarding life. I am going to believe you when you say that you are doing all those things.

"It was not a total shock to learn that Circe is back in your life. Your behavior and attitude had changed toward us (me, anyway), so I had already begun to wonder, and then, when the same old arguments started, it became pretty clear. It was just a matter of you admitting it. In any case, she is obviously very important to you, and it is the right thing to finally acknowledge her. It's not fair to her not to. If she loves you, she will encourage you to have a happy and healthy relationship with your family and do her best to make us see her love and devotion to you. I would be greatly relieved if I could see that in her. The last thing she should do is allow you to divorce your family.

"I will follow your lead, and if the only way I can be a part of your life is to also include Circe, then so be it, I can do that. I will do my best to give her the benefit of the doubt that she is back in your life because she truly cares about you and is sincere in her agenda. At the very least, I hope you will keep in touch. The ball is in your court. You have the ability to set up the play, to determine a yokey-doke, a lob, or a clean, straight shot down center court.

"You aren't the only one making life's choices and moving on. Your brother is in the middle of a major move, and I need to make some decisions myself, so it behooves each of us to show caring, understanding, and support for what each needs to do to make their way."

David was not one to hold a grudge. He immediately emailed back:

"Hi, Mom, I think Reston will continue to grow. That is why I chose Reston. The metro is coming this way. Northrop Grumman is putting in a huge facility by the town center. Eventually from equity combined with my savings from work and eBay, I will have the capital to open my first barber shop.

"Reston has the nicest tennis courts I have seen. There is one right by my house that is beautiful. It has sliding nets in between courts, lights, and benches, and they are in excellent condition. There is a Reston Tennis league. I am thinking about joining it next year. That way I can get into tournaments. They also have mixed doubles tournaments. I was thinking that we could team up and enter the tournament.

"I want you to understand that I have relieved the strain of my narcissism. I am not on edge, drugs, or depression. I am just living happy. I have goals, but they aren't desperate necessities. But, the most important thing I am relieved of is the need to explain myself and justify my actions. I believe in myself and don't have to convince anyone that I know what I am doing. I know that I do. Eventually we will all accept each other and be happy!"

MARRIAGE AND A TRUE STORY ABOUT A HAIRCUT

Most of our communication throughout the rest of 2006 was by email or telephone. I found out a few years later that David and Circe were married in a civil ceremony at their condo on December 12, 2006. In late December, David emailed a contract to his father, who was loaning him $5,000 for the purpose of capital for a business venture, to be repaid monthly. His dad emailed back that the contract looked fine and told David he hoped his hand was better. I was reading this email after David died, and I wondered how David hurt his hand. Then I found a Facebook message David sent to a girlfriend in March of 2012. The girlfriend was unhappy with her hair and asked David if he would fix it for her. David responded with a factual story about cutting another girlfriend's hair:

"I want to tell you a story. An ex-girlfriend wanted me to cut her hair, so I did. She monitored every cut I made. When I finished, she was messin with it and said it was right. I said, 'Good, I'm glad I did it right.'

"She said, 'Well, you really didn't do anything, cuz I told you what to do.'

"I said, 'I really don't care about getting the credit. I just want you to be happy with your hair, honey, and it really doesn't matter who gets the credit.'

"Then she went into the bathroom and started to style it. She was in the bathroom for about 20 minutes and all of a sudden I could hear her screaming through the bathroom door. She came out and started screaming, saying her hair is ruined and that she hated me.

"I said, 'Hold up now, first of ALL, the way you are yelling at me is completely unacceptable. Tell me what the problem is and I will see if I can fix it.'

"She screamed back in my face, 'Fuck you! You will never touch my hair again and you will never touch me again!'

"Then she started telling me that I was a loser and a stupid dope fiend. I wasn't going to listen to her shit, 'Fuck this, I'm leaving. I'm not gonna sit here and listen to you talk to me like this.' I headed for the door.

"She ran in front of the door and wouldn't let me leave. So I went into the bedroom. She kept yelling at me and putting me down while fuckin with her hair. She said I gave her a mullet. I said, 'Look, cutting hair, like everything, is not a magic trick. Let's fix the problem and get it right.' But she didn't want to do that. She just wanted to be a bitch.

"She continued with her crazy shit talk and I said, 'Fuck this, I'm packing my shit. You got the wrong motherfucker if you want to be with someone you can talk to like you're talking to me.'

"I started packing my clothes and putting them in suitcases. I carried two of the suitcases, opened the sliding door of our condo and put them on the patio. I closed the screen but left the glass door open. I went back into our bedroom and packed two more suitcases with her screaming and calling me a loser the whole time. I stopped responding to her and that made her even madder. Finally I said, 'I'm fucking leaving you, and I don't care what else you have to say. You have gone too far, and I am done.'

"I had the suitcases in my hands when I got to the screen door. I set them down to open the screen door as she said something really fucked up, and it fuckin pissed me off so much I went to punch the screen. I swung very hard and had no idea that she had closed and locked the sliding glass door. I guess she was trying to lock my stuff out there so I couldn't get to it. I will never know the reason why she closed the glass door, but I slammed my fist into the glass door—it hurt sooooo fucking BAD.

"Of course, I had to go to the hospital. They set my hand and put it in a cast. She was all apologizing and shit. I didn't give a shit. I was so done with her. I was very cold and mean to her. She continued apologizing, and I didn't want to hear it. She thought I was mad because I broke my hand and blamed her for it, but I didn't blame her for my hand. She didn't know I was gonna punch the screen. Hell, I didn't know I was gonna punch the screen. I tried to be very clear about why I was so angry.

"I told her, 'After we get home from the hospital, I am grabbing the shit I have packed and I'm leaving. I'm not leaving because of my hand, I'm leaving because I will not be talked to like you were talking to me. I don't care what the situation is, I simply do not believe that is the right way to communicate and since you seem to believe it is, and since a relationship requires communication between two people, these two people have to have some sort of agreement on how they intend to communicate. I will not yell and scream like you fucking do. If you want to do that then you have to find a man who also communicates that way, but I promise you . . . I will not do it!'

"We got home, and I went to a hotel for a couple days. She called me up being all sweet and I agreed to come home. We looked at her hair and figured out what she believed was the problem. The layers I put in were a little fucked up. So I just took the back up one more inch and the layers looked great. Then we dealt with what she had called a mullet. I changed the shape some and brought it up a little more and her hair was great and she loved it. About three months later, she had the nerve to ask me to cut her hair again, but I said, 'Hell no, Baaaaabeeee! I love you, but I am not putting myself in that situation again!'

"Anyway, my point in telling you this story is to tell you a couple things. First, I'm not a stylist, I'm a barber. Second, and most importantly, if you are going to be mean and spiteful and want to communicate with me via arguments while you generalize me with all other guys, then I'm not the guy for you. I think you need to learn that a boyfriend doesn't have to be an enemy or someone you are always having these ups and downs with. Breaking up, then making up, then loving each other, then hating each other. I think this is the only kind of relationship you have ever had. I think it is time for you to learn that that is not what a relationship is supposed to be. That is never how mine are and why I am still close with all my exes. I want to still see you and will help you with your hair if you want."

WEDDINGS / TREATMENT / LEARNING TO COPE

During the first few months of 2007, David stayed occupied with barbering and running his eBay business. He and Circe seemed happy at the condo and said they wanted to invite me over for shrimp on the grill. The shrimp dinner never materialized, but I saw David periodically for dinner out or a movie. We continued to communicate mostly by phone and email. David's eBay business slowly came to a halt in April after more problems with distributors, product quality, and lack of payments.

The year 2007 was the year of weddings. David's brother, Bill, was due to get married in April. As one of his brother's two best men, David was actively involved, in particular, planning for the bachelor party. Held in the Florida Keys on a beautiful beach, the wedding was lovely. David, Circe, my niece Dawn, Greg, and I stayed in a house on a canal where we hosted the rehearsal dinner and party. It was the perfect setting for a fun evening as we gathered with friends and family. The night before Bill's wedding was the last time I slept under the same roof as both my sons.

On the morning of Bill's wedding, watching Dave give the groom a haircut outside on the patio warmed my heart. I could see that David was not quite right, but I ignored it. If the beast was beating up on him inside, he kept it to himself. On the outside, he was a fun, helpful, loving, and excellent best man and brother. He was agreeable with all the plans save one . . . David told his brother, "I will not wear flip flops at the wedding unless my toes grow back!"

My husband, Greg, and I married a few months later in September. By then, David had relapsed again into active heroin use. In May, Circe was frantic when she called me to say that David had taken her car and was on his way to D.C. to buy drugs. I was not surprised. The signs that David was using heroin again had been there for some time, but of course, he denied it. On my wedding day, I would have liked nothing better than to have walked down the aisle between my two sons, but I couldn't risk that David might be a no show or show up bleary-eyed or dopesick. As it turned out, all was fine. David was helpful and caring on the day of the wedding. He attended all of the wedding festivities with Circe. I was fine, too, and managed to deny the beast in the room as long as I ignored David's red-rimmed, glassy eyes set behind dark circles.

COLEMAN INSTITUTE

Dave and I didn't communicate much during the rest of 2007 and most of 2008. Emails show that he discovered online pharmacies, collection agencies were calling, his bank account was shut down, he was denied new bank accounts, and he searched online for information to declare bankruptcy. In April, he was arrested in D.C. for attempted possession of heroin, and his drivers' license was revoked. On September 2, 2008, he gave his probation officer a dirty urine sample. He was back on the crazy addiction train to nowhere.

After failing the urine test, Dave called me and said that he had relapsed. He asked if I would take him to the Coleman Institute in Richmond, VA, for a Naltrexone[19] implant. With the implant, the Coleman Institute offers accelerated detoxification from painkillers, methadone, Suboxone, heroin, other opioids, and alcohol.[20] David was given explicit instructions to follow prior to the implant procedure. He could not use any drugs, specifically heroin, within a certain number of days of the procedure.

During the 1½ hour drive to Richmond, David and I discussed the procedure and the importance of not using heroin prior to getting the implant. David *adamantly* assured me that, as instructed, he had not used heroin. He *lied*. Mr. "I Can Handle It and I Don't Need to Follow Instructions" used heroin the day before we went to Richmond.

We left the institute right after David got the implant. There was no requirement to wait around to ensure that he was not going to have a negative reaction. It took us about five minutes to walk back to where we parked the car and another 10 minutes to drive through town to the interstate. Five minutes later we were back on I-95 headed home when David was "sent" into acute opiate withdrawal. When I say "sent," I mean it was like a bullet hit him.

I was driving, and David was in the passenger seat. Suddenly and without any warning, his whole body jolted up and out of the seat. I was driving 65 miles per hour, surrounded by four lanes of speeding cars and trucks. I could not just pull over. I didn't know if my son was having a seizure, a heart attack, or an allergic reaction that was going to kill him right then and there. I started to sweat and shake all over. I gripped the steering wheel and tried to steer toward the shoulder of the highway, while at the same time watching my son clutch his body and scream out in excruciating pain. David crawled over the console and fell into the back seat. He knew what was happening to him and shouted at me, "Just drive, Mom! Don't pull over! Don't stop! I can handle this. I just need for you to get me home!"

When I felt sure David was not going to die, I was indescribably *pissed*! I lost every ounce of compassion and screamed at him in the rearview mirror, "You promised me, David! You promised me in this car less than two hours ago that you didn't use! This is so typical of you, always thinking Mr. Special David doesn't have to follow instructions or do what he is told to do. You got the warning! How could you do this?! Always pushing the buttons and testing the limits—you blatantly lied to me and put me in the middle of a very dangerous and terrible situation."

There have been few other times that I lost it with him like I did on that day. For the rest of the drive, David moaned and cried out as he twisted and turned his body and struggled to find comfort, balled up in the small back seat of my sedan. I dropped him off at his condo. I didn't even see to it that he got settled. I was still fuming and shaking when I arrived home.

The implant worked for two months just as the Coleman Institute promised.

Once the implant wore off, David immediately started using heroin again and relapsed. In December, David asked if I would take him for the three-month implant, and we made a second trip to Richmond. This time, David did not have the extreme immediate reaction he had after the two-month implant; however, he wrote in a letter that he (again) lied to the doctor about being clean. When the three months were up and the implant wore off, David once again immediately started using heroin and relapsed.

3CS / REALITY / SERENITY PRAYER

I was angry and disgusted with David, but I was even angrier at myself because nothing I did or said affected his behavior. Like many loved ones of addicts, I both loved too much and failed at tough love. I learned about the 3Cs at a Nar-Anon meeting:

> I didn't cause it.
> I can't control it.
> I can't cure it.

I also couldn't accept it. After nine years of heroin addiction, we were still barreling down the tracks to nowhere.

I knew my son loved his family, but the cruel reality was that he was controlled by heroin. In fact, the real reality was that heroin controlled us all. There was *nothing* I could do to make David stop using heroin or to change his behavior. All I could do was change my reactions to his actions and be there to talk or to take him to detox or treatment if he asked. I hadn't given him money or paid any of his expenses for years. At this point, it was rare that we even met up for a meal. If anything, I felt like a lousy parent because life goes on. There were times when I would be on a trip or out with friends, and I would catch myself laughing or having fun. I would immediately feel guilty.

Addicts are masters of manipulation and adept at putting guilt on others as they travel through the phases of addiction. It takes courage to say "no" when someone you love needs money, a place to sleep, or even groceries. But, a firm, loving "no" has power. It is a first step to separating the anger and hurt, and to loving and supporting your loved one without being controlled by the addict's drug yourself. I had to guard against becoming addicted to the addict.

To gather strength, I often found myself repeating the Serenity Prayer:

> God, grant me the Serenity to accept
> the things I cannot change,
> the Courage to change the things I can,
> and the Wisdom to know the difference.

This meant sometimes losing communication with David for long periods of time. Not being in communication was brutal. During those times, I just waited. Eventually something would happen to bring about reconnection.

ENABLING

It wasn't clear when Circe officially moved out of the condo that she and David bought in 2006. After she left, she continued to pay the rent, utilities, and home owner dues. Even though Circe constantly threatened David with divorce, she said she would not divorce him because, if she did, he would not have health insurance. I did not know or ask where she went to live, but I soon found out that she was living with another man.

After David's funeral, a friend of Circe's told me that Circe moved in with her "boyfriend" so that she would have enough money to keep supporting David. Another friend told me that Circe kept supporting David out of hate, because he'd gotten her addicted to heroin and ruined her life. I do not know the truth regarding either of these claims. But I do know that supporting him and paying for his health insurance was not helping him. David needed all the crutches taken away if he was going to stand strong and free himself from addiction.

Rule #2 from "14 Rules You Must Never Break when Dealing with Addiction"[21] addresses the dangers of enabling:

> Don't be an Enabler: Enablers might believe they are helping when, in fact, they are contributing to a person's self-destruction. As hard as it might be for some people to accept, an enabler actually makes it possible for a person to continue to abuse drugs or alcohol. Enabling can come in an infinite number of variations. Instead of insisting a person get professional help, an enabler might let a drug-using person who is falling out the bottom live in the home, may help him find a job, lend him a car (which he uses to go get drugs), or bring food over to his house day after day.

Bobby Newman supports this rule and writes that giving/loaning money, providing a vehicle, paying bills, or finding a job for an addict are the most common ways families enable their loved ones to continue using drugs. Mr. Newman goes on to say:

> Don't be an Enabler: Doing so only makes it easier for the addicted to continue their destructive behavior. Being soft on the addict is about the most significant mistake people make. You are never going to love an addiction away (Newman, *Secrets*, 2020. Kindle p. 44).

JAIL VS. TREATMENT

According to Washington, D.C.'s automated probation records and comments by David's probation officer, on March 17, 2009, David was placed on daily sanction reporting due to his positive drug tests. He had been testing positive for drugs from March 10 to March 26. On March 26, he provided proof that he was receiving both outpatient drug treatment and mental health treatment.

David and I didn't have much contact during early 2009. When I talked to him during the week of March 16, I recognized he was in terrible shape. I suggested he get another implant and offered to pay for it. I said I would drive him as long as he was clean when we went to get it. He declined my offer and said, "I will never have an implant put in again. Withdrawal after the last implant lasted five days. I was very sick, and I'm never going through that kind of pain again. I've signed up as an outpatient for the Comprehensive Addiction Treatment Services (CATS) program at Fairfax INOVA Hospital. I've also seen a psychiatrist and started on the medication Prozac."[22]

On Saturday afternoon, March 28, David was arrested again in D.C. for possession of heroin, possession of drug paraphernalia, and failure to obey the officer. David sat in jail the rest of the weekend. His court-appointed attorney, Circe, and I attended court with him on Monday afternoon. The judge made it clear that she did not want to release David, but because he recently made the effort to get the Naltrexone implants—giving him five months clean—and had enrolled in the CATS program the week before, the judge was open for discussion and negotiation. Circe approached and pleaded with the judge and promised that, if released to us, David would go directly from the courthouse to detox and then to a 28-day treatment program—one of the best in the country—courtesy of her employer's health insurance program. As David's case was being heard, Circe spoke by phone with the health insurance provider, confirming they would cover the cost of treatment.

Horrible as it was, I was sadly of the mind that David should face the music and go to jail. I did not have an ounce of faith that another treatment facility—no matter how renowned—was the answer. However, I stayed quiet. Before we could leave the courthouse, Circe's first promise that David would go directly from the courthouse to detox fell into my lap. Once out of the courtroom and away from the judge, Circe started to panic. It was late and her boyfriend was calling and wondering where she was. She had to get home, pronto! I delivered David to the detox unit at Fairfax INOVA Hospital that night as promised.

A couple days later, David's attorney sent me an email to let me know his case would be going to community court, which was a special court set up to adjudicate misdemeanor cases. If David had not had extensive or violent priors, he could have qualified for a diversion program (drug treatment, community service, etc.) to get the case dismissed. But because David was on probation at the time of his March 28 arrest, there was a chance he would not qualify for a diversion program. She also informed me that, because David was arrested while he was on probation, there would most likely be a "show cause" hearing soon and that the judge for that hearing would most definitely give David every bit of 150 days to serve if he did not follow through with Circe's promised treatment plan.

As frustrated as I was with David, I was more frustrated with his wife and her need to control him. It happened time and time again that Circe would give David every material thing he asked for (even after she left him), but when he messed up and needed drug money, got locked up, or was discovered with another woman, she would call me scared and sobbing that she didn't know what to do. Before her tears could dry, she would be searching the want-ads for a new car to buy him or for their next place to live when they got back together.

For years I encouraged Circe to leave David, not only because her actions enabled him to keep using heroin but also because he treated her terribly. They had a codependent and turbulent relationship that erupted often. Although David's addiction was a huge problem, he couldn't keep his hands off other women. If heroin was his physical addiction, sex was his emotional addiction. When asked during treatment, "Have you ever substituted one addiction or compulsion behavior for another?" David answered, "Yes, heroin for women."[23]

David expressed his "trouble" with women in a Facebook message:

> "Yeah that is what I meant by new addictions. Women. I gotta slow it down but I am having trouble. I just wanna fuck em all. Gettin' too old for this shit. Still doin it, though. Seems like I am always hooked on something."

Circe always circled back to David, regardless of whether he was using heroin, screwing other women, stealing from her purse, or screaming obscenities in her face. She would give him a shitload of grief first, but she always went back to him. It was pathetic to witness their behavior. David let her control him.

On his second day in Fairfax detox, I attended an evening family meeting with him. I had hoped Circe would attend, too, because it focused on enabling and codependency, but she said she could not be there due to a work commitment. David agreed it was a good meeting and promised to give Circe a copy of the handout. Even though David and I had sat together in these family meetings multiple times and had already heard and learned most of what was said, it gave us another opportunity to fight the beast together, or so I thought at the time. But by April 2009, it was all up to David. He was in his 10th year of using. Was it still a matter of his wanting to stop? Or was the dopamine in his brain so diminished that any ability to stop was gone?

David wrote in his journal about his second day in detox, unfortunately not as a positive outlook for recovery from heroin addiction but to keep from going to jail.

"April 1, 2009. Second day in detox. Feel good, thanks to Suboxone. Mom came to visit. Got a letter through her from new lawyer that says I am definitely going to be violated. NOT good at all. My only hope is to completely give myself to the idea of a treatment program. Then, maybe, I could keep from going to jail. WE SHALL SEE. I feel I need this anyway. I have lost my way and need to find it again. I believe this to be the correct path. Forget work and anything else. I need to find my way."

David was receiving Suboxone to help ease withdrawal and he was feeling better. He was saying all the right things. Was I convinced that this detox would be any different from other times in detox? No, but unlike other times when I'd taken David to detox, he hadn't walked out yet, and, as he promised the judge, he remained committed to attending a 28-day in-house treatment program. David was well aware that, if he didn't go for treatment, he was going directly to D.C. jail. His attorney encouraged me and Circe to attend an Al-Anon group meeting and recommended the book, *A Beautiful Boy*. I had already read it. Circe promised she would read it.

David stayed for the full seven days of detoxing at Fairfax INOVA, got things in order with his probation officer, and notified the barber shop that he would be away for the next 30 days. David, Circe, and I had dinner the evening before he left for the Hazelden Treatment Center in Center City, Minnesota. At the restaurant, I felt like I was sitting across from a stranger. The past several months of heavy heroin use had left David thin as a rail, probably 30 pounds lighter, and worn out. His hands shook as he sugared his tea and he constantly squirmed in his chair. This past drug binge had indeed beaten him up. He was anxious and on edge but resolute that he was done with drugs. He promised us that this last drug binge and arrest put a permanent stop to his heroin use, and repeated over and over that he couldn't physically do it anymore. Circe was ecstatic and in her element for saving the day and getting David released from court so he could go to the "best" treatment facility in the country.

I could only hope Hazelden's 28-day treatment program would give him the foundation and desire he needed to stop using heroin... to *want* to stop using heroin.

On April 8, I sent a short note to Dave before he left for Hazelden:

> Dave, I wish I had some magic words to send you off with. Words that would snap you back when urges plague you, when your brain defies you, when confidence eludes you, and old habits mask contentment like house pants and warm slippers on a snowy night. But all I can do is tell you that I love you. I'm here if you need to be reminded of who you are and who you aren't, and to replace evil voices that think they can rule your soul. I can listen, too. Please keep in touch while you are away. I've really missed you these past few years.

Flying out to Minneapolis was a giant step. David was apprehensive but also relieved to go—the treatment center was certainly better than D.C. Jail. He flew out from National Airport on Thursday, April 9, 2009, and began 28 days of what was promised to be the best intensive drug treatment available.

HAZELDEN

Each time David got locked up, he promised himself and me this lock up would be his last, and this new stint in jail would give him time to concentrate on getting clean and staying clean. He often questioned himself: "What happened to me?"

Each time David attended drug treatment, he again promised himself and assured me he was going to work hard to make that treatment program his last. He would say he was grateful for the opportunity to attend treatment and would do everything he could to stop using heroin.

Going to Hazelden was no different. David was adamant he was going to get clean and stay clean this time. He filled out the following drug screening inventory when he entered Hazelden. The questions required a yes or no answer. David answered "yes" to all the questions, which have a numerical rating from 1-39. He scored a 39, which is the severe level and an indicator that he was dependent on drugs. His comments follow the questions.

HAZELDEN'S DRUG SCREENING INVENTORY

1. Has your drug use affected your ability to take care of your responsibilities (e.g., affected school/work performance or household duties)?

2. Have you used drugs in situations where you could have been physically hurt (e.g., driving under the influence)?

3. Has your drug use resulted in problems with the law?

4. Have you kept using drugs even though it caused problems with family, friends, or other people?

5. Have you had to use larger amounts of a drug to get the same effect as before?

6. Have you experienced withdrawal symptoms (such as shakes, DTs, sleeping problems) or used drugs to make withdrawal symptoms go away?

7. Have you used larger amounts of drugs or for a longer time than you meant to?

8. Have you often wanted to cut down on your drug use, or tried to cut down and couldn't?

9. Have you spent a great deal of time getting, using, or getting over the effects of drugs?

10. Have you given up important activities because of drug use (e.g., given up work-related activities, doing things with friends, or hobbies)?

11. Have you kept using drugs even though you knew it could make you more physically sick or emotionally upset than usual?

DAVID'S COMMENTS ON THE DRUG SCREENING QUESTIONS

"I look at the numbers, and I know exactly how it got like that. First, I was experimenting with a substance that I thought I would be able to enjoy. I was aware of the dangers. Everyone has an image in their mind of a junkie. It was my arrogance that told me that I was too good to reflect that image. The thing is, for me, heroin gives a feeling like no other drug. The more I use it, the less other things matter to me. I could see myself spiraling downward, but I didn't care. At some point, I didn't even care what I looked like. I told myself, who cares what people think? I am the smart one. With heroin, I get to live on a puffy cloud and everyone else can kiss my ass.

"Problem is, no matter what I did, I couldn't stay on the cloud. The comedowns got more and more painful and it became more and more difficult to get on that cloud. Some days I would. Some days I wouldn't. The days I didn't get there were so terrible. I am not even talking about withdrawal—I was just so preoccupied with the cloud I could not stand anything else. I eventually managed to find a little more balance the second go around. (I was actually a fiend two different times, and they were very different.) Still, I just didn't care about anything else, and the only way I could function was to stop completely. You just can't do heroin part time. To survive, I had to say goodbye to it."

GETTING SETTLED AT HAZELDEN

I did not have much communication with David while he was at Hazelden. He was only there for 28 days. It was too far away to visit, and I welcomed the break from addict chaos. Based on our conversations, a couple of letters, and his journal entries, David seemed to thoroughly enjoy his stay at Hazelden. He came away with new friends and fond memories.

"April 11, 2009. It is Saturday evening. I am feeling good about where I'm at. I will chill tomorrow and, come Monday, I need to start really takin' care of business. I need to make lists, check things off when I do them and write things down when I think of them!! Find out when all of my court dates are: (a) Fairfax date 5-16-09, 2:00 p.m.; (b) Probation violation; (c) New charge 5-28-09."

"April 2009. Hi Mom, thank you for the letter. I have been writing in my journal regularly. I find that it really helps me think more clearly. I write things down so they don't get forgotten, inspiration is not lost, and tasks get completed.

"I feel so much better here. I know this is an important opportunity that I must take advantage of. The future inspires fear in me, so I try not to think of it too much. I am doing my best to BE HERE NOW! I must take advantage of this place. It isn't like jail whose only purpose is to end. This place is very different than 2nd G, it's more like a college campus, where that place was more like a prison.

"I am sorry that I haven't called. The phone cards I have don't work. I mainly want to tell you how much I appreciate your support. I can't tell you how difficult this would be without having someone on the outside, or feeling that there is no one who cares about me.

"It's strange, people don't seem to always take my problem seriously. They roll their eyes and say, 'Stop that stupid stuff!' Then they pretend that it's not there. Maybe I'm just not missing enough teeth or don't look pathetic enough. But I know that if they truly knew who I have been, they would probably be disgusted by me and I don't want to disgust people. So I play on their assumption that I am not what I claim to be. I have even come to expect that people will not believe me, even when I tell them the truth. I cannot allow myself to believe that though, because I know!

"I am still at the beginning and for that I am grateful. I already feel like I have been here quite some time. For now, I am just gonna take one day at a time, listen to these people, and try to find a way to move forward with my life.

"THANK YOU FOR BEING THERE FOR ME!"

The following entries from David's journal describe life and some of the people he met while he was at Hazelden:

"April 24, 2009. Did my short story today. It was a pretty intense experience. I had plans to deliver it like I do when I tell my [fictional] stories. It turns out, though, that when I tell my story in terms of my drug problem, it's not so funny. I got rolling, and I went way over time. Everyone was so mesmerized by my insane life they just let me go. I must say, it felt good to tell a good portion of the tale to a group of people. These people don't want me to shoot dope anymore, neither do I. I WILL DIE IF I DO!!"

"April 26, 2009. It is Sunday afternoon. Lots of people have visitors. It is nice to see them. Although I haven't had any visitors, just seeing the love makes me happy. L has five kids, and they are soooo beautiful. I was just playing a hand slapping game with all of them. I hope soooo much to have children. I have so much love to give and no one to give it to. Since I have always been the youngest; I have never had a young'un to love and teach. I want that so bad, I can taste it."

"April 28, 2009. Well, J and S are leaving. C, T, and D left last night. A bunch of new people came in. I still have over a week left. Kind of ready to go now."

"April 30, 2009. Had a 45-minute discussion with A. It was much better than previous conversations. He said a lot about my capabilities and that I am a leader and could be a positive leader here if I want to be. He had said that before, but this time he really seemed to mean it. He said I am a narcissist. Not that I never heard that before!! I will try to internalize the things he says. I said (and he agreed) that I seek affirmation from others. I know that true power must come from within. So I need to start practicing what I preach. BE THE MAN YOU KNOW YOU SHOULD BE!!! Tonight G is leaving; me, Z, and B are next. One week to go."

"May 6, 2009 [large scrawled writing]. Leavin' mañana, went to alumni breakfast this a.m. Now it is my exit nurse visit with the nicest lady in the world, M. She is very helpful. T is in there now, so I am waiting.

"Graduated last night! It was pretty lame because some guys went to an outside AA meeting and got back at 9:45 or so. So, everyone was tired. Plus I graduated with Z and B. Z wanted to make it as fast as possible so he could go to sleep and B was ---, so we didn't pass the pig, and no one really got an opportunity to say anything. People wanted to, too. If I had graduated alone, it would have been a party!! But those lame ass fuckers killed it. Anyway, B (the old redneck drunk, who is such a great and funny guy) really said the nicest thing to me. He said that he wishes I was his next door neighbor. He said it several times."

"May 7, 2009 [large scrawled writing]. Leavin' early!! Took the first shuttle smokin' out of there. It was a bittersweet departure. Everyone continuously told me how much they will miss me. I will miss them, too. Just soooo many GREAT GUYS!! I truly loved most all of them."

THE FLIGHT NOT TAKEN

David's flight home from Hazelden was scheduled to land at National Airport on May 7, at 6:30 p.m. Circe wasn't available to pick David up, so I drove over to get him. His flight landed and 30 minutes later, I was still driving in circles around the airport waiting for him to appear. He didn't have a cell phone. Another 30 minutes went by and still no David. I parked and went into the airport terminal to make sure the flight had landed on time. It had, but the agents would not give me any information about whether David was on the flight. Finally, I went into the baggage terminal and a nice man helped me confirm that he was not on board. After a couple hours, I drove home.

The sixth sense I had developed during David's addiction kicked in, and I feared what had happened. I didn't want to think it. I didn't want to know... but I knew. My excitement to see David turned to sadness and disappointment, then to anger. I waited.

After I got home, I called Circe to see if she had heard from David. She had not. I went back into wait mode. Around 10:30 p.m., David called with a crystal clear and very cheery, "Hey Ma!"

I wasn't so cheery. "Hi, David. Where are you?"

"I'm still in Minnesota. I rescheduled my flight. Can you pick me up when I land at National a little later tonight?"

"I already spent hours at the airport, waiting for you and trying to figure out why you weren't on the 6:30 flight. What happened?"

David explained, "Mom, we decided to have a last lunch together—great group of guys! I'm sorry that I forgot to let you know that I would be later than planned, but I was so excited to be leaving and also sad to be leaving so many great and new friends. I am really going to miss those guys!"

I was furious and minced no words when I responded, "Dave, really? You're full of crap! I don't believe a word of what you're telling me. Thirty grand, Dave, thirty grand to send you to what's touted as the best drug treatment facility in the world and all you can say is sorry, I forgot to let you know I'd be late and you're really going to miss such a great group of guys. You weren't sent to Hazelden to make great friends! You had such a fun time that you couldn't get your act together to get to the plane on time?! Do you think I'm a complete idiot?!"

My gut knew he was lying and already dirty with his favorite drug. After 10 years of his addict behavior, this was easy to figure out. Before David could even get home, we were screaming at each other. And I was screaming at myself for walking him out of that courtroom. David denied everything I accused him of and became angry, too. We were back to square one.

I did not go back to the airport to pick him up, and I do not know how he got home to his condo. I didn't ask. I didn't care. My worries and concerns and happiness at the thought of welcoming back a clean and ready to get back-on-track David had turned to resentment and frustration.

Based on one of David's journal entries, he did have lunch with a couple of his new Hazelden friends. I learned later that "dessert" was black tar heroin. Based on his scrawled handwriting in his journal, my guess is that he was using while at Hazelden.

POST HAZELDEN

On May 9, David described in his journal how he felt being back home from Hazelden and his thoughts on his legal situation.

"Two days out of treatment, and I feel good. I am cleaning this place [Reston condo] up. Getting unpacked, doin' laundry, etc. Feel great, although my legal situation has worsened. Spoke to both lawyers yesterday. It seems that I do indeed have a bench warrant.

"It is amazing how much different the two lawyers are. Attorney A will spend "hours talking to me on the phone. The other guy required four calls before he called me back. Then after talking for five minutes, he said he had an appointment and couldn't talk anymore. He called me. He should have called when he had some time to speak to his client. I had to repeatedly tell him that I am serious about this and need his help. I felt like those words bounced right off him. He has no personality and couldn't seem to care less about me. I told him that I was in rehab, etc. He had no information about me, and he didn't care. I asked him why I got a bench warrant and he said "because you weren't there." I told him that I had written permission from my PO. He acted all surprised. I asked him why my PO didn't speak up and say where I was . . . he couldn't even remember if she was there!!!"

OUT OF CONTROL

Some would say that David was fortunate to have a home to go to and a car to drive. I think maybe not. In less than a week after leaving Hazelden, David was once again out of control and immersed in uncontrollable heroin addiction. There were no discussions between us, just the return to huge arguments every time I talked to him. David received Hazelden alumni emails and sometimes forwarded them to me to discuss, but overall he was done with Hazelden and did not follow their recommended aftercare. I felt sure he would never stop using heroin. David obviously knew he was out of control and needed help when he questioned himself in his journal a few days later on May 22:

"Wrecked the Jeep last Sunday. I feel sick just writing that down. I've been fuckin up BAD!! Too much bad stuff. CAN'T FIND IT IN ME TO WRITE IT. I can't ignore it, though. By writing I free myself and open myself to fix it. Things progressively get worse as I continue to use [heroin]. It is a fascinating phenomenon. Someday I intend to analyze this whole thing. Unfortunately, as of now, I am immersed in it. This list of issues I have [for] myself is enormous. It is horribly painful. It is outrageous. People wouldn't even believe it. I am SOOOO FUCKED! I would list these things but it is just too painful. I can't take it. WHAT DO I DO?

"Just had a vision of Circe. I love her so much but she has had it with me. She didn't come home last night. I took the bus to a doctor in Falls Church today. I got a prescription for Suboxone. I will begin on it this weekend.

"Got court Tuesday morning.

"Need to call D.C. attorney!!!

"CAN'T THINK STRAIGHT NOW.

"ALL IS LOST.

"I'LL COME BACK LATER

"EMPTINESS IS FILLING ME."

During this critical time, Circe and I talked and emailed often. I had to try to work with her. Surely, now, she would recognize the severity of David's addiction. Though Circe was depressed and overcome with guilt that Hazelden had been such a waste of time and money, she still didn't seem to understand that she couldn't fix David. She had been so sure sending him to Hazelden was going to magically clean him up. I pleaded with her to stop enabling him, if for no other reason than for her safety and sanity. I again tried to drill the 3Cs of family recovery into her head, but she wouldn't let go.

David was using his manipulation talents on Circe full force, demanding she buy him another car and an iPhone. I told her not to buy him anything and again pleaded with her to stop enabling his drug use by supporting him. Circe was a smart woman, and as far as I knew, she had overcome her own addiction several years ago. I couldn't understand her inability to recognize the damage she was doing, especially when his demands turned into threats and instilled fear in her. Circe promised me she would read the books on addiction I'd recommended and join a Nar-Anon support group.

On David's 35th birthday, I sent an email to AC, David's D.C. court-appointed attorney for his March arrest, to check in and find out if David had shown up for court the day before. Circe had dropped him off at the courthouse in the morning, so we knew he'd made it there, but we weren't so sure he'd actually gone in. He told Circe that he met with AC, but he decided that it was best that he not appear in court, so he left.

AC responded to my email and said she could not discuss his case with me but I could look up the docket information online, which said David failed to appear for the probation case or the possession case. AC also said that "they [the cases] are non-extraditable. (i.e., if he's picked up in Virginia or anywhere else, D.C. won't come to pick him up)."

Bottom line: All David needed to do to avoid going to jail on these cases was to stay out of D.C.

David's brother moved to the Florida Keys a few months before he got married. He was home visiting during the weekend of July 26, 2009. Bill and I made plans to meet David at a restaurant for dinner. As usual, David was late. We waited. When David finally arrived, he was staggering and about to fall off his puffy cloud. It was apparent he was on a serious drug binge and using heavily. He was emaciated and looked like an old man at death's door. His skin was greasy, eyes popping, red, and glassy, and his hands shook so bad he could barely hold a fork or drink from a glass. Although drink he did. The waiter could not keep his glasses of water and iced tea full. We watched as David consumed his water and tea, drinking so fast and furiously that his mouth couldn't hold his gulps. Liquid rolled out of the sides of his mouth, down his chin, and onto the front of his shirt as he had difficulty swallowing.

Seeing David like this was physically and emotionally painful. He had no clue what he looked like or how sick he was. He adamantly denied he was actively using heroin. Conversation was difficult during dinner, but he told us he was about to lose his job at the barber shop. They had warned him about being late, money was missing from the cash drawer, and he was no longer able to hide his drug use.

After dinner, as dusk rolled in, a calmer Dave and I sat outside the restaurant on a bench. Talking became easier. Losing his job was his main concern throughout the evening and all he wanted to talk about. Bill was distraught, pacing back and forth in front of us. I could feel his mind spinning; his face showed his anguish. He took out his phone and took pictures of David and me sitting on the bench. A few months later, Bill showed the pictures to a sober David. Those photos spoke louder than words. David couldn't believe what he looked like and he had little memory about meeting us for dinner.

David was driving an old beat up car he bought for a couple hundred dollars. The inspection sticker was going to expire on August 1, and it needed a new driver side window. We asked about the window. He said it just blew out. This was weird, but apparently not an uncommon problem for an addict. As Bill and I watched David drive away, the solemnity of the evening overwhelmed both of us, and I could no longer hold back my tears—for both of my sons—and heavy worries I would never see my younger son again. I was terrified David wouldn't even make it home and this would be the last time the three of us would be together.

Bill and I tried to make contact with David every day. We encouraged him to get help, but David continued to insist that he was in control, saying to us, "Please just stop pestering me! I know what I'm doing and will stop when I'm good and ready!"

David was out of control and beyond capable of helping himself. Nothing we said or did made a positive impact toward getting him to sober up. We were helpless other than to answer the phone and listen if he called, which he rarely did. I did the only thing left to do . . . I waited.

The next Saturday, David crashed his car. I never got the details about what happened. David told Bill he got some "really strong stuff" and nodded out while driving. He acknowledged that this car crash scared him, but he still refused to go to detox or to get help.

A few days later and still without a car, David was dopesick and desperate. It was evening and Circe was doing her volunteer work, caring for cats at a local pet store. David went to the store and caused a terrible scene. Circe called me and screamed into the phone, "David is here! He wants money and the keys to my car! He's strung out and threatening to hurt me if I don't give him what he wants!"

I told Circe, "Get someone to help you get him out of the store. Do not let him back in. Do not give him anything. Do not leave the store with him. Call the police if you can't get him under control."

I could hear David angrily yelling at her for calling me, demanding that she hang up the phone. David was manic and totally out of control. Circe exclaimed, "He's threatening me with his fist . . . this is so embarrassing! I can't have him doing this where I volunteer! People here don't know that I'm married to a drug addict!"

Circe ended up giving David $45, which prevented her from being slugged in the face. Once David had the money, he immediately left the store and used the money to get to D.C. to buy a fix. The only good that came out of this incident was having Circe publicly exposed to the depth of his relapse. Now, she had to acknowledge addiction had taken over his life. She also admitted what little effect she had on him when he was desperate. Mostly, he embarrassed and scared the shit out of her in front of other people. The last thing she wanted was to be openly associated with the truth of what David had become.

Bill and I continued to keep in touch with David. I gave David hell about the pet store incident and told him I was ashamed of him but my admonishment had no effect. When an addict is coming down and all they feel is the pain of withdrawal, they will do anything to anyone to make the pain stop. As Beth Macy describes in *Dopesick,* ". . . the most important thing for the morphine-hijacked brain is, always, not to experience the crushing physical and psychological pain of withdrawal: to avoid dope sickness at any cost."

David remained on a heroin binge. His world—losing his wife, work, health, home, and the life he knew he could have if he could just stop using heroin— was collapsing around him. It was excruciating having to stand on the sidelines, watching and waiting . . . and waiting. Whenever I was able to find him and talk to him, I begged and pleaded with him to see a doctor or to go to detox. He was steadfast that he didn't need help.

Later the next week, David told me, "I'm detoxing at home with Suboxone."

He lied. His very dangerous heroin binge continued and so did the unanswered phone calls. Circe was again away for the weekend, which seemed to drive David even harder to use. Sometimes when he wouldn't answer the phone, I would drive to his barber shop and hope to see him working through the window. Oftentimes he was there, just not answering my call. I would sit in the car, parked in the back of the parking lot, and watch him work. I needed so badly just to see him and to know he was alive. If he looked approachable, I would pull the car to the front of the barber shop where he could see me. One time when he came out and sat in the car with me for a few minutes, he said, "Hey Ma, what are you doing out here sitting in the car?"

"Watching you."

"What do you mean, watching me? That's weird."

"Just that. I want to see what my boy looks like today and maybe get a hug."

That would usually get a smile out of him and perhaps a decent conversation. Our interactions during these times were tenuous, to say the least. The last thing I wanted when I went looking for him under these circumstances was another argument. I had to be very careful how I approached him. If I confronted him with, "I'm so worried about you. Where have you been? I've called and called and you don't answer!" I would get a snarl and denials that there's no good reason on God's green earth I should worry about him, and I would lose him.

David wrote and said many times that using heroin didn't harm anyone but him. He claimed he could not understand why the people who loved him kept getting so angry about his drug use. I once suggested to him, "Ok, here's what we'll do. Next time you come over to the house, bring your tool kit and some heroin, and we'll shoot up together."

"What the fuuuuuucccck?! I know you don't mean that. I'm not going to shoot you up, and I know you don't want me to."

I think for a split second, as the "uuuucccckkk" came out of his mouth, he considered my suggestion. I replied, "How do you know what I want? Maybe I want to know what it is about heroin that you love so much. What makes it worthwhile to destroy your life? Why wouldn't it be a good idea for me to try it so I can better understand why you keep chasing it? Seems a reasonable idea to me. Maybe if I use heroin and enjoy it too, we'll have one of those special mother/son moments and we can finally stop arguing all the time. Oh, hey, wait a minute . . . maybe you just don't want to share with me. That's OK, I'll buy."

His eyes squinted almost closed and his nose squeezed up tight, in a look that reminded me of little David in his highchair. "Yeah, right," he snarled and looked at me. "Now I know you're just trying to bait me. I know what I'm doing to myself. I just don't understand why you feel so affected by it."

"Because you are a part of me, and I love you." Silence.

"I love you too."

David was right, I didn't mean it, and I knew he knew I didn't mean what I was suggesting, but it was one way to change the conversation and to make my point without the same old useless argument. Weird, yes, if you've never been on the crazy addiction train going nowhere. But for me, it was just another tactic to try to spark in my addict son the realization of how heroin was making him a walking disaster, and that if I shouldn't do it, then why should he. This is the kind of crazy stuff I found myself saying, thinking, and doing after many years of addict madness. David understood what his addiction was doing to him and to his family. He just couldn't make it stop.

I missed my son and desperately wanted him back. Ten years of using heroin had taken him to a place that didn't allow me in. I had to find a way to accept who he had become. I also had to accept I didn't like "David the addict" so much. My fantasy for who I thought he was or who he could be had to die. Though it was hard to love the addict he evolved into, I was slowly realizing the young man I raised might never come back. He had done all the bad things addicts do and broken my heart many times over. To survive and not completely lose him, I had to face reality. And, I had to return my addict son to himself, an idea eloquently expressed by a mom in an essay titled, "Reality vs. Fantasy," posted on *NarAnon.org* and reprinted in the Epilogue.

SUBOXONE

Suboxone is a Medication-Assisted Treatment (MAT) used to treat opioid (narcotic) addiction. It contains a combination of buprenorphine and naloxone. Unlike opioids, Suboxone is not for use as a pain medication. Like opioids, Suboxone should only be used under a doctor's care and is highly addictive. Buprenorphine is an opioid medication, sometimes called a narcotic. Naloxone blocks the effects of opioid medication, including pain relief or feelings of well-being that can lead to opioid abuse.[24]

David was prescribed Suboxone many times when he entered detox or treatment to help curb the painful effects of withdrawal. Over the years, Suboxone was prescribed by David's primary care doctor as a maintenance drug to slowly wean him off heroin. Misuse of Suboxone is dangerous and can cause overdose or death if taken while using other drugs or alcohol. Circe sent me emails showing that David was regularly having Suboxone prescriptions filled while actively using heroin. She suspected he had begun selling Suboxone to support his heroin habit. David's Suboxone use in 2009, from March to October, was a rocky experience.

In November 2011, David entered the following essay, "A Method to End the Suffering," in a contest sponsored by the Addiction Technology Transfer Center Network (ATTC), an organization that invited individuals who had been supported by MAT (Suboxone), to write about their experiences. David sent me a text on November 24, to let me know his essay placed in the top 20 out of 128 entries and was published in the commemorative booklet, *In My Own Words* . . . Unfortunately, David's essay is mostly addict speak, just giving the sponsors of the contest what they wanted to hear.

A METHOD TO END THE SUFFERING

"Fourteen months ago, I began my journey away from a place of unimaginable ignorance and chaos. Suffering from the cost of my own indulgences, I discovered that at my weakest point, this was when I was to be my strongest. I have now emerged from this place with my mind free and my path clear. The Gorilla that goes by the name of Heroin does not get fed, and this is how I have done it.

"First, I am maintaining a lifestyle that includes people who also suffer from this illness and wish to remain free of opiates. It is paramount that I have people I can trust to talk openly and honestly about my struggle. Before treatment I suffered from a belief that I was able to decipher my own personal issues. It is now clear to me that this thinking was misguided.

"Second, Suboxone. The most profound conclusion I have come to in dealing with this illness is that time is the most effective tool to arrest my heroin use. The more time I have away from a shot of heroin, the further my mind drifts from its grip. Suboxone eliminates my powerful cravings and affords me the time I need to keep this savage affliction at bay.

"For fourteen years, I tried every method I could engineer to arrest my affliction. Finally, I believe I can have a future without limits, provided I maintain my commitment to recovery."

THE CAR HEIST

Among the many realities running through my head was that David was going to kill himself or innocent people if he continued driving high or nodding off while on heroin. I became obsessed with worry. I had discussed my concerns with Circe numerous times. Still shaken from the pet store incident, Circe agreed to help me get his car keys and to take and hide his car. We made a plan and chose the evening of Tuesday, August 11. We met at their condo.

As far as I know, David did not know we were coming. Using Circe's key, we let ourselves into the condo and found David in bed wrapped up in blankets. When we walked into the bedroom, he was immediately angry. When he saw me, he shouted at Circe, "Get her out of here! What the fuck are you doing here?! GET OUT!"

David was severely dopesick and in withdrawals. When he spoke, his words were filled with spit, slurred, mean, and nasty. He had difficulty completing a sentence and kept nodding off as he fell back into the pillows. Finding him so sick was a shock. All I wanted to do was to hold him and cry, but I needed to be strong.

The condo was filthy. The stink made me want to gag. Drug paraphernalia littered every surface. The bathroom sink and floor were covered with blood splatters. I had never seen anything like this. It was difficult not to go soft, but I reminded myself that we were there specifically to get David's car keys.

I pleaded with him, "David, you're sick. Please let us take you to the hospital for help to get you through this."

David spit back at me, "What the fuck are you doing here? Get the fuck out! I don't need you to tell me what to do! This is none of your damn business! Leave me alone!"

He glared at Circe. "Are you fucking crazy, bringing her here?! Get out!"

I screamed back at David as he tried unsuccessfully to get out of bed. "We can't let you stay here like this. You're killing yourself!"

"I said, get the fuck out! I'm not going to any fucking hospital. Who do you think you are coming into my home and demanding that I do what you want me to do! This is my home! I know what I'm doing!" David sunk back into his blankets and nodded off.

When it was clear that he wasn't going to let us take him to the hospital or detox, we threatened to call the police, which just brought out more anger and obscenities. While I screamed back and forth with him, Circe searched through his stuff for his car keys. When she found the keys, we waited until he nodded off again and left.

Given David's state of incoherence and seeming lack of strength, we thought we were in the free and clear. We were wrong. David realized we had taken his car keys. I had just backed out of the parking space in front of his condo and was driving in the parking lot when I saw David in the rearview mirror, chasing the car and yelling at us, "STOP! STOP THE FUCKING CAR!"

David was barefoot and only wearing an A-shirt[25] and house (pajama) pants. I was still in the parking lot and could not speed up. He caught up with the car and jumped on the hood. He lay on the hood and banged on the windshield with his fists while continuing to shout obscenities at us. He then swung himself around and began pounding on the side windows and demanded we give him his keys back. Words cannot describe how terrified I was for him and for us. I was still trying to drive, swerving all over the parking lot, as he swung side-to-side on top of the car. I could see people in the parking lot, watching us and running for cover.

Finally, David dropped off the hood, and I sped away. I was shaking uncontrollably . . . he could have fallen off and I could have run over him . . . I could have killed my own son. What the hell was I doing?! The madness had to stop! I couldn't believe I left him standing barefoot in that parking lot. His fisted hands and angry red face faded in my rearview mirror as I drove away. Trying to deal with David's addiction had made me do and say a lot of crazy stuff, but this event topped them all.

The only consolation was that we got the car keys. We drove a short distance from the condo to where David parked his car. I don't know why he didn't park his car at the condo but Circe knew exactly where it would be parked. Then to hide it, Circe drove the car to a friend's house. The only relief was that David could not hurt himself or anyone else while driving to buy and use heroin, which was important because, given his current state, he was desperate for a fix. Without a car and with Circe's promise that she would not give the car back to him, he would be forced to endure withdrawals and either get help on his own or get sober on his own.

The next morning, David was up early, showered, and ready when Circe arrived to drive him to work. He told both of us that our taking his car was the best thing we could have done for him. He made it through the day. Thursday was his day off. I called and asked if he wanted to get a bite to eat. When I arrived at the condo to pick him up, he was ready to go. We had a nice, relaxing dinner sitting outside at Clyde's in Reston. David looked remarkably better and we talked easily. I was suspicious and amazed that this was the same person who, two days before, had been completely out of control and sick, drooling all over himself, and barely able to put together a legible sentence. Could he possibly have gotten through withdrawals and become calm and sober so quickly? No. He had found a way to use.

Even though I had my suspicions, I didn't want to do or say anything to disturb the calm. I just wanted to see my son and spend time with him without an argument. Without my asking questions or bringing up Tuesday's car incident, David blurted out, "Mom, I mean it, I'm going to quit this time. I've had it." I very much wanted to believe him.

The calm and the promise were short lived. Monday, August 17, was a BAD day. Circe called Bill in a panic and told him that David was missing. She demanded Bill and I start calling hospitals, because she was sure David had overdosed. I called several local hospitals but David had not been admitted. We continued calling David all day, but there was no answer. Our fears mounted. He finally answered Circe's call and said he was on a bus. He refused to tell her his destination. A little while later, he called me from a Mexican restaurant in Reston.

"David, where have you been? Why haven't you answered our calls? Circe was frantic, thinking you had overdosed. I've been calling hospitals, trying to find you. What the hell is going on? Where are you now?"

David responded, "Mom, You won't like this, but I'm going to tell you the truth . . . I was trying to find my dealer."

"What in hell do you mean, 'Trying to find my dealer?!'"

"Yeah, Mom, trying to find my dealer, but it was too complicated without a car and it's too expensive to get around D.C. using cabs—I got very frustrated! So I gave up and came back to Reston."

"Do you really expect me to believe you spent all day looking for your dealer and when you couldn't find him just gave up?"

"That's what happened, Mom. Believe what you want."

Based on an emailed client intake form, Circe filed for a "fast divorce." She listed August 19, 2009, as their date of separation, even though she'd moved out of the condo long before. She had threatened divorce so many times, I have no idea whether or not this was real or just another scare tactic.

A couple of weeks later, Circe returned the car to David.

Later in September, when David and I met for dinner, I was sure he was under the influence of heroin, but he wasn't strung out. He had gotten his car inspected and done a few repairs, which was a good sign. When he's in the midst of heavy use, he doesn't take care of anything, especially himself or his possessions. I still had not talked to Circe since she'd returned the car to David. I could not forgive her.

INSOMNIA / ENDORPHINS / ENKEPHALINS

At this stage of David's addiction, he researched and requested information online about whether taking aminos would help him sleep. His concern was combining aminos with Suboxone. According to his source, he could take Suboxone with aminos, and the amino DLPA (D-Phenylalanine (known as nature's pain pill) was recommended. David was told that sleep disturbance is the number one symptom of addiction, and individuals who are genetically programmed to prefer opiates (heroin) are found to be deficient in endorphins/enkephalins (the body's natural painkillers). Endorphins are thought to block pain principally at the brain stem; enkephalins block pain signals in the spinal cord. Both are morphine-like substances whose functions are similar to those of opium-based drugs.[26]

David's September 5 email to his source for information on insomnia expressed his need to get better sleep and to start eating regularly if he intended to overcome his addiction to opiates. He goes on to say that he is "done" and is looking for a natural solution to begin functioning better, and he describes his relationship with his co-workers and why getting "clean" this time is going to be different than other times when he knew he would fail.

"September 5, 2009. I am going to go to GNC tomorrow to pick up those amino acids. I definitely need something to help me start sleeping like a normal person again. I will be able to start functioning better with some regular sleep. As a result of my lack of sleep, I pretty much walk around in a fog right now. I need to start eatin' regular, too. My co-workers wonder why I never eat lunch. They know something is wrong with me. Fortunately we all get along real well, and they like me, so they don't hold what I think they consider my eccentricities against me. Nevertheless, if I can get some regular sleep and eat well, my "strange" behavior will cease.

"I tell [you] what, the whole process is difficult, but it is amazing how supportive people have been. Even the people who don't know exactly what has been wrong with me can tell that I am making changes in my behavior. Everyone just seems to want me to get better. Usually when I get clean, I am much less public about it. You see, I know that I will fail so I don't want to let people down. (Obviously, this isn't the first time I have gotten clean.) This time though, I have made public declarations that my behavior is about to change and really put myself out there. Unlike what I usually do. I am doing this naturally and I think it's because I know that I am done and fully intend to make it work. Conversely, before, when I knew I would fail, I stayed more secluded so I wouldn't let people down when I relapsed.

"Anyway, I appreciate your help. There are so many little things, like eating and sleeping, that need to be fixed. The solutions are out there and I appreciate all of the resources I have at my disposal and resources that I can acquire."

JILL

In a September 9 Facebook message, David reconnects with a young woman whom I'll call Jill. He knew Jill in high school and formed a relationship with her while incarcerated in Arlington. They became "boyfriend" and "girlfriend" while they were both serving time. Jill was incarcerated for check fraud. I happened to meet her in 2007, when she was working at my doctor's office. She recognized my name and realized I was David's mom. She sought me out after one of my appointments and bravely introduced herself. She was a lovely young woman. Her telling me about how she and Dave helped each other get through serving time in jail was weirdly heartwarming. It was obvious talking to her that they cared deeply for each other; reading their messages many years later leaves no doubt. David sent her a Facebook message on September 9, and another on September 16.

"September 9, 2009. Helllooooo, I was on Myspace and I looked for u there but couldn't find ya. It is great to hear from you. You look real good and your daughter is beautiful. My mom told me that she used to see you. She really liked you and wanted me to call you. I wanted to, too, but I am married now. My wife knows about you. I told [her] that we are good friends and that is more important than anything. Right? I would love to see you and your daughter some time. Are you married? Boyfriend? I just hope you are happy. I think about you and all that you had to go through. Such a shame. Have you had trouble getting a job? What are you doing? Here is my phone number. Please call me any time. At least, write me back here. Great to hear from you, Love Always, Dave"

"September 16, 2009. I don't know where to start. Right now isn't a great time for me. My wife and I are separated. We have been having some difficulties. Basically, she has left me. This is the girl I have been with, on & off, for over 11 years. I love her but it is one of those things that . . . you know . . . I just don't know if it is gonna work out. Things just aren't goin so great. I am in debt pretty bad. I am at a different barber shop. Same company but different shop. Work is really slow. It's a newer shop, and the customer base just isn't there. We have busy days that are good, but then we'll have days (like today) where we just sit around watching TV. I don't make money unless I'm cuttin' hair. I am like an independent contractor. There is no limit on how much I can make, which is good when it's busy, but if no one comes in, then I don't make money. I was making good money at the other shop but I had to switch. I had to take some time off.

"I am embarrassed to tell you this but I had to check myself into a rehab. I went to a place called Hazelden in Minnesota. It was a really good experience. Things have gotten better since then, but I have slipped up a few times and this is the main reason why my wife has left me. Things got pretty bad. I wrecked 3 cars. My mustang, which was a very nice car. Then I wrecked my wife's VW. She got a new car before I went to Minnesota. Then I bought a 2005 Jeep Liberty and went to Minnesota shortly after. I got a great deal on it. I paid $8000 and they were going for $12,500. When I came back from Minn., I slipped up, fell asleep behind the wheel, and totaled it. It was soooo horrible. My wife was just disgusted with me. She really liked that car. She didn't leave me right away, but I think at that point she decided that I was a lost cause.

"I hate telling you these things but I feel like I can be honest w/ you. I bought another car from my co-worker. It's a '95 Honda civic. I paid cash for it so no payment, which is good, but it is definitely a step back. It leaks oil so I have to put in like 2 quarts a week and the paint is all faded. It is a pretty good metaphor for where I am in my life. I have a job, just not as good as it used to be. I have a car, not as good. I am staying at the condo all alone. My wife is staying w/ some guy she met. I think he lives in Chicago and just has a house here so she is staying in his house. He is an older guy. I know she doesn't love him, but I do know that he is in love w/ her, and I am pretty sure he is married. I'm not sure about any of this, though. It's just what I've been able to piece together.

"Really, all I know is that she has left and he sends her text messages that he loves her, etc. The hardest thing to deal w/ is that it is all my fault. Plus, we have this condo that we bought together in March 2006, at the height of the Real Estate boom. We paid $268,000 for it. Now, similar condos are selling for $130,000 and lower. So we are stuck w/ this condo and huge mortgage for a place that isn't worth it. The bills are piling up and I'm not making shit. Which makes her resent me even more.

"Anyway, sorry to drop all of this on you. I was just gonna be superficial and tell you everything is all right, but I don't think you would want that. Maybe I shouldn't have said so much. You don't want to hear that shit. I am just confused right now, and I don't know what to do. I am not real depressed or anything. I am just confused and overwhelmed. And I feel all alone in this place."

Jill responded to Dave:

"Please don't worry—it should go unsaid. Though you may not realize it, YOU got me through the most horrible experience of my life. From your letters you held my hand when it just needed to be held—embraced me when I just needed to feel loved— and made love to me when I needed to escape it all. All from your words and if I never said thank you, THANK YOU!"

On October 13, David was arrested at a toll booth on the Dulles Toll Road for drug possession and driving without a license. Trooper M of the VA State Police reported that David was stopped under suspicion of driving while intoxicated. During the trooper's investigation of the car, she found several tiny bags, metal cups, and needles, each containing suspected heroin residue. David was then placed under arrest for possession of heroin. Each of these items was transported to the VA Department of Forensic Science where several tested positive for heroin residue.

David gave his car keys back to Circe and declared, "This is it!"

He was going to get sober and stay sober this time. He said that not having a car to make the drug trip into D.C. was the answer. A few days later on Friday, I received a frantic phone call and a voicemail from Circe:

"I picked David up from work and now he is trying to take my car! I can't make him stop!"

I ignored the call and the voicemail.

A couple days later, I tried to call Circe, but her phone was disconnected. I reached David the same night. He was whacked out and though his speech was slow and slurred, we talked for a long time. David mostly ranted and raved about Circe's boyfriend, who he got into a fight with the previous Friday night. When I learned about the boyfriend, I cautioned Circe not to let her boyfriend get involved. I had no idea what Circe's relationship was with her boyfriend or how she framed her relationship with David, but allowing them to meet spelled disaster.

The next day, I couldn't reach David until the evening. He had spent the day in D.C., getting loaded with dope because he was going to the doctor the next morning for help to detox. He asked if I would take him. I said I would and drove him to Dr. K, his primary care physician.

David's main purpose for the visit was to ask Dr. K to renew his prescription for Suboxone. I didn't know until that day that Dr. K had been prescribing Suboxone to treat David's addiction for some time. When David asked me to take him to the doctor, I assumed I was just his transportation and was surprised when he asked me to go in with him while he met with the doctor. Dr. K greeted me warmly and took the time to review David's medical history with me. It was evident that he cared about David, not just as a patient or an addict, but as a person. I also was surprised at how kind and considerate Dr. K was toward me.

As the mother of an addict, I had become accustomed to being treated with suspicion that there surely must be something wrong with me to produce a drug-addled son. I got used to it; however, it was a welcome relief to discuss my son's addiction without feelings of shame or embarrassment. For once, I didn't feel the need to prove my decency.

Dr. K was firm when he told David he would only give him one more Suboxone prescription. He said David had relapsed back to using heroin too many times. He also emphasized and assured us that he would always be there to help David with his addiction as long as David stuck with the program.

After the appointment, I drove David to the pharmacy to have the prescription filled. He was angry. He didn't like losing an unlimited stream of Suboxone and thought Dr. K talked down to him. He didn't like that at all, especially in front of me. Maybe Dave thought having me at the appointment would soften Dr. K up. What he didn't anticipate was that I would learn so much about his medical history and relapses. I don't know what David was thinking, but I was somewhat relieved. Maybe I finally had an ally in this crazy addiction war. Maybe Dr. K was on to David and suspected as I did that David was selling Suboxone to support his heroin habit. I took David to Dr. K again in November, and as far as I could tell, he stuck to Dr. K's program and hadn't used heroin for a while.

CHAPTER 8: 2010

LEGAL PROBLEMS MOUNT / JAIL / PLEASURE VS. PAIN

In February 2010, David spent 30 days in jail for the October 13 DWI arrest. As the arrests and court dates mounted up again, it was difficult to keep up with what he was arrested for and when he served time for what offense. In an April 25 Facebook message, David told a friend, "I just spent a little time in the Fairfax County spa for fuckin up."

By May, David was struggling with the pain vs. pleasure dilemma using heroin creates. He reached out to an addict friend for help to stay clean after a 70-day jail term:

> "May, 14, 2010, Facebook. Hey man, sorry to take so long to get back atcha. I just had to [do] another stint in jail. 70 days, man. Got out about 2 weeks ago. I went in 4 days before you sent this message. I tell you what man . . . I can't take it anymore. I've been clean since I got out. It's pretty easy at first but that freshly released from jail optimism is wearin' off and the old thoughts are doin what they do. I tell you what man . . . I want what you have. (I'm assumin' you still have it.) I want to really and truly surrender. I don't want to put you on the spot, but I would be very appreciative if you would take me to a meeting with you sometime. I'm tryin' to do this all alone and, as you know, it grows increasingly more difficult by the day. Anyway, I'm not tryin' to be a wet blanket, but I think you could understand and hope you could at least point me in a proppa direction! Peace, Bruva!!! (V)"

David's poem, "My Timing is Good," describes his attempt to get and stay clean, and it speaks to his pain and inability to stop the cycle of addiction. The poem is signed Socrates H. Dillinger, May 26, 2010—the day before David's 36th birthday.

MY TIMING IS GOOD

My timing is good
But my brain's not thinkin' like it should
Cuz I'm thinkin' 'bout all the losses

The jobs I've had
The times I was sad
All those horrible bosses

Pain is all I feel
It's all that is real
Though I know it is wrong

A prisoner of time
Even enslaved by this rhyme
And the day, it is oh so long

So I laugh and I joke
In a hot bath I soak
Anything to ease the pain

The good days are still bad
I'm miserable and sad
Even sunny days, they feel like rain

I could write a thousand songs
Each an hour long
And each would make you cry

What is the point?
My soul don't anoint
Regardless, I'm just gonna die

So why participate?
Engage or initiate
Smile or cry or see red

It all goes away
Just like the day
Without the Pain,
I'm Cold and Dead

So I tried a new way
I stepped out to the day
I faced it, with a new way of thinking

Stopped with the drugs
Gave up on cheap love
Quit all that goddamn drinking

At first it was ruff
Even though I'm tuff
I wanted to cash in my chips

For once it wasn't lies
And artificial cries
The sounds comin' from my lips

Before I had tried
To myself I had lied
So this time, I made a firm resolution

Even though it would be mean
At times it would be lean
I knew, this to be my final solution

Get myself rich
Get away from that bitch
I can start to put things in order

Find a practical way
To fill each day
Never leave a task's completion at the border

I'll think things all the way thru
Won't give in to blue
The pain will start to fade away

I'll stand up real strong
And stay up real long
Accomplish a goal each day

As each day comes
I will pass by the bums
I used to call my friends

I pass on by
Wave to them "hi"
But, stay away to protect my mends

Then eventually I stop
While they are duckin' the cops
I join in, do a shot, pop a pill

Even though time has passed
And I'm happy at last
I give in, to a little cheap thrill

The cycle resumes
I'm back with the pain
My freedom and peace I bleed

When truth defies reason
Once again, it is that season
Without the Pain, I'm Cold and Dead.

On David's 36th birthday, I talked to him on the phone and asked if he wanted to come over for dinner. He declined, said he was having dinner with Circe, and sounded excited because she was giving him exercise equipment for his birthday. It was hard to tell how he was really doing, but his speech was clear. Our communications had deteriorated over the past few months, and I didn't see him much.

He posted on his Facebook page that Memorial Day weekend was his favorite time of the year, but that this year he was lonely. I tried to get him to come for a cook-out on Memorial Day, but he said that without a car, it was too difficult and buses don't run on Memorial Day. Hearing him tell me he couldn't get to my house when I knew he was making almost daily trips to D.C. to buy heroin was infuriating. I offered to drive out and pick him up, but he declined.

On June 1, David and a buddy were planning via Facebook to "party" at David's condo. His friend said he would help with the costs if David would go pick up the "party favors." David was still without a car and told his friend, "We'll have to make a trip to D.C.; it's a long, arduous journey w/ no car. I do it a couple times a week though." As it turned out, the party didn't happen. David didn't hear back from his friend, so he made the trip to D.C. by himself and then learned his friend didn't show up for their party because he had passed out.

LEGAL PROBLEMS

In June 2010, David got caught up with Rita, another old friend from high school, through Facebook messages. Here, he tells her about the consequences of using drugs, his dislike of being labeled a drug addict, conforming to the rules of society, and TRUTH.

"June 26, 2010. I have legal problems as a result of drug use. This has been a horrible consequence from using drugs, but I don't consider myself to be in Recovery. I know it may be confusing, but I will not let the government and their malicious tactics decide that I am a drug addict. I am only a man. The labels they want to put on me are their labels. I refuse to allow them to tell me who I am.

"Also, I know I said that I use cocaine, and although I have used it some, cocaine is not my drug of choice. I won't go any further into it, because it only matters that 'I' know who I am. I feel that I have been persecuted for something I have done that hurts no one else. I have never stolen for drugs. I have never hurt anyone for drugs. And I don't sell them. The judge said to me that I am a menace to society . . . This couldn't be further from the truth. I do recognize, however, that I truly do deserve to be punished for driving while intoxicated. That one I accept as being fundamentally wrong, and I paid my debt to society.

"This possession charge, however, is fundamentally wrong. I didn't even have any drugs. I had drug paraphernalia that had drug residue on it. So to them, that constitutes possession . . . I get sentenced for that on Friday, July the 2nd. Pray for me cuz I don't want any more trouble. I have been clean since this all happened, and I believe that if I continue to do the right thing then this burden should, eventually, be lifted!

"Anyway, despite my objections with their labeling of me, I do know that I cannot use drugs anymore. If I were to continue to use them given all of these consequences, then they would be stronger than me. That is not the case. So therefore, I am clean and will have to stay that way. Like it or not, I must be strong and remember what is truly important and drugs are not what is important. I simply must conform to the rules of society whether I agree with them or not.

"I am generally an open book, as long as I deem that my audience can understand what I have to say. This is not the usual shallow Facebook talk. You must know that I am not one for shallow, superficial talk. I seek only to get to the actual nature of things. TRUTH. The problem is, once you break through the illusion, there is no going back."

Attorney K, David's Fairfax attorney, sent me an email on July 1 and attached the Virginia Department of Correction's Pre-Sentence Investigation Report, Offender Information, on David. Though grim, it provided a brief and accurate status report of David's addiction for the previous five years. On April 26, he was tried for Schedule 1 drug possession. Sentencing was scheduled for July 2. David entered an Alford Plea, which, based on Attorney K's email, is a guilty plea in criminal court, whereby a defendant in a criminal case does not admit the criminal act and asserts innocence. By entering an Alford plea, the defendant admits that the evidence the prosecution has would be likely to persuade a judge or jury to find the defendant guilty beyond a reasonable doubt. At the time the report was completed, June 21, 2010, it was noted that David was six feet tall, 175 pounds.

VA DEPARTMENT OF CORRECTIONS
INVESTIGATIVE REPORT

Substance Abuse Information Narrative: David reported a poly-substance abuse history that began when he was 18 years old. Subject has a history of using Percocet, opium, codeine, OxyContin, benzodiazepines, Xanax and Valium; has had multiple overdose episodes that required medical interventions. Completed Second Genesis Drug Treatment Program in 2003 and Hazelden Treatment Program in Minnesota in 2009. Subsequent to these programs, David completed a Steps to

Recovery relapse prevention program in Falls Church. He lived in an Oxford House Recovery program for about five months after he completed Steps to Recovery. David characterizes present substance abuse as sporadic. He has had a significant challenge with respect to his sobriety in the last five years. Reports relapse on heroin one week before his arrest for this offense. David reports that addiction has had a significant negative impact on his family. His wife has extended her patience but she maintains her support despite the intermittent drug use and employment. David appears to be aware of all the tools needed for sobriety but does not project confidence in his ability to stay clean and sober.

Recommendation: (by Probation Officer J) David is a 35 year old married man, who stands before the court for sentencing on a charge of Possession of a Controlled Drug. He entered an Alford plea on April 26, 2010. This represents the subject's second felony conviction for Possession of a Controlled Drug. The defendant has a chronic and progressive addiction that spans over 15 years. He has had multiple treatment interventions, including a commitment at Second Genesis and Hazelden facilities. He is presently receiving treatment from a private substance abuse counselor in Fairfax County.

The defendant appears to have moderate remorse, and he takes minimal responsibility for this offense. He is not presently attending Narcotic's Anonymous, and he does not have a sponsor. Subject reports his family as his system with respect to sobriety. Subject reports his abuse cycle as sporadic. His longest period of sobriety has been two years. Subject presents as a high functioning addict who believes he has control of his addiction. It is this officer's opinion that subject's addiction and related issues are severe enough for intense and long term intervention.

> A plea agreement has been entered in this case. This officer recommends a period of incarceration with probation to follow. Subject would benefit from substance abuse treatment as a special condition of proposed probation.

SENTENCED TO D.C. JAIL

July 16, 2010, three weeks after his June assessment in Fairfax, David was arrested for possession of drugs and paraphernalia. He was taken to D.C. Central Detention. Now that D.C. had him back, they could enforce bench warrants from a year ago. On July 17, David was arraigned before D.C. Judge S to schedule the July 16 drug case and the bench warrants. On July 20, D.C. Judge R held a bench warrant hearing; David was given no bond. On July 21, David was arraigned before D.C. Judge C for failure to show at the April 30, 2009 "show cause" hearing; plea judgment guilty. Judge C revoked David's probation and sentenced him to 180 days in D.C. jail. He got credit for 30 days currently served; his expected release date was December 13, 2010. None of this was a surprise. It was made clear to David a year ago that D.C. would not "come and get him." All he had to do to avoid jail in D.C. was to stay out of D.C., but heroin's grip on David was too tight.

On July 30, David stood before D.C. Judge R for the July 16 possession case. He pled guilty. He was sentenced to an additional 40 days, extending his stay in D.C. jail to sometime in February 2011. David served this time at D.C.'s Correctional Treatment Facility. During this process, I communicated with David's D.C. attorney, but there was little she would share with me, citing attorney-client privilege. David was right back to where he was a year ago before he left for Hazelden, but this time Circe could not rescue him. He was very angry.

Unlike earlier times when David was in Arlington and Fairfax jails and I visited regularly, I only visited Dave a few times by myself and once with his brother while he was incarcerated in D.C. Each time he was angry and belligerent. Our visits were miserable. It's ironic that he talks about a hug in his August 17 letter; there were no hugs, or maybe my memory doesn't serve me well about hugs during that horrific time. One of our visits turned so tense and ugly, I had to leave before time was up. The time his brother went with me was better. I don't know if he had any other visitors. Visiting any jail was not a pleasant experience; visiting D.C. jail was dreadful.

Circe was filing for bankruptcy, and according to David's August 1 letter, she was not having anything to do with him, including providing funds for his commissary purchases. I sent what I thought was enough for David's basic needs, but he complained that I wasn't sending enough. No doubt David felt abandoned.

Though I knew his letters were full of BS, manipulations, and what he thought I would want to hear, they were heartbreaking to read. David could not fathom how difficult it was for his family to live a "good" life while he lived in such an appalling place. Like so many parents of addicted sons and daughters in jail, I kept up the front of a "good" life. No one realized how alone and afraid I felt. Regardless of where I was, what I was doing, or who I was with, my anger about David's addiction stayed on a low simmer. Looking back, I should have gotten professional help. I was stubborn and determined to stay strong, tough it out, beat the beast. I was wrong.

As before when Dave was incarcerated, he needed support from the outside to survive inside the D.C. jail. I knew the drill. Although I was angry with him, I was more scared for him.

"August 1, 2010, D.C. Jail. Hi Mom—I just spoke to you. It was nice to finally speak to you after being here over two weeks and either not being allowed to use the phone or when I do, not being able to get ahold of you. It has been a very difficult two weeks, but I haven't been in any danger. I have a case manager in the jail and she is helping me to make sure I am placed in the safest housing units.

"I am waiting to go to the Residents Substance Abuse Treatment (RSAT) program. It is a safe, secure block, and it will allow me to make good use of my time. I will be able to really work on my problem as well as make good, well thought out plans for the future. I want you to know, I don't have to go to this program. My time won't get reduced. I'm doing it, because I choose to. I'll probably be the only one in there who chose to go there, and not to impress a judge or parole board.

"Anyway, I want to say that I am sorry for not being in your life like I should. I'm the one who really misses out though. You have a good life, doing good things and living well. I am sad and all alone. I am that [way] because I have chosen to be. I have chosen this pain. All I have to do is choose not to suffer anymore. I hope that you will be there for me. It kills me that I can't be there today for the retirement party. These are the things I miss so much. Tell [your husband] I am happy for him in his retirement, and I'm sorry I can't be there. Also, tell Bill I will write and call him as soon as I get his number and address.

"Mom, I'm sorry I haven't given you what you deserve, and that's a good happy relationship with a good happy son that you put so much time and effort into raising. You should have someone you can count on! Someone who cares about you and what you are doing. Someone who wants to be there to share life with. Play tennis, go out to dinner, and attend retirement parties. I want to be that son to you. I miss when we used to play tennis. I really was starting to become happy back then. I threw it all away for nothing. My own selfish desire for immediate satisfaction. Mom, I love you, and I want to be part of your life. Anyway, it really was nice to finally talk to you. I am safe right now. It is better to be locked down 23 hours a day with nothing to do than in danger. So, I will face my situation like a man and not complain.

"You need to set up a phone account so I can call you. Bill, too. You both have to call to set it up. Visiting is Mondays and Fridays, 12–7 p.m. Sure would love a visit from you and Bill.

"I hope you will correspond with me and not be too negative all the time. I don't mean to be like this. I don't know what happened. I don't fully understand it, but I do know that I can change it. It is in my power, and I will if it takes everything I have. Like the Phoenix, I'll rise from the ashes and be strong again. I love you, Mom, and I hope to hear from you soon :)"

David's August 16 letter is about his system for getting accepted and respected in his new environment. He assures me he is safe, and he explains the need for him to immediately establish himself as strong, likeable, and a respected member of his new "community."

"August 16, 2010. Hi Mom, it was nice to finally get your letter last night. Getting mail is always exciting in here. First, I am safe. This is a bad place, probably the worst I can think of, but you have to realize that I am a very strong and likable person. The key is in the beginning. Unfortunately, since I have done this a few times, I have a system for getting myself accepted and respected (even among so many blacks).

"The key for me is cards. I am proficient at just about all games, card and board. Chess, spades, pinochle, rummy, Scrabble, Monopoly, checkers—everything. And, believe me, they play everything. Usually, though, the biggest game in any jail is the game of spades. At this game, I am an expert. So, what I do when I come in a place with 160 people, almost all black, I have to show no fear. I go straight to the spade table and try to get in a game. Usually early in the day when not everyone that day is playing yet. Being new and white, it is very difficult to get into a game. This is when I must be strong and not give up. (This may sound foolish, but it is vital for me establishing myself as a strong, likeable, and respected member of the community.) Then, when I finally get into a game, I showcase my skill at the game. Believe me, everyone will be watching so there is no room for error. Once they see how good I am at the game, I become an asset to anyone looking to win. Plus, during these games I get to showcase my personality, which people like. The key is that I don't play too good or gloat when I win. People resent that. I play just good enough to win and be humble about it.

"Within a couple of days everyone wants to be my friend. Then, I can navigate my way and associate with only the good people, but the bad people won't mess with me because I now have too many friends and have become well respected. So, although this IS a terrible place, I am safe and will remain that way because I am smart and strong.

"Now, if I could just find a way to use my skills in a practical way in the real world. I know I can. I just have to stay clean. I will. I have no doubt. I must believe. This is essential to my success. I know you probably don't care about the social hierarchy in a jail setting, I am basically trying to tell you that I am safe.

"I understand that you don't want to visit. I don't blame you, but I am going to be here six months, ten days. Maybe you will come sometime during that period. Bill could come, too. Maybe once, sometime :) And, no, I can't get on the Internet. The only thing I can think of is that I left Facebook and my email open on my computer. Circe probably did it.

"I also hope you'll send some books. Something similar to Carl Sagan's, Cosmos. Has to be paperback. I know you probably think I don't deserve anything, but I am not some criminal. I am a person who can come out of this better and stronger. I cannot let this place take away my desire to live. I must keep good spirits. I must be strong. I must keep my mind focused on being a positive, strong person. I will persevere. I will be a good son. I will see you in about five more months. You will see me and you will see my strength.

"But, for now, and for a long while, I am here and I must be strong. (I wouldn't even want to count how many times I said 'I must be strong.' I guess it seems corny but very, very true.) Anyway, I hope all is well in your world. How are my cousins, especially Jim? I'm gonna write Bill next. I'll talk to you soon!"

David's August 19 letter brings the good news that he has been moved and assigned to work in the barber shop.

"August 19. 2010. Hi Mom—I have good news!! I have been moved! There is another jail right next to the place where I was. It is called CTF and considered a major privilege to be over here. Gone are the orange jumpsuits. I now have a dark blue 2-piece outfit. There are many other perks, too. Mainly, it is considered great fortune to be here and only the most compliant and lowest security levels come here so it will be safe. I will list some good things about it:

—Cable TV, including HBO.

—With that, I will now be able to watch football games in the coming season. I was going to miss them over where I was.

—Soft chairs (no more sitting on steel and concrete all day).

—I'll get to go outside and a gym with basketball, weights. I haven't been out there yet but it sounds good.

—Way better commissary. They have deodorant that actually works (supposedly), regular sized toothbrushes (instead of the little teeny ones), and better food.

—Plus, I could buy a Walkman over here. They cost $39 though.

—Porcelain toilets and sinks, instead of ice cold steel.

"The only problem is that I have to go through the whole intake process again, which is a 72-hour lockdown and then wait however long it takes to move to where I'm gonna be. I talked to the case manager lady today. She asked me what I do for a living. I told her. She immediately made a phone call and had me placed in the barber shop. So that will be a decent job. Plus, I'll go to AA/NA a couple times a week, and I signed up for Relapse Prevention classes. I'm sure I won't learn anything new but it might help reinforce what I know, plus help to keep my mind right.

"I know you just set up an account so I can call you. That one won't work now. Sorry!! You have to set up another one. Plus, the visits are contact and one-hour long. No glass or phones. You set up a time by calling ---. Then you come and we can hug, sit at a table like normal people. They have vending machines for sodas and snacks, and it lasts an hour. You and Bill could come together one day. That would be nice!! The address is also different. My inmate # is the same.

"Well, back to my book. Been reading a lot. The windows aren't covered. I can actually see outside. A huge graveyard where people walk their dogs. That's nice, plus I watched a rainstorm the other night. I hope everything is well with you. I would like to hear from you again. Let me know what's up."

David's August 21 letter finds him trying to stay positive and strong in a crazy place, locked down in his cell because of a "huge gladiator-style melee" among the inmates.

"August 21, 2010. Hey Mom—Still locked in this cell. They sure do make things difficult. I haven't been able to send this letter off, because I can't get to the mailbox. There was a huge gladiator-style melee with weapons and everything. Muslims against people trying to steal from one of them. It was ridiculous. I am being forced to be around complete idiots. It solves nothing. Then, they took everyone involved and took them to the hole. About 20 of them. Now, we have been locked in our cells for two days. Even though the perpetrators are gone. This place (hopefully) will be better but sure isn't yet.

"It's kind of hard to stay positive in a crazy situation like this. I have to be strong. I have to believe that things will get better with time. I HAVE TO! I believe that I must keep my mind positive. I MUST.

"I just have to let it all go . . . I have to control my thoughts and not allow negativity in. I can and will survive and persevere. It won't be easy. Thanks for listening."

IF WE CAN FREE OUR MINDS, WE CAN FREE OURSELVES

David was desperate to maintain freedom for himself and his mind. Freeing one's mind became his mantra. He never fully thought I understood his concept of freeing his mind, but I did. What I thought David couldn't let himself believe was that his mind would never be free as long as he numbed it with heroin—our never ending argument. "If we can free our minds, we can free ourselves" is inscribed on David's grave plaque as a tribute to his philosophy and determination to make others understand his ideas and thoughts.

It was impossible to predict what mood David would be in day-to-day. He was argumentative—with me and himself—in his November 3 letter. He describes his need to control his thoughts and to stay positive as he tries to convince me and himself that he is strong, honest, interesting, and special.

"November 3, 2010. Hi Mom, I just want to tell you that I do not intend to explain myself to anyone anymore. I do not intend to lie, to conform to what I believe to be expected. The purest and most fundamental truth is that I know who I am. I am a special person. I am aware that this is not evident to outsiders, although people around can always see it. This fact will become more and more evident as time goes by until someday, not too far off, it will be clear to all. I say this not because I need the approval of everyone. I do not. It will be clear because the light inside me cannot stay hidden, it is destined to shine. And it will. I do not require anyone to believe me, or in me. (Although it does not hurt.) I do not require anyone to take care of me. My suffering is a temporary state and has never and will never be motivation enough for me to be something other than what I am; an honest, strong and interesting person. I like who I am. I understand that using heroin is not the correct path for me. But, although this is wrong, it does not mean that all is wrong. My mind is free and I will not have anyone around me who wishes to liberate me from this freedom and force me to conform to something I can never be.

"I do believe though, that it is important that I state that. This is part of the reason I am special. Someday you will say, 'That's my boy.' But, it won't be because I became someone different and had this great change. It will be because I mastered the use of my own unique and beautiful mind. You see, this is the path . . .

"I know you want what's best for me. But, ultimately what's best for me is not what's best for you. You would like me to be happy, humble, and normal in terms of appearances. That, I can be. But the path to that, will look, and has looked, strikingly different. This is because you don't truly wish freedom for me. My mind and myself must be free. Free from anything and anyone who would wish me to close my mind and myself. Suffer I must. A free mind does not come free. The price to pay is high. But the fruit my mind will bear will be beautiful and unique. Just like me.

"I am not seeking your approval. I am only telling you this because you are my mother and I love you without condition. Thanks for listening."

On November 11, my visit with Dave was not good. He was angry I got the November 11 visitor spot. He told me that when he found out he had a visitor coming, he was hoping someone else was coming and made it clear that he was disappointed it was me. I felt bad, too, but I had no control over who went to see him that day. I got up and left. The following poem was undated, but considering the content, David may have written it around this time.

WITHOUT THE PAIN I'D BE COLD AND DEAD

Everyone who surrounds me, seems as crazy as can be
Sometimes I fear, the crazy one is me.

I think one way today, tomorrow something new
How am I supposed to know what is true?

My thoughts are in flux, my opinions the same
How is it I have, only one name?

The confusion runs deep, nothing is clear
The only thing certain, is the pain and the fear.

All that I've given and all that I've bled
It seems without the pain, I'd be cold and dead.

So I hold strong to my fear and tight to my pain
Standing alone, in the pouring rain.

If I were to be left without the two of these
I would be a forest, without any trees.

CHAPTER 9: 2011

RECONNECTING

In January 2011, David was released from D.C. jail after 190 days of incarceration.* I was parked outside the jail, anxiously waiting for him when he walked out into the cold, sunny day. I wasn't sure whether to expect a still angry David, who would storm out and head straight for his dealer, or a David who would welcome the sight of me. My worries flew away when he spotted me and his face broke into a wide grin. I was so glad to see him! He looked great. He had put on weight, his skin was clear, and his brown eyes shined. We shared big hugs and happy tears; relief washed over me. I took him back to my house to stay until he could get into an Oxford House (residential sober house). His brother, Bill, joined us for lunch. I cannot express the joy I felt having both of my sons healthy and together again.

After lunch, I drove David to his barber shop to see about getting his job back. I watched through the front window as Kathy, his friend and co-worker, greeted him with a big smile and hug. Her welcome warmed my heart and brought more tears. Not only did the barber shop want David to come back to work, but Kathy asked David to begin working that afternoon. David was unsure about what to do, so much had happened that day, but he decided to stay and work. I left David at the shop, giving thanks and with fingers crossed that he would take advantage of this new beginning and achieve the life he claimed to be capable of.

Now that his job was secure, David's next steps were to call his probation officer, get new eyeglasses, and find an Oxford House close enough to the shop so he could use public transportation and not need a car. David wrote on Facebook, "Hopefully, I am now done with all the jail time I will ever

---

* David's fictional story, "When a Man Must Face the World Alone," reflects his leaving D.C. jail in 2011.

have to do. I am living in Fairfax at an Oxford House (sober house)."

Within days, Circe began sending David realtor emails for houses they could share.

REBA

David immediately began reconnecting with old friends on social media. One of the first was his longtime high school girlfriend, Reba. She was as glad to hear from David as he was to find her. Over the next year and a half they shared through Facebook their lives, music, old friends, future hopes and dreams, and what could have been, if only. They found each other in a more mature place and easily resumed a caring relationship online. David's messages to Reba are endearing and give more clues about his addiction, who he was as a young man, and who he thought he could be.

On January 13, 2011, Dave wrote:

> "It is good to see your face again. I was waiting for you to join Facebook so I could see you. It's been too long and that ain't right. I have been away for a while. I wasn't ignoring you. I looked at your pictures and came across something that stunned me . . . I couldn't believe my eyes. Your daughter is like a little woman now, huh? You know, the last time I saw her she was a baby. She was sooo cute. I can remember it all so clear. You being pregnant. I remember you naming her, then you changed it. Me & U taking the baby to the Dr. She probably doesn't even know I exist. That's ok, though. I am at my mother's house right now. I showed her your daughter's pic. She couldn't believe it. Then she pulled out our prom pics. Man, we sure do look young. My haircut is retarded but you were just so pretty. You really were. So many things I could say. I sure do hope you guys are happy. Anyway, I hope to hear from ya soon, David"

> May 11, 2011: "I was thinking about our relationship . . . good or bad . . . you were the person I had my first Love with. I truly was in love with you, too. It's weird. I have had many relationships since then. But I don't experience love in the same way. That

complete and total attraction to another person. It's just not that way anymore. Maybe I just grew up and that is how kids experience love. I don't know . . . good or bad, you were the one that I loved. You were the one who made me really feel the pain that love songs are written about. I can't deny that. You will always hold a special place in my heart. Sometimes I think how foolish I was and how stupid I behaved but the reality is that things happened the way they did and nothing can change that. And, I am who I am as a result. That is what I will never regret because I am happy with who I am. I sure hope that you are, too, honey. I loved you then, and I always will . . . I hope you are happy, and I am glad to see your daughter is becoming a happy, well-adjusted young woman. I don't have any kids and always wished she had been mine, so I kind of feel like that's the closest I have ever come."

In another message on October 16, Dave wrote:

"I'm rebuilding my life because I pretty much lost everything when I went to prison. The best thing was the fact that my job was waiting for me when I got out. They have been good to me. Nevertheless, I am trying to save enough to start my own Barber Shop. I have had several setbacks along the way, but it is pretty amazing how much I have accomplished in the 10 months I have been out. I impress myself sometimes at all I can do when I don't have drugs holding me back. If I hadn't relapsed back in 2005, I would really be somewhere. Back then I was taking 12 credits at NOVA, got my barbers license, and ran an eBay business. But I did it one time, I did one shot of heroin and that was it. I gave it all up. I got too cocky, because I was doing so well that I thought I could just sneak a shot every now and then. I know now that I cannot do that. So I can do anything as long as I don't do that."

KNOW THYSELF

In January 201, David was Facebooking with another old friend when he wrote:

"You said that knowledge is key. I hope you realize how profound that is. Specifically self-knowledge. You know, The Ancient Greek Oracle at Delphi had something written on the wall in her Chamber. It said, (in Greek) 'know thyself.' When Socrates went to see her he came to the conclusion that no matter what you asked the Oracle, the answer lay in those two words. The Oracle proclaimed Socrates to be the wisest man in the land, because he claimed he knew that he knew nothing. He definitely knew enough to recognize the wisdom in 'know thyself.'"

RITA

In February, David responded to a Facebook message from his friend, Rita:

"I am well. I just completed 190 days for D.C. Hopefully, I am now done w/ all the jail time I will ever have to do. I am living in Fairfax at an Oxford House (sober house). I still have my condo in Reston, but I have chosen to live here cuz I know I need a fresh start away from anyone who may tempt me. Last time I got out, I went by to see old buddies. I did one shot of morphine, and I was right back. I think the key is that I never do it even once. If I don't do it that first time, then I'll quit fucking up my life. So I am taking steps to do that. I feel real good, though. My mind is clear. I read about 50 more books and am now a master chess player. These things I enjoy. I love being alive, and I like who I am. It is not clear why I would want to be numb all of the time. I think it has a lot to do with the fact that heroin is just so addictive that stopping alone is impossible for almost anyone. But now that I have been clean for some time, if I were to start back up, then that would be my foolishness. This is a critical time in my life. I intend to succeed and move forward. Things are good and if I am off that shit, I know that I can be the person I want to be."

It wasn't until after David died that I learned of his friendship with Rita. Getting to know Rita was getting to know another side of my son. David didn't try to manipulate, trick, or deny who he was with Rita. As far as I know, she was probably the one person he was most honest with. After David died, Rita, an avid writer and blogger, compiled her communications with him and sent them to us. I am forever grateful to her for her support and for sharing her personal memories.

Mid-April 2011, David attended court-ordered outpatient drug treatment. He sent a Facebook message to Rita to let her know what he was up to:

"April 12, 2011. Hello, Sorry I haven't responded. I have not been Facebookin it the last few days. I've been busy with all sorts of bullshit. Today, I am stuck in downtown Fairfax all day. I am now enrolled in INOVA Fairfax Hospital's outpatient drug treatment they call CATS that the courts are making me do. I just spent three hours in this counselor guy's office. It should not have taken so long, but I can't just sit there and let somebody tell me some bullshit. I guess I can for a little while but at some point, I have to let the guy know exactly the caliber of mind he is dealing with. That is the only way I can benefit from what these people have to offer. You know? They are not gonna sit there and tell me that I am just the same as every other junkie out there. I don't think I am better, just different. I expect to be handled accordingly.

"Then I have to go through the long drawn out process of unveiling to these people just what is and where my perspective lies. This always happens to me. Then they start to realize that I am smart . . . call me Einstein and shit . . . then I have to shut that down and let him know that I am open to new information. I am just not gonna sit there and listen to ridiculous bullshit . . . just cuz everybody else goes for it, that's cool . . . I don't want to influence them or turn anybody against you guys, as I could if I chose to. You just have to work with me on my level . . . that's all. I mean, you don't teach a master carpenter how to use a hammer, and you can't spend all day telling him that he is using it wrong, when he knows otherwise through experience. That doesn't mean that a master carpenter has nothing left to learn. There are always things to learn . . . I just have to establish these things when I deal with these people, and I always say that I am just gonna go in there and keep my mouth shut, go through whatever kind of bullshit I gotta go through and get the hell out of there. But I just can't seem to do it. I can't seem to keep my mouth shut.

"Anyway, then during that process, a bond between me and the other person begins to develop, and he enjoys the conversation so it gets longer and longer. It's OK, though. I have to go to ASAP [Alcohol Safety Action Program] tonight, which is also here in Fairfax so I am pretty much stuck here all day. Pretty good place to be stuck though. Plenty of food and a great library. So killing time here is really better spent than at home anyway. Plus the tattoo shop I go to is right here. I was gonna go get one but my guy is all booked. Anyway, that is all about my day :) I just needed to rant and you got it. Sorry."

WHO AM I?

David often wrote about playing a role and feeling the need to be who others wanted him to be. He would rhetorically ask and write, "Who am I?" He wondered if he was crazy, fooling himself, or maybe he had another person inside of him. Choosing to write under a pseudonym indicates he struggled with his identity. Selfies that David posted on Facebook and other pictures found on his laptop ranged from a clean-cut, good-looking regular guy to a mean and tough dude in his A-shirt. It was almost like he was running through his personalities. In an April 16 Facebook message, David commiserated with a female friend about his problems finding the "right" girl:

"April 16, 2011. I have a couple girls I talk to, that is what I am saying. I just don't really like them that much . . . I just can't seem to find a good one. That is all I want. I don't want to keep going from girl to girl. But I also am not gonna settle for anything less than . . . well, she doesn't have to be perfect but . . . All the girls I meet just don't meet all my criteria. I just can't stand being around a dumb chick for very long. And then the ones who wouldn't know funny if it hit them over the head. I like to laugh, have fun, have interesting conversations, be attracted to each other, have great sex, and fall asleep together. Most girls fit some part of that, but most don't fit all."

His friend responded that she didn't think his criteria were too strict and that it sounded like a personal ad, which may have given David an idea. She also put David in his place when she wrote:

"I am sure most people want the same thing. I think you might be in trouble, though . . . only the dumb chicks are gonna find you funny!"

Within a few days, David joined SpeedDate, and on May 11, 2011, posted a personal ad on Craig's List:

"I am just looking for someone who is easy to talk to and is easy on the eyes. I am both of those things, so if such a person sees this then hit me up. The bottom line is that I can't find a girl who is attractive, fun to be around, and knows about enough to carry on an intelligent and funny conversation. I can tell you about me. I am a very smart person, very interesting, and fun, but I am also a bit of a bad-boy. I am never violent, or even rude . . . I just don't conform unless I deem that is the correct path. I never conform just because everyone else is. I am a free thinker. I have read many, many books. All kinds, and I am a philosophy buff. I am a bit of an existentialist mixed with Buddhist. I have tattooed on both of my forearms the words JUST BE. I feel that in any situation, for me to make the correct action, I must completely let go of the noise and confusion, and JUST BE. Then I can take the correct action to move forward. I have several other tattoos, too, but I am not covered with them. I cut hair for a living and do well, although I intend to move forward beyond that . . . I am a VERY happy person and will not let anyone threaten my happiness. I am looking for a good woman to help me grow and be my friend and lover . . . I am a sexual person but it does not define me or my relationships . . . sex will be a part of our relationship, though. If you don't like good healthy sex, then I'm not your man. I don't do kinky shit or anal shit. I am a passionate lover, and I revel in the connection made during sex. I also like sports, chess, and cards. I like all kinds of cool shit. I love life and the things it has to offer . . . so, look at my pictures and if you think we are a good fit then put 'BADD BOY' on the subject line and hit me back. Love, David"

TRUTH, KNOWLEDGE & A KISS

On April 28, 2011, David was Facebooking with Rita and wrote:

"You are talking mostly about accepting that you don't have certain knowledge. I think that is very important. So often we delude ourselves into believing we know something that we do not know. This is one of the worst things a person can do. If we do that then we can never gain that knowledge since we have not accepted that we do not possess it. This is the path to ignorance, the enemy of enlightenment.

"Truth is a very big deal to me. It sets us free. It isn't even the great things that happen when we accept the truth (because they do not.) It is more about the terrible things we do to ourselves in the process of avoiding it. Then these delusions pile up on us, and this results in a state of confusion. Debilitating confusion. This confusion is actually going to be a major point in my next essay.""[*]

Rita responded with, "EXACTLY! Muah!!"

David asked, "I have seen 'muah' several times, what does it mean?"

"It's a kiss, silly . . . the sound of giving one."

"Oh! I get it . . . kisses are good. Do you like kisses? Did you know it is not necessary to be wearing clothes when you kiss?"

---

[*] "Cure for Confusion" can be found with David's collection of writings following the memoir.

WOMEN / DRUGS / FRIENDSHIP

Social media gave David a way to feed another of his addictions. Facebook and Craig's List became David's primary venues for finding women. He wanted to woo and screw them all. He signed up for dating websites, found online porn, and flirted endlessly to satisfy his hunger for sex, which he compared to his hunger for drugs, neither of which he could stop.

David wrote about women, relationships, and friendship in various Facebook and email messages during 2011. Most of his messages were flirty and light, with humor, providing relief from his sad and serious writing about darkness and addiction. In a Facebook message about friendship, David reveals his "Beware the Righteous" concept, which was so important to him that he had it tattooed across his chest, and an event that inspired one of his short stories. By January 2012, he was women weary and wrote:

> "It's a strange phenomenon, friendship is. Often we end up in friendships with people for the wrong reasons. I know that I am probably not like other male friends you have. I am not very outwardly nice and agreeable. Sometimes women want to be around people who are very agreeable. The problem is that those people are often playing a role in front of you. Many men are like this, and women tend to seek them out and then they wonder why they get hurt.

> "I am not a 'yes man.' I am your friend. I hope you understand what I mean by this. To me, the physical act of love is a wonderful thing, and I have never been one to take advantage of women. I know people think differently, but they are wrong. That is why I am still friends with almost every woman I have been with, and the nice guy friends they had at the time warning them about me are long gone. I very much believe in loyalty. Those agreeable people are just lying, and they are bad people. That argument also solidifies my Beware the Righteous concept."

The previous Fall David wrote on Facebook:

"September 7, 2011.* I have been having some trouble with women lately. It isn't anything I am doing, because I try to keep to myself. But I have been seeing a woman who I care a great deal for. She lives with another guy now, and I am ok with that. But she always comes over to my house. I don't mind, but she fills my head with lies. Normally she keeps me away from her friends, (who used to be my friends, too), but we all went out Saturday night. I couldn't believe the things that were coming out of this one girl's mouth. She was just casually revealing to me just how complex and deep all of these lies are. I normally just let her lie, because I am over her anyway. But it made me mad as shit.

"She has another friend who was there and always hits on me when she drinks. Anyway, I said fuck it. I am single and she supposedly loves this other guy so I took her friend home with me. Well, she has freaked out. She is just harassing me so bad. I don't understand how I got myself mixed up with these crazy people. They all have been told I am still on drugs and were surprised to see that I am clean and healthy. The real problem is that I think they liked me more when I was on heroin, because I would let them take advantage of me and they felt like they were better than me. I know I have to just let these people go . . . they don't care about me. However, I feel very alone at this prospect. She also has been successful at making me feel that I am a fool with my stupid philosophical ideas."

Facebook messages multiplied. A good friend left a Facebook message listing several reasons why she was upset with David about his "erratic and selfish behavior" and questioned why he had stopped responding to her. He wrote back:

"I just can't do it right now. I am sorry you don't respect me. I am trying to get myself together right now, and I am gonna just cancel my Facebook."*

---

* David's fictional story, "When a Man Must Face the World Alone," reflects the event described in this September 7 Facebook message.
* It was around this time that David wrote his poems, "Plague of Confusion" and "Facebook Confusion."

WRITING / WRITERS' BLOCK

Most of David's stories were written during the 2011 to 2012 timeframe. He expresses frustration in Facebook messages about losing some of his work, experiencing writers' block, and the inability to stay focused.

"April 2011. I just wrote about 500 words . . . Then got interrupted by an idiot and lost it all. Not only did I lose the words but I lost the state of mind necessary to rewrite them. Let me find my way back there.

"I find myself in a place of peace. I will not try to rewrite what I wrote. It was pure, true poetry, but it is gone. This is of little matter because the words come with ease in the Free State . . . Fleetwood Mac's 'Dreams' just came on my MP3 random. This is good. My back door is open and it is cool but not cold. When the song goes off, there is a pause and I can hear my neighbors upstairs; they are loud but it is not a distraction . . . it actually adds to the dreamlike state I seek. A little wine helps, too. Ahhh, 'Gold Dust Woman,' Nice . . ."

David continued to struggle creatively and wrote:

"The other failure is that I have the book I want to write in my head, but for some reason I cannot seem to sit down and write it. I am tired and lazy all the time. I am confused about this. I don't know what it is. I work on it constantly in my mind. I think it's fear, but I don't know what I am afraid of. Success, I guess. I have never been successful. I never visualize myself that way. I don't know, but that is where I am at.

"I have been in a meditative state for two days now. I have not left the house. I will find my way, but I wanted to spend these, actually two and a half days, writing. But that is not what I did. Instead, I have read and tried to find my path. My failures recently were causing confusion in my mind and anger in my heart . . . I had to let that go. I just hope I can find the strength to start writing soon."

David very much wanted to be a published author. In late summer, he confidently drafted a letter to "The Potential Agent of the Next Great American Author":

"August 2011. My name is David. Going by the pseudonym, Socrates H. Dillinger, I have written a novel. This is a piece I have been preparing for some time and it is now complete. It is a true work of art. It is very well written, interesting and dynamic. I have written it in a style completely unique to me. I have no specific influences in an attempt to create a work that is to set a new precedent in the world of fiction.

"I am aware that this is a bold statement. As my agent, though, you should know that my aim as a writer is not only to tell an entertaining and interesting story; it must be well written. Complex characters, interesting dialogue, and a story that says something interesting and unique. Most important to me is my ability to play the English language like the violin I see it to be. I am a lover of the English language. I like to relay multiple pieces of dynamic information using easy to understand and dense language.

"I believe that this book will be successful. Specifically, it will be successful with people who love great literature and critics alike. Not to say the latter is always the former, but I am sure it will be a critical success.

"The bottom line for an agent, though, is that it will sell. People will talk about it because it is good. They will buy it and it will generate money for us both. The good news also is that I have creative ideas* flowing through me like water. I have many more ideas, and I have the ability to articulate them well.

"In short, I need an agent to represent me in selling this book and all of my future books."

---

* Dave's Creative Writing Ideas List is in his collection of writings following this memoir.

At the end of August, David rediscovered his journal and documented where he was with life and writing:

"I just came across this book and read it. Amazing how writing things down brings back memories. Well, I am living alone at the condo! Working at the Barber Shop. I feel very good. My wife doesn't live with me but I see her every day. I am 10,000 words into my book!!

"It's amazing how, when I look back at this journal, I realize I haven't changed at all. I still want the same things and have similar ideas. I have been trading in the stock market, but I have not been doing well. It's a tough market right now. I have learned a whole lot, though. I can read charts. I fully understand how it works. That's good. I know this, too—those penny stocks are almost all fake companies. It is an interesting scam people have going on. I plan to investigate how they create a fake company; take it public (on pink sheets or OTC BB); and pump and dump it using message boards, chat rooms, and emails.

"It is very interesting. I wouldn't want to run a scam like that though. Rippin' people off like that. I would do it for a little while though to get some start-up capital to get a business going. I am now studying the FOREX market. See if I can't make some money trading currency. I just need about $30K to start a barber shop.

"Well, I am gonna go back to writing. If I can ever finish this book, I look forward to trying to sell it. This could be a DREAMS COME TRUE kind of thing so I should be working on it constantly. It is very difficult, though. Writing a book is HARD, VERY HARD. I HAVE TO GO OVER IT AND OVER IT TO GET ALL OF THE WORDS RIGHT. THEN KEEP WRITING FURTHER IT COULD TAKE A YEAR IF I'M NOT DILIGENT!"

PHILOSOPHIES

Reba wrote to Dave on Facebook:

> "Thank God for rules and blinders, for me ignorance is bliss."

Upset with her statement, Dave responded:

> "This is so wrong, so fundamentally flawed and very sad. If you really feel that way, then you will miss the beauty and majesty that lies in the details of life. You will miss the metaphors and symbolism in movies and books. You have to open your mind to truly appreciate life. There is just sooooo much out there to learn and know. The rewards for this knowledge continue to pay dividends forever. Please don't embrace ignorance. That is not the life I want for you."

David had numerous philosophical discussions with me, friends, and anyone else who would listen and offer commentary. Favorite topics included know thyself; analyzing truth; putting thoughts into perspective; knowledge and power; and enlightenment. When he and I had these discussions, we usually ended up in a realist vs. idealist debate. I, the realist, was no match for David. It saddens me still that I let his addiction overshadow the creative and knowledgeable man he was struggling to become. Taking from Socrates's quote "The only true wisdom is in knowing you know nothing," Dave often said, "Know that we know nothing, then we are freed to find the truth."

We think we know the truth about our addict. We don't. Addiction robs us of the ability to see beyond their cruel actions and mean words. Our truth becomes a stranger and we are lost.

On June 21, 2011, David posted the following about truth on his blog, *Constructs of a Feeble Human Intellect*. This short untitled narrative is presented exactly as David posted it on his blog.

> "... and for a moment I knew what it was all about. But then it was gone ...."

> ". . . That's when she said to me. A shadow is not the blocking of light by an object, rather, the darkness is the natural state. The light imposes on the dark its will. The object protects the spot,

keeps the spot in its true state. The darkness does not need to be illuminated. It does not need to be seen. It is us that needs to see it. So we naturally assume that the illumination of a spot is the truth of it. The truth is that the spot remains itself with or without our ability to see it. First, the light imposes on it. Then, our ability to see it causes us to impose our will on the spot.

"I then responded, but our mere awareness of something can cause it to change. It may exist, just based simply on the fact that someone knows it does. This is the way of all things. Right or wrong. This is the way . . .

". . . and for a moment I knew what it was all about.....but then it was gone . . ."

GOTTA MOVE

David and Circe's condo sold in a short sale in September, 2011. He had to find a new place to live. Their codependent, love/hate relationship continued as it had for years. Circe's emails toggled between love and fierce anger because David continued to see other women. David's emails toggled between love and anger because Circe had left him to live with another guy. He repeatedly promised that he loved only Circe and would be true blue if she would just come back to live with him. Circe did not go back to David, even though she returned his love and bombarded him with realtor emails for houses they could share. Meanwhile, David continued to cheat on her and use heroin, and Circe threatened to take away his health insurance and sent divorce papers asking for damages. Their destructive psycho drama and codependent behavior never ended.

David described his situation in a Facebook message:

"October 27, 2011. I really wanna open my own shop but this is a good place for now. I am pretty much rebuilding right now. I caught some drug charges a while back and went to prison for a year so I lost a lot. I still had my job when I got out, so things have gone well. I am selling my condo cuz it lost all its value in this market, but it worked out because it sat waiting for me the whole time I was gone. So I had a job and a home right away when I got out. It could be a lot worse. Things are great, though. I have been out 10 months, no drugs, I am single, and things are good! Haircuts are $16 and yes, I am happy!

"I would love to have some land with my own garage and maybe get an old car I could restore in the garage. Get a 4-wheeler, have a couple dogs, etc., or move to the city by myself. I won't be able to get as big of a place but I will have my freedom and I have always wanted to live in the city."

David's relationship with family during most of 2011 was good. He continued to write stories, joined online writing websites, and downloaded *How to Publish Your Own Book* from Apple. He continued to reconnect with old friends and sent writing samples to people for review. As far as I know, he was not actively using heroin, but he was having a lot of sex. In fact, regardless of what David told Circe, he was obsessed with women and sex, regularly meeting and communicating with women, mostly online.

BARBER TOOLS

David's description of what barber tools he used and his "designer" haircuts comes from a Facebook message he sent to a friend who was thinking about becoming a barber. Sometimes David would send me pictures of his designer cuts. They were usually of pre-teen boys who wanted a star, a stripe, or some type of symbol shaved into the side or back of their head. David developed a reputation as a skilled barber and for his designer haircuts.

"October 27, 2011. I use Wahl detailers and cut freehand. Be careful of the gimmick clippers. Most of the time they don't work and you end up doing it freehand anyway. Sometimes, I will make up a stencil. The most important thing is to really think out the cut BEFORE you begin. Experience helps cuz cutting into hair can be strange depending on the way the grain of the hair goes and the type of hair the person has—thin, thick, curly, straight. Also, it is very important to decide if you are going to cut an image in the hair or create an image with the hair and clean around it. It usually looks better when the image is with the hair and not in the hair. Just make sure you visualize the image in the head before you start . . . then proceed.

"Once you start cutting, you can't turn back. This may have you staring at the side of someone's head for a while, and they will think you're weird. But I have to see in my own head the picture on the person's head before I can begin to cut. Placement is important, too. If you start too low then you are stuck down there and the same with too high. I do that all the time. I never remember to take pictures. I gotta remember that, but even when I do, my brain doesn't really function on things like that. It's a strange thing, actually, cuz I can't even do simple math after cutting hair. I guess it's the other side of my brain that is active and my mind has to adjust. If you think it through, then anyone can do it."

On the same day, Dave offered advice to another friend on the best way to cope with drugs and addiction:

"The best way to cope with these vices—drugs—is to look deep inside yourself and accept who and what you are. Then strive to be the best you can be . . . the universe will just give you everything you want and maybe even more.

"The longer you indulge your angst, the harder it becomes to let it go. That is no different than opiate addiction. It is an addiction that is inherent to the human condition placed there to give us strength, but we must use our strength to overcome it. It isn't easy. Eventually you will have to Free Yourself. Maybe not today, but that day is coming and when it does, remember that you know people who can relate and are willing to assist."

MOVE FROM THE CONDO

In November, David moved from the Reston condo and rented a small room in a house in Vienna. I helped him move his few things and knew that he would not be happy there, but his options were limited. He kept in touch and attended family outings and dinners until mid-November when he didn't make it for his brother's birthday dinner. David canceled at the last minute—a first indicator of addict behavior returning. He called and said he was out shopping for a car with Circe and wouldn't be able to make it back to my house in time for dinner. I didn't know it then, but Circe had bombarded David's email inbox with *Auto Trader* emails throughout the day.

David was also a no show for Thanksgiving, 2011. We had planned for me to pick him up at 12:45, but when I texted that morning to confirm, he texted back that 12:45 was too early and he would have to miss dinner. He gave no other excuse. There was also no mention about the 2007 Ford Escape that Circe bought him. On Thanksgiving Day, Circe was upset and sent David a detailed email listing his expenses she had paid for—totaling over $20K—including the Ford Escape; judgment payment; rent; HOA for the condo; bankruptcy lawyer; trustee payment; and association documents. I have no idea if these charges are accurate. David emailed her back, "I can't do anything about this, but you can have the car back."

David texted on Christmas morning and said he would be late because he forgot about his phone bill and had to stop to pay it. After a couple of hours, he finally arrived, and we exchanged gifts and had brunch at my house. He seemed to be OK but was groggy and had obviously lost weight. After brunch we drove to my niece's house, an hour away, for Christmas dinner. I realized soon after we arrived that the walls were caving in around David. By the time we sat down to eat dinner, he had a difficult time functioning well enough to use his fork.

I could see other family members were closely watching him and were disgusted by his spastic behavior even though he wasn't being mean, loud or disruptive. He also wasn't his usual talkative self. He was trying to be "normal." I was trying to be "normal." It was useless. I blamed myself for allowing family members to be exposed to David and his slow dive to drugged lethargy and dysfunction. I felt worse for David, who didn't seem to have a clue what was going on around him. The next Christmas, David was not welcome to attend dinner. I understood. Addicts scare people.

In a Facebook message, David described what he did on Christmas Eve, which helps explain why he was in such bad shape on Christmas Day. Stopping to "pay his phone bill" earlier that morning was a typical addict excuse for a trip to his dealer and, I suspect, the real reason for his inability to function by dinner time.

> "December 24, 2011. I went to David's BBQ after work to eat and there were so many people there whose hair I cut that my meal was free, and people bought me all my beers and 3 shots. I only paid for one beer when I left. Except I drank more than I planned on drinking. Now I am at Reston Town Center cuz I really don't have anything else to do. I'm goin' to see family tomorrow, but I'm all alone tonight. Just a gigolo everywhere I go."

David must have been feeling philosophical when he penned his Christmas greeting to me and my husband:

> "Sometimes the path is not always clear and knowing what to do is sometimes hard. But if we resist revelations of confusion and fear and use this correctly, the truth can be found. Merry Christmas, David."

Circe wasn't so cheery when she sent a Facebook message to Dave on Christmas Day 2011 and told him to get his mother or one of his other girlfriends to buy him a house, to move his [health] insurance [payments] from her bank account, and to transfer the car to his name. She asked for his address so she could send divorce papers. Circe exclaimed that she was no longer going to let him drag her into more debt and misery. Now, she said, he could enjoy all the sleepovers he wanted.

By year's end, David was partying hard, mixing pills and alcohol, and getting "hammered," as he put it in messages to a woman he was seeing and another friend:

> "I think I know why I passed out like that. It was the Valium. That shit makes me sleep hard as shit. I'm at home now. It was a long day at work. I am a tired white boy . . . I took another Valium and two Roxies so I am gonna be out real soon."

A couple days later:

> "I got fucking screwed last night. This girl who is a friend of mine got a room at the Hyatt, which is a beautiful hotel right in Reston Town Center. It is right next to Clyde's, a restaurant, and they had a huge party. It was awesome. I ran into a shitload of people I know. But at some point, this girl and her friend went back to the room without telling me. People kept buying me shots on the ice luge. I ended up hammered. When I went back to the room, these two bitches were fucking passed out and didn't open the door. I got stranded."

BULL SHITTERS ANONYMOUS

Circe was not happy when she found out where David was on New Year's Eve. In early January, she emailed David and said that along with his NA [Narcotics Anonymous], he should start a BSA, Bull Shitters Anonymous. She was fed up and closing the door on him. She told him that he would never use her again.

CHAPTER 10: 2012

WOMEN WEARY

On January 16, 2012, David marked the one-year anniversary of his release from D.C. jail by posting on Facebook:

"I let January 12 go by without even noticing. Exactly one year before I was released from the DC DOC. It is strange but looking out the window of a prison cell is kind of like looking outward from the summit of a mountain on a clear day. I could see my path so clearly. I could see the obstacles and navigate a path to avoid them. But on my release date I had to come down from that summit and its clear view to actually walk this path. It was easy at first, but the further away I get from that view and the more immersed I become in this path, the less I can remember what I saw. I no longer know what I knew, but I can still remember that I knew something and it seems that I must rely on that to navigate further. What a strange year it has been. I've lost my way at times, but ultimately it has been great and I have lived free. Hopefully I can continue to do that."

On January 2, David sent contradicting Facebook messages about using drugs to a woman he was dating and another friend.

"I took 2 Roxies, which is actually the strongest Percocet out there. I then took a Valium, which has really sent me to a beautiful place. Wow! What an adventure this weekend was . . . I am tired. Gotta work, though!! I am still on that cloud, floating around the barber shop. I feel good today. I'm not gonna drink for a while though. I know what is wrong with me. I took one of those Ambiens last night, and I have not been able to keep my eyes open all day. God, that shit is strong. Dilaudid is a beautiful thing. One of my favorites."

January 2, 30 minutes later, to another friend:

> "Oh. I will stay out of jail. No more drugs for me. That, along with a positive outlook, allows me to have a wonderful life that is without limits."

By mid-January, his head was spinning with too many women:

> "January 18, 2012. My real problem right now, though, is the women. I have just gotten myself caught up with so many different women at one time, my head is spinning. It is causing me to lie and to constantly have to respond to their texts. And then I am going out all the time, so I am drinking a lot, which I really don't wanna be doing but it is just part of going out. Then the girl thinks I have been super busy all week (cuz that is what I tell them) and I should be excited about a night out but the truth is I have been out every night with a different girl.

> "There are just so many different ways it causes me to suffer and not feel free but it is very hard for me to let any of them go. Then when I do, I keep getting new ones. I can't resist. I know this sounds pretty stupid. Too many women. That's like saying too much money, right? No, it isn't. These women are very demanding and they are draining me so I know what I gotta do. I also knew what I had to do when I was doin' drugs, but I couldn't stop that either."

As angry and frustrated as Circe was with David, she continued sending realtor emails for houses they could share and, at the same time, email threats to divorce him if he didn't stop with all the women. She berated him unrelentingly about all the money she had given him and the Ford Escape that she didn't take back. When Dave blocked Circe from his Facebook profile, she sent him a Facebook message and said that since he continued to block her from his profile, to change his relationship status to "divorced." Nevertheless, Circe continued blasting realtor emails for days.

By this time, there were many women, and he continued looking for more. His drinking, pill popping, and dangerous behavior continued through February as noted in messages to one of the women he was dating:

"February 19. Hey Honey. I'm sorry about the whole thing. It was craziness, and I just hate myself for taking those pills. That just isn't me anymore, and I slipped. Although it wasn't my fault the cab hit me, bad things happen to me when I do stupid drugs like that. It always does and there is no justification for my behavior."

"February 28. I had a bad day today cuz a dog (or possibly a coyote) came darting out in front of my car and I hit it. I searched everywhere for it, but couldn't find it. I feel sooooo terrible about it."

She responded to his messages writing, "You were real fucked up last night. Sorry that your car got hit."

On February 19, Circe emailed Dave again about signing the divorce papers and how lucky he was to have her give him $12K to pay his fines, rent, and a car. She warned him that was his last chance to get his life together. Ten days later, Circe emailed David a link to a 2000 Cadillac Escalade for sale on *Auto Trader*.

WORST THING THAT EVER HAPPENED

In March 2012, David was searching for a new place to live. The Vienna room was small, and David didn't like his housemates. To complicate life, on March 20, David and his lady friend were out partying, big time. She was supposed to be the designated driver but got too trashed to drive. David drove and was pulled over and arrested for DUI, which caused him significant grief with the courts.

Dave sent an email to the bail bondsman to thank him after the DUI arrest:

"March 21, 2012. This is David, the Barber. I just wanted to thank you for your help yesterday. You're a good man, James. Saved my ass twice now. I wish I wasn't such a good customer, but I appreciate the fact that you sat down there all day, then drove me out of your way. You went above and beyond, and I appreciate that!"

In large sprawled writing, he made notes to himself about the arrest and his case in his journal:

"I need to see the police report. Possibly contest the stop. Why was I stopped? Read the police report. Allegation of swerving? Is there a dash-mounted camera? Where is the video of the arrest? Was I pulled over just because of the time?

"My case: I had no drinks for two hours before leaving the bar. The girl was supposed to drive, but she was too intoxicated. I played a game of chess against the bouncer at the end of the night. We can subpoena him to say that I was not drinking during this game and was of sound, sober mind. We can subpoena the girl to say that I stopped drinking several hours before we left and was drinking water. She can also say that she was supposed to drive but she drank too much, so to be safe, I drove. The nurse can also testify that I was sober at the hospital. Witnesses: Bouncer, girl, nurse at the hospital, the cop.

"I have Hepatitis C. There have been many cases where it was shown that the BAC [blood alcohol content] level was higher than it should be as a result of having Hep C.

"Another Possible Strategy: Speak to the judge myself. Articulate to him the exact situation and why I am able to feel good about the choices I made in this situation. The girl who was supposed to drive was heavily intoxicated and certainly it would not have been prudent to allow her to drive. I had three Capt. and Cokes. I will grant that the bartender made them strong. Something I was not particularly happy about because I am not a drinker. I will note that my other DUI did not involve alcohol. I think that is important, because I am opposed to driving drunk."

When Circe heard about the DUI, she rolled into action and took charge to save Dave. She immediately started sending him emails with information about a DUI attorney who also handled probation violations. It wasn't long before Dave sought out his "best friend" to escape his troubles and relapsed back into active heroin addiction.

PERFECT BASEMENT APARTMENT

David eventually found what he described to me in a text as the "perfect" place for him to live. Attached to the text were pictures of a basement apartment and the nearby tennis courts. David was excited and happy to have found a place of his own on his own. Little did he know that this "perfect" apartment would be the scene of his death. He also sent along the title for his next novel, *The Dopefiend Messiah!*

> "March 28, 2012. A great little basement apartment! I have my own entrance with a nice patio with a grill and chairs on it. Fireplace in my room. My own full bathroom. The landlord lives in Maryland. I met him yesterday. Great Guy. 4 other guys in the house all renting rooms independently. All young cool people. My rent is $650 a month. It is perfect."

In April, there was a chance one of David's ladies was pregnant. When she told him she was pregnant but that she didn't think it was his, David replied with his ego: "I hope it isn't mine. I do. But if that baby comes out super awesome, brilliant, and handsome as shit then u know u got a little Dave on your hands, and I am gonna wanna know about it."

YOU OWE ME

On June 1, Circe sent an email to both David and me. In it was an extensive list of what she had paid out for him—now totaling over $25,000. The list included condo expenses and repairs, car and health insurance, attorney fees and court fines, and car payments. She insisted that she did all this to help him get back on his feet, but she was upset that he had not kept any of his promises to her. In her very long email, she laid out a plan for him to pay her back and the terms she was willing to accept. Circe included me on the email for two reasons: 1) she thought, as his mother, I should pay David's attorneys' fees; and 2) she wanted me to agree to have David's payments to her funneled through me.

What Circe didn't understand was I was not going to pay any of David's debts, including his attorneys' fees. And, even if I wanted to, there was no way I could or would ensure he paid monthly payments to her. I responded I was not going to become David's keeper, and she must stop thinking that by paying his debts, she was "helping" him.

I had no way of knowing if what Circe wrote in this email was true or when she supposedly did all these things, but I assume it was sometime after David returned from D.C. jail in January. I do know that her actions and behavior are classic traits of enabling and codependency and are destructive for an addict. Could she really believe she was helping Dave when she did these things? Weren't the last 12 years of addict madness enough to convince her that continuing to support David and to pay his debts was the opposite of what he needed? Even without knowing the details of "all" she was doing for him, I knew that if she continued to "help" him in any way, it hindered Dave from stopping his heroin use.

On June 3, David joined "SaucyDates" online and set up his profile. He continued regularly "dating" several women and texting or Facebook messaging numerous others. Circe was relentless. She continued to keep tabs on David's whereabouts and who he was talking to. In addition to breaking into his online accounts, she often went to his apartment to search through his things. David knew this because emails were sent from his account while he was in jail or he would get an email notice that his accounts had been accessed from another computer. For the most part, he didn't seem to care. But sometimes she crossed the line and interfered in his "personal" business.

That's when he got annoyed. As with most of their battles and throughout their relationship, the animosity between Dave and Circe didn't last.

FACIAL TICS & HEROIN

As a young child, when David got mad or didn't get his way, he would squint his eyes almost closed, squeeze up his nose, and turn red. It appeared to be a controlled action and response. As he got older, he developed a facial tic that included a rapid eye blink and scrunching up his nose and cheek, and it appeared to be an uncontrollable action. He seemed to enjoy it. I don't remember making too much of it. Most of the time, though, his tic was just a mild twitch and barely noticeable. However, as he got older and deeper into addiction, his facial tics became more prominent and one of my cues that if his tic was especially noticeable, I could be pretty sure he was using.

According to *The Merck Manual of Medical Information*, "Tourette's syndrome is a disorder in which motor and vocal tics occur frequently and often begin with simple tics (repetitive, unwanted, purposeless, jerking muscle movements) in early childhood and progresses to bursts of complex movements." *Merck* goes on to say, "Tourette's syndrome is a hereditary disorder that is three times more common in men than in women. The precise cause isn't known but is thought to be an abnormality in dopamine or other brain neurotransmitters (substances that nerve cells use to communicate)."[27] To my knowledge, David was never diagnosed with Tourette's syndrome, but he liked to tell others that Tourette's caused his tics. Considering the impact heroin use has on dopamine in brains, it would not be surprising.

So, it was especially interesting to find in his journal an essay about the similarity between facial tics and heroin. The essay is also important because it explains his "key" to stopping both facial tics and using heroin.

"June 2012. There's a fascinating similarity between heroin addiction and facial tics. My experience with both have given me a unique perspective, allowing me to find a true and complete cure for both. Not all heroin addicts are the same. First, a person must be diagnosed as to what kind of heroin addict they are. Many people have overcome their afflictions without truly understanding how they did it. The key to stopping both is that they become so intrusive that the person actually wants to stop. That is the 'key.'

"Example: I always received somewhat of a reward from my tics but when they would start to give me a headache, the reward stopped being worth it. Also, the power of time away from these afflictions allows me to move past the affliction. This could last forever and for many people it does. But if I give in to a tic or dope after overcoming it, I will find myself once again enveloped by the addiction . . . just like before."

MY REVELATION OF TRUTH

Based on the essay's theory, heroin had not become intrusive enough on David's life to make the reward for stopping greater than the reward for using. First, David's almighty brain must have promised a better reward for using heroin than not using it, because he couldn't stop using even when he knew heroin was destroying him physically and mentally. Second, although he had multiple opportunities, he never found the "power" within himself to stop using through abstinence. From this perspective, David was telling the truth when he said, "I will stop when I'm ready." David's "bottom" or "cure" would only come when the reward for not using heroin outweighed the reward for using heroin. Looking at it now seems simple.

While I did not fully understand David's perspective on how to "cure" his addiction in these terms, I did know that the cure had to come from within and on his own. I also knew that neither my pleading with him nor Circe's funding his life was going to be his cure. I held out hope that a spark out of nowhere would ignite his recovery. As Dave said, and as I've read, many people do overcome addiction without knowing how. For whatever reason, the day finally comes for some addicts when the reward for stopping is greater than the reward for using. It wasn't to be for David, but families should *never* give up hope.

The good news: "'Scientists have made a major advance in untangling the brain circuits that lead to the powerful addictive effects of heroin,' a study in the open-access journal *eLife* reports. The study could lead to more effective treatments for addiction and a new generation of less addictive painkilling medications."[*]

The untitled poem below followed the "Tic vs. Heroin" essay in David's journal, which his brother would later modify to close his eulogy at David's funeral.

I laid there on my back
Looking up at the sky

Over and over thinking
Why, why, why?

The sky looks the same
As when I was young

The same as it was
Before I was lost

Everything in my life is different
I am so confused

Everything is gone
Everything has been used

Yet the sky is the same
And the grass and the trees

The only thing different
Is poor ole me.

Circe followed up her June 1 email with another email to David and me on June 4, wherein she said she had to have our "arrangements" witnessed and in writing. She also wanted to be "crystal clear" to both of us that she was going to hold him to it and not be "aggravated" again. She wanted to be paid back, pronto.

[*] www.medicalxpress.com

David responded back to Circe and me with an amount of what he thought he could pay monthly. That wasn't good enough. Circe had him tight in her grip. She wasn't going to let go. She responded by naming items she didn't address earlier. She was ruthless, sending multiple emails to both of us throughout the day that were full of drama and agonizing to read. Neither David nor I responded. At the end of the day, when it appeared she had exhausted all her grievances, David sent her a short email that read:

> "Ok, I agree to everything. I will pay $400 to Circe on the 15th of every month. Signed, David"

Dave's response prompted more Circe emails regurgitating how badly he treated her, the money he owed her, and the only terms she would accept for payment. Then, on June 22, Circe sent an email to both of us after she received a mailed notice that on June 5, the Ford Explorer she bought for David got a camera ticket for speeding on the Dulles toll road at 9:30 in the morning, obviously headed for its daily trip to D.C. Because the Explorer was in Circe's name, her name was on the ticket, and she was livid. She threatened to call the police if David didn't return the Explorer immediately.

Circe's June 22 email, Subject line:

> "BRING BACK MY CAR—PRONTO!!!!!!!!!!!!!!!!!!"

Dave's email response:

> "I AM NOT USING!!!! That specific moment in time was horribly stressful. Things are not going great right now and Circe, you are hell bent on making sure I am unhappy."

A new round of Circe's emails, demands, and threats circulated among the three of us throughout the day. She said she was going to remove him from her health insurance and proceed with a divorce immediately. I was filled with hope that she would. I sent a short response that I was disappointed and rebuked David for his behavior, but I couldn't take the drama anymore. By then, we had been on the crazy addiction train for 13 years. I was out of patience with both of them.

David was irate with Circe for including me on her June 22 email, and out of patience with her demands. He struck back at Circe with harsh words, and she backed down. I just wanted her to stop bombarding us with emails. She would not let go. Circe emailed me directly, looking for sympathy and support. She found none.

As much as I wanted to totally wipe Circe out of my life, I also was aware she knew more about David's life than I did. It was during all these June emails that I learned David had Hepatitis C. There was also the constant worry about AIDS. Even so, the only benefit David seemed to be getting from health insurance was a never-ending prescription for Suboxone, which I began to suspect he was selling to support his heroin habit. Circe's emails kept coming, filled with all of the bad things David had done and what she thought he should be doing.

David's only defense when he wrote back to both of us was that he got the ticket because he was caught in a speed trap, and he further defended himself by writing:

> "I am a good person and not a criminal. The insanity I had to endure that day from Circe was not justified. I have had some setbacks and definitely should not use drugs to cope but that does not make me a bad person. I am flawed but I have a good heart. I do not deserve to be treated this way. So everyone can just leave me alone. I am better off alone than to be continuously persecuted."

Excuse or not, David's defense of himself and having to say he was a good person and would be better off alone broke my heart. His behavior was atrocious and he deserved what he got. But to me, David had become mentally unable to make responsible choices and his behavior was a product of his addiction. This switch in feelings caused me inner turmoil. Even so, I couldn't allow myself to accept his excuses. However, I know how frustrated I got the day before he got the ticket—Circe's emails, the demands, the inconsistency of "generosity" and blame. No one should have to endure insanity like we did on June 4. David was an addict but also a human being.

Our June email drama finally came to a close. David and I talked on the phone the next evening. He sounded good and said he was taking Suboxone and not using heroin. Circe had confirmed that David got a refill for Suboxone on June 1 and had been refilling it regularly since January, paid for by health insurance. I was skeptical because, just a few weeks earlier, I noticed his neck had broken out with small red nicks. When I pointed the nicks out to him in the mirror, he said they were caused by bad clippers. However, speeding down the toll road early in the morning, the Suboxone prescriptions, and his drained bank account were signs of another heroin relapse. Despite his claims to the contrary, David must have been selling Suboxone to pay for heroin.

In the midst of the Circe drama and in addition to the DUI, David missed scheduled appointments with his probation officer. On June 26, he texted me that he was sentenced to what amounted to 20 days in jail for the March DUI. His driver's license was suspended for three years.

David entered Prince William County Jail at 9:00 a.m. on June 27. When he was released, he texted:

> "There will be no more driving, drinking, or drugs. I'm lucky to still have what I have. No more messing around! I'm too old for this mess!"

REBA'S DEATH

In August 2012, Reba had a fatal car accident. David posted a message on her Facebook timeline when he heard the news and shared a YouTube link on his Facebook timeline:

> "August 16, 2012. My sweet darling . . . Many years have passed since I looked into your eyes but the wellness of those eyes are my paramount concern right now. You must open them and find your way back to us. I know it's hard, but it is when we are at our weakest that we must be our strongest. It's a strange thing cuz it's easy to be strong when all is well and we are healthy, wealthy, and everyone likes us. But it is when things go bad and we lie there alone, and we are weak that we must find strength

when there is very little strength to be found. I know the strength lies within you, so open your eyes and come back to us.

"The most beautiful video on YouTube. Through the void I send you this in HOPES that you might see . . . ~ Pink Floyd, 'Coming Back to Life'"

Reba died a few days later. David and his friends were devastated. He asked me to send him their high school prom and homecoming pictures to take with him to the funeral. After the funeral, David and several of his old high school friends gathered together at the beach. He posted the following "good-bye" note to her on his Facebook page:

"You weren't just my high school sweetheart, you were my friend for the past 25 years. I am truly broken-hearted. Some of the most pivotal moments of my life I shared with you. Good-bye."

Over the next several days, messages such as the following flew back and forth on social media as David received condolences and shared his sadness:

"August 19, 2012. Hi. You said some nice things. It's very sad. Things aren't great for me. I am pretty upset about this. I am drinking, smoking, and listening to sad music and thinking about life. I am at a pretty low point in life right now. At least I always knew she cared, but she is gone. I just got out of jail, again, coming off yet another heroin bender, my wife is at VA beach with her boyfriend, my car is gone so I have to take cabs everywhere, my mother hates me and I am all alone. I know that's a lot to put on you but it is a lot to handle.

"It's very sad. Several people have hit me up since it happened. To be honest with you, it has hit me kind of hard. I've never had anyone that I knew so well die. It's a strange thing, so final. Since FB, I have heard from her on the regular. Anyway, I just want everyone to be happy and do good, life is short.

"She was driving a Jeep, took a turn too fast and flipped it. It crushed her skull. She survived a few days but the injury was just too bad and she died. The fucked up thing is she always took curves too fast. I told her a thousand times to slow the fuck down and now it killed her. It's very sad, she just had a baby eight months ago."

SUICIDE

Reba's dying was a reality check for her former classmates about life and death. One friend told David about a fellow classmate who had committed suicide. David's response: "Life can be hard and people feel all alone sometimes. I do not think a person could do that if they feel loved."

The first question the detective asked me on the day we found David was whether he was suicidal. I was completely taken by surprise, because David committing suicide was never a worry. Yes, I had constant worry that he was going to kill himself by overdosing or contracting AIDS or in a fatal car crash, but suicide? No.

At the end of August 2012, David was in a spiral of depression. In a Facebook message he told a friend,

> "Unfortunately, my mind is all congested with so much that it seems to have just shut down. The clarity I once possessed has given way to confusion. I have just had so much to deal with lately that I just shut down."

Circe was sending David email links for information on compression devices for legs. I didn't know David had begun having problems with his legs swelling and varicose veins or that he had started wearing support socks. Circe also emailed David an article ("Skin and Soft Tissue Infections and Vascular Disease among Drug Users, England") about re-emerging infectious diseases and deep venous thrombosis (blood clots in the legs).

DAILY RITUAL

So many years of IV drug use had worn out David's veins. David injected heroin into his neck, and he had begun injecting into his groin, an infected site that ultimately caused a staph infection to grow in his back. In September 2012, David wrote the following iPad note to himself that describes a trip to buy drugs and his inability to stop himself:

> "It is Saturday, September 29th. I just got off work, and I took a
> cab up to the East Falls Church metro station. I had to spend
> extra to come all the way up here because Vienna-West Falls
> Church is closed all weekend. I am headed to see KB, something
> that has become a daily ritual. I have been spending $120-$180
> a day on dope. I have court Friday. I need to have my rent and
> utilities paid before I go, in case I go to jail. It is unbelievable
> how much I spend on dope, but even more amazing how much I
> make at work. I really do make good money. The problem is I
> have left myself one weekend to come up with all of my
> monthly bills. And now I am going downtown again today. I am
> screwing myself, but I will figure something out. I'm just not
> ready to quit today. Tomorrow!"

I talked with David earlier the same day to thank him for the tomatoes he
gave me the day before from a small garden he planted at his house. He
sounded so good. It was difficult to discover years later that he'd gone to see
KB, his dealer, that same afternoon. I had no idea at the time that he had
relapsed so badly.

In another iPad note and email to himself, David lashes out for his failure to
believe in himself, and he acknowledges time is running out to make "the
change." He knows he has to "let it all go," but unfortunately, heroin kept
him tightly wound and unable to lift the weight of his addiction.

> "I must start anew as of this very day, October 14, 2012!!! No
> more fuckin around. No more games. This is it. I must get this
> wasted existence in order. Every single thing I could have
> possibly done the correct way, I have done wrong, since I was 14
> years old. I am a complete failure. It is sickening what I have
> done with my life. That is the bad news, but the good news is
> that I am still alive, and although I squandered my youth, if I
> decide to make the change necessary right now, then I just
> might be able to turn this wasted existence around. I cannot get
> that lost time back, but I also cannot afford to waste any more
> time. To do this, I must be strong and believe in myself. Now is

the time!!! NO MORE FUCKIN AROUND!!!"

In early November, a friend emailed Dave that she was worried about him. He responded:

"I have lost my way. The path I seek is complex and elusive. So many variables litter the path that this simple concept gives way to confusion. Therefore, my moves might make no sense but they are necessary. Mainly, I want you to know that none of this is in any way a personal attack on you! I hope not to strain our friendship, I just need space from most everyone in hopes that I may find my way! Wish me the clarity I will need to overcome this challenge! Furthermore, I need you to know that I am not in a dark place, I don't know what I did or said to make you come to that conclusion but it is anything but accurate! If you really knew me, you would know that I am too much of a nihilist to ever fall into a depression like that, I carry no overt sadness within me. What I am dealing with is more of an existential crisis."

Most of our communication the last few months of 2012 was through texting or telephone calls. We shared and talked through a thunderstorm one evening. He sent a text to share his excitement over a Washington Redskins football victory and joined us to celebrate Thanksgiving and Christmas.

On December 17, Circe submitted her third emailed client intake form for "A Fast Divorce."

CHAPTER 11: 2013

THE YEAR OF "LASTS"

David was scheduled to be back in court on January 4. I texted him the day before and wished him luck. He sent back a text, "Keep your fingers crossed for me! I really do not want to go back to jail. I feel like I have done everything I was supposed to do. I am very nervous."

Later, Dave texted, "I got very lucky! My case was dismissed on a technicality."

In an email to himself, Dave warns himself to "let it all go":

> "January 13, 2013. You just have to let it all go—attachments, the need for validation, the feeling that you do not exist if there isn't someone there to verify it. You have to let all of it go, and when you do, when everything finally just falls away, and the weight that caused so much strain, weighs you down no more . . . and you are left there, bare naked and pure, not alone, but with yourself . . . that is when you will see just how beautiful you are. It won't be easy."

On January 16, David put an ad on Craig's List, "A very small retail space wanted for a one chair Barber Shop." To my knowledge, he received no response to the ad.

On January 27, David and I emailed back and forth. He was just getting off work and seemed to be OK. We talked about the weather and the forecast for snow. He asked if I was going skiing anytime soon. I said no because I was saving my leave for when I retired in August. He responded, "Wow, I can't believe you are retiring. That's awesome. I am so happy for you!!!"

In February, David's Fairfax probation officer was trying unsuccessfully to reach him by phone about his missed urine screen. David sent him an email, letting him know that he had relapsed but that he was not "so far gone."

"February 20, 2012. Hey . . . sorry about this morning, I left a message. I am going into detox on Tuesday. I don't really feel like I am so far gone that I need to detoxify myself, but clearly my life is headed in the wrong direction and I need to get on top of it before it gets worse. Plus, my wife is very unhappy with me, and she is insisting I do it. I would go in sooner, but there is a waitlist for a bed, plus I need to arrange it with work. I will be at the CATS detox in Fairfax Hospital and will be there for a week. As far as my phone goes, it was on all day. Do you have the number right?"

Based on email exchanges, Circe must have been well aware of David's relapse and known about the infection in his groin, but none of this, including the current relapse, was shared with me. She continued to send David emails and talked to him daily about names and contact phone numbers for psychiatrists; medical information; realtor emails for houses and rustic cabins; and copies of the drafted divorce documents her attorney had drawn up.

Easter came early in 2013, March 31. David initiated a family gathering for Sunday dinner at my house; Circe attended with him. Things between them seemed to be rolling along amicably until the morning of April 3, when Circe emailed David with only text in the subject line, "You are married to heroin and to all of the low lifes you hung with." I have no idea what prompted her email. Of course, David denied it and responded with an apology and a promise:

"I am sorry for everything, honey. I truly am. I understand why you feel this way. I just called the CATS people. They are supposed to call me back. I really am gonna get my shit together. But I understand why you don't have any faith in me to do the right thing. I just want my wife and my home back. It will break my heart to sign those divorce papers."

Later in the afternoon of April 3, Circe forwarded David an email from her attorney with the drafted divorce documents attached. Throughout the rest of April and in tandem with divorce threats, Circe continued to email David links to properties for sale and rustic cabins to buy. She also emailed David's probation officer a copy of an insurance claim for David, showing that he was in Fairfax INOVA Hospital the night of February 28, but no detail on why. Overdose?

It is difficult to look back and realize how much I didn't know about my son's life. I never got the full story from David or Circe, and I never knew who or what to believe when they did communicate, all of which added to the insanity of riding on the crazy addiction train to nowhere.

LAST MOTHER'S DAY

For Mother's Day, 2013, Dave, Bill, my husband Greg, and I made plans to have an early dinner outside in the garden of a Greek restaurant we all liked. It was a beautiful warm day as we settled at our table surrounded by red geraniums and pink petunias. We had a nice dinner and easy conversation. As I write this, I am looking at the picture of the three of us taken that afternoon—Bill to my right and David to my left with his arm draped across my back and his hand resting on my shoulder. Bill and I are smiling, David looks a little like he has been startled but stands steady. It's easy to see he wasn't doing well—his eyes are dark rimmed, red, and sunken. There hasn't been much in my life that has given me as much pleasure as standing between my two tall and beautiful sons. I wasn't about to ruin the day with accusations or worries.

After we left the restaurant and returned to my house, David told me for the first time about the pain he was having in his back. He said he had seen a doctor who told him the pain was caused by muscle spasms, but the medication prescribed by the doctor was not giving him any relief. I looked David's symptoms up in my big red *Merck Manual of Medical Information* and found Osteomyelitis—my heart sank as I read *Merck's* description out loud to David:

> Osteomyelitis is a bone infection usually caused by bacteria but sometimes by a fungus . . . Bones, which usually are well

protected from infection, can become infected through three routes: the bloodstream, direct invasion, and adjacent soft tissue infections. The bloodstream may carry an infection from another part of the body to the bones. An infection usually occurs in the ends of the leg and arm bones in children and in the spine (vertebrae) in adults. People who undergo kidney dialysis and those who inject illegal drugs are particularly susceptible to an infection of the vertebrae (Vertebral Osteomyelitis). These infections may not cause fever and blood test results may be normal.[28]

Even though Merck's description accurately reflected David's symptoms, right down to no fever, and blood tests had been normal, he unequivocally insisted that the pain in his back could not be vertebral osteomyelitis. What he didn't say was he had been repeatedly injecting heroin into an infected area of his groin because he had run out of veins. As he shot more and more heroin from the infected injection site, the infection moved through David's bloodstream up into his spine and ate away two vertebrae (T11 and T12). David was either in denial to himself about the cause of his back pain or unable to admit the truth. Knowing what I know now, David may have been in denial, but Circe must have suspected something when she emailed him the article about skin and soft tissue infections the previous August. Dave didn't want to talk about it anymore and said he would continue seeing the doctor and "get to the bottom" of what was wrong with his back.

RELAPSE / ARREST

David did not go back to see the doctor about his back but began to self-medicate with heavy doses of ibuprofen (10 at a time) to manage his pain. He also rearranged his work schedule to attend Fairfax INOVA's CATS treatment program* on Mondays, Wednesdays, and Fridays for outpatient drug treatment. David quietly celebrated his 39th birthday in late May. On

---

* David's 2013 CATS Treatment Worksheet follows his collection of writings.

June 1, he was arrested again in D.C. for possession of heroin. It came to light that the only reason David enrolled in the CATS program was because he had given his Fairfax probation officer dirty urine. And, as he did so many other times, he went to D.C. for "just one more fix" before he was forced to start another round of treatment.

David was arraigned for the June 1 arrest in D.C. court on June 3. He was released and told to report to his Fairfax probation officer and to begin the CATS program he had signed up for, which was a blessing. They could have just thrown him back into D.C. jail. His trial was set for Tuesday, June 25.

Circe was in full panic mode when she called me on the morning of his arraignment to tell me David was missing. She was screaming into the phone and sobbing out of control. She said she had already called David's Fairfax probation officer and checked jail sites but couldn't find him anywhere. She was convinced that David was dead. It was then that she told me about his dirty urine reports, that he was ordered to attend CATS by the courts, and that he was not going to treatment by choice. She also told me she had given him her car so he could get around. Every drop of compassion drained right out of me.

David texted me that same evening. He was very upset. Not because he went missing the last couple of days and Circe was in a tailspin over his disappearance or because his attempts to stop using heroin had failed. No, David was upset because he got caught . . . again. He told me his version of why he had to go to D.C. on June 1, which was the same "last fix" justification he'd used so many times. Probably the only truths he admitted to being upset about were his fear that he would lose his basement apartment, because he didn't have enough money to pay for his share of the utilities that month, and because the barber shop had done an audit and some cash was missing—fingers were pointing at David.

David's roommates gave him a couple extra days to pay his share of the utilities, so his immediate worries about losing his apartment were resolved. He admitted to his boss that he had "borrowed" cash, which wasn't unusual, but had paid it back. As far as I know, that issue was resolved, too.

I was tired of being angry with David, fed up with his lies, and unable take any more of Circe's drama and threats. David and I mostly texted and phoned to keep in touch. We avoided subjects that ignited arguments and conversations that required admission of guilt or answers. I could not make him or Circe change. The only person I could change or control was myself. I went into wait mode.

BACK IN D.C. COURT

I promised myself that, after the March, 2009 D.C. court hearing, I would not go to court with David again, but I found myself sitting in the D.C. courthouse hallway one morning in June, 2013. I hadn't planned to go. In fact, I made no conscious decision to go. But when I arrived at work early that morning, it was as though I was drawn into some kind of twilight zone. I just automatically put on my tennis shoes and walked over to the courthouse.

When I arrived, it was so early in the morning that the hallways were still somewhat dark and there were only a few people milling around. For a courthouse that gets very active, it was eerily nice to witness the quiet and the calm before the chaos a courthouse becomes. About midway down the long, wide hallway, I sat on one of the benches lining the wall and waited.

The morning had turned sunny and bright as a few people shuffled in. It wasn't long before I saw a bent, shadowy figure enter through the double doors. I knew it was Dave. I was surprised because he was early. I watched as he ambled down the hallway. I was apprehensive that he would not welcome my presence. In the semi-light of the corridor, David did not see me until he was very close. He sat next to me and quietly said, "I'm surprised to see you here."

I looked into his sad brown eyes, nodded, and said, "I'm surprised, too."

A subdued David patted my hand and replied, "I'm glad you're here," and settled back on the bench. I breathed a sigh of relief. We talked a little but mostly sat quietly together and waited until his case was called. The judge assigned his case to Drug Court, which would take place in July. I did not interfere with the court proceedings or let the court know I was there. Following the court date, I relied on David to keep me in the loop about how his case proceeded. Later that afternoon, David texted:

> "Thank you for your concern and especially coming to court. I have really messed up this time. I don't know what is going to happen, and I am really scared. It is nice to know that there are people who care, though. Thank you, Mom! My basement apartment probably won't be my home much longer. It's such a shame cuz it is such a great spot for me. I'm pretty low right now."

I answered that I was afraid that he would never win his battle with addiction and that he had to focus on how to rise above it. I told him I felt useless, encouraged him to make this a new start, and assured him he was not alone. He responded:

> "I don't know if I will ever be able to beat it. I hope I can. I can never give up though, that much I know. I am down but I still want to live a good life so I must fight on . . . "

On June 15, David appeared in D.C.'s Drug Court. I met him there, wished him well, and then waited outside in front of the courthouse. Afterwards he had to fill out paperwork for a psychological assessment; I returned to my office. That evening, Dave texted to thank me for my support and to ask if I looked up "Drug Court" on the Internet.

Drug courts are all over the country and geared toward non-violent offenders who need treatment more than incarceration. David was fortunate that D.C. was giving him the opportunity to have his case decided in Drug Court rather than Criminal Court. And it was certainly better than being thrown back in jail when what he really needed was treatment. I reiterated to David that recovery was the most important thing he could be doing right now and emailed him a link to a National Institute of Defense research paper on D.C.'s drug court.[29]

Circe chose June 17 to email me the article, "Spinal Infection in Intravenous Drug Abusers," which basically confirmed what we had already read in the

Merck manual on Mother's Day. I emailed her back and asked her again to please read Beverly Conyers's book, *Addict in the Family*. She said she would. David's back pain was to the point where he could barely walk.

In early July, Dave met with his case worker to sort out plans for attending D.C.'s Drug Court. He also started attending the CATS program and said that it would work much better for him, insinuating that attending CATS was in place of Drug Court. However, the CATS treatment program in INOVA Fairfax Hospital was totally separate from D.C.'s Drug Court. Jurisdictions often worked together but not in this case. David was trying to manipulate the system by attending CATS, hoping that D.C.'s Drug Court would forget about him, but they didn't. When he didn't show up for Drug Court, D.C. issued a warrant for his arrest.

I received an early morning text from David on July 10, his second day at CATS. He said he felt good about the CATS program, but he was concerned because he hadn't heard from Circe; she was out of the country, visiting family. David emailed her with his concerns:

> "July 10, 2013. Helllllooooo. Are you alive?? I haven't heard from you at all!! I know you are in --- and probably busy, but I would have at least thought you would have tried to call me once just to let me know you made it there safe & sound and are having a good time. What if something happened to you? I'll bet your family wouldn't even contact me. They all [probably] think you are with --- and I am long gone. That really hurts me, honey. I know it's all my fault, but it doesn't change the fact that I love you and I miss you!

> "PS: My mother has asked about how you [are] every time I've talked to her. I feel foolish when I have to tell her that you haven't cared enough to call me. Especially when I recently told her how important you are to me and that we both are working to live together again because we want this marriage to work. I just miss you, honey, and I am worried you are just gonna forget about me. I would understand if you did. I have been a terrible husband. I'm sorry, honey."

What David tells Circe in his email isn't exactly what he told me, but he did think she was coming back to live with him if he could stop using heroin and give up other women. A few days later, David again pleaded in an email for Circe to contact him.

In mid-July, David enrolled in CATS's Intensive Outpatient Program (IOP), which consisted of three groups weekly, three hours per group for 10 weeks. His back pain continued to be excruciating, and he said he made an appointment to see a neurologist. I questioned his going to a neurologist for his back pain, and he said a friend of his had shoulder pain that was caused by a nerve issue. He thought maybe his pain could also be a nerve issue. At the end of July, David saw the neurologist, who recommended he see an orthopedist.

David was due back in Fairfax County Court on August 2 for violating his probation, submitting dirty urine samples, and failing to enter the CATS program at Fairfax Hospital in February. I attended court with him. David's court appointed attorney, TK, was a godsend. He spoke with David's probation officer and the prosecuting attorney, and all agreed and recommended to the judge that David's case be continued to give him time to complete the CATS program. The judge immediately agreed and continued David's case to October 4. Attorney TK took an active interest in David's case, and he spent time talking with both of us while we waited for the judge to hear his case. TK had a unique way of humanizing David as separate from his addiction and resulting situation, which opened up an avenue for constructive discussion and deliberation about how David should proceed. I didn't realize until then that TK had previously represented David. It was apparent David respected and trusted him. They had become friends.

It was very important now for David to complete the CATS program with flying colors, get drug free, wean off Suboxone, and maintain his work schedule. The orthopedic doctor thought David might have a tumor causing the pain in his back. He scheduled David for bloodwork and a CT in early August—luckily, both appointments were at Fairfax Hospital, where David attended CATS.

DIAGNOSIS: VERTEBRAL OSTEOMYELITIS[30]

On August 6, Circe called and told me that David was in Fairfax INOVA Hospital's emergency room. I immediately called David, "Circe just called—what's happening?"

"I'm in the ER, Room 22."

"Do they know what's wrong?"

"Spinal infection. It looks like the infection thing we looked up on Mother's Day. Not a tumor or muscle spasms. As of now, they are saying a few days of strong antibiotics, not surgery. Hopefully, that is the case."

July 31 was my last day at work. I was officially retired and free to come and go as I pleased. I immediately left home for the hospital. The MRI and CT scans confirmed David's back pain was caused by a bone infection, vertebral osteomyelitis. The bacteria causing the infection was identified as staphylo-coccus, which entered David's bloodstream because of his continual heroin injections into the infected area of his groin. A robust regiment of IV antibiotics was started, he was fitted with a back brace and used a walker to get around. Because finding a usable vein was difficult, the doctors inserted a PICC line into his arm to administer the antibiotics. David remained at Fairfax INOVA Hospital for six days.

Following his hospital stay, David was sent for a two-week stay at a nursing facility and then sent home with the PICC line to be administered by a visiting nurse. As far as I know, David did not abuse the PICC line; although, we did have to make an emergency room visit in early September to have the PICC line re-inserted.

I began driving David to and from CATS and doctor appointments, to run errands, and to just about anywhere he needed to go. Circe would drive him when she was available. David created a file cabinet out of a box and began organizing his court documents, medical records, and bills into folders. In his journal, he expressed his thoughts about what he missed the most during this time:

"It's interesting the things I always miss the most when I am removed from

my world. Coffee the way I like it. I miss the people I see every day. I don't even miss heroin; although, with the way I have lived you would think that would be the thing I missed the most. But I don't. Love, even though I neglect all of my relationships. It's amazing how many people care about such a selfish person. I will digress now, though. I don't sleep very well but what's new?

"I just hope I can stay the course and never have to deal with any of these types of things again. There is so much more I want from life than that numb existence."

On August 15, while still in the nursing facility, Dave texted me:

> "Positive thinking, every morning I need to create my own positive reality by willing it into manifestation. This is how I will repair my 'brain damage.' I believe I can do that."

Hope for his recovery was springing from me like a tall, strong, and freshly bloomed, beautiful sunflower. I told myself, this has to be David's bottom! He's going to dig out this time! I had not felt this hopeful in many years.

On August 16, David texted me his 10 Keys to Success:

1. Believe when others doubt.
2. Learn while others loaf.
3. Decide while others delay.
4. Begin while others procrastinate.
5. Work while others wish.
6. Save while others spend.
7. Listen while others talk.
8. Smile while others scowl.
9. Commend while others criticize.
10. Persist when others quit.

After David left the nursing facility, he re-entered CATS's treatment program and filled out a treatment worksheet. David's answers on the worksheet give a thorough and accurate account of the progression of his addiction and his current status.

OUR NEW ROUTINE

After David left the nursing facility and returned to his apartment, he started a daily "must do" list in his journal to help him stop procrastinating—a major ongoing problem—and to start getting things done. I picked David up every Monday, Wednesday, and Friday morning and drove him to CATS for outpatient drug treatment. He was upbeat and positive, and he greeted me with a big grin and "Good Morning, Mom!"

I was absolutely giddy to have my son back. For years, when we had plans to do something or to go somewhere, David would either be late or a last minute no-show. What a delight to find him clean and dressed each morning, promptly waiting for me on the curb outside of his house, holding his backpack and coffee cup with vanilla creamer ready for the hot coffee I brought in a thermos. If I surprised him with a banana or a muffin, he was always grateful and happy. This was the David whom I hadn't seen in a long, long while. My optimism grew that, as serious and painful as the infection was, it might be his "bottom" and the spark that would ignite and get him to the last stop on the crazy addiction train before heroin killed him.

At noon when I would pick Dave up from CATS, we ran errands, attended doctor appointments (in addition to the orthopedic doctor who attended him at the hospital, he was under the care of an infectious disease doctor), or did whatever he needed to get done, and then I delivered him back to his house. My fingers were crossed, white-knuckle tight, with hope that this miracle change in him would continue to evolve into a drug-free lifestyle. Most important, David and I were re-establishing a good relationship with communication and trust.

GETTING BACK TO WORK

Returning to work was David's major goal, but until the infection cleared up, he could not stand long hours and cut hair. However, his wallet was empty. I contacted his landlord and began to pay his monthly rent. Although I cut off all such assistance years ago for fear of enabling him to buy heroin, I justified helping him during his recovery as long as he was physically unable to work and actively attending drug recovery treatment. I also knew if I didn't pay his rent, Circe would, and I didn't want his dependence on her to continue.

David applied for and received food stamps. I hated that he had to ask for assistance, but I reminded myself this was a step in the right direction for David to take care of David, even if it was in the form of public assistance. I recognized I was walking the tightrope between "helping" and "enabling."

David and I talked or texted every day. On a Sunday in mid-September, he said two of his roommates had asked him several times to give them haircuts. He said he had already put them off but was thinking that maybe giving them haircuts would be a good test run for whether he was ready to return to work. He also liked that the shop was closed, and he could work at his own pace. He asked me, "Do you think it's a good or bad idea?"

I said, "I don't think it's a good idea health-wise. Also, what is your boss going to think about you going into the shop when it's closed?"

Dave responded, "He won't even know I came by, but even if he did, I need to go in there and try to cut hair to see where I am at so I can determine when I will be capable of going back to work. I can't go there during work hours because, as soon as customers see me, they will think I am back and want me to cut their hair. I think I should try."

David texted a few hours later:

> "I went to the shop and cut my roommates' hair to see if I could do it. I did my first roommate, no problem, but then on the second guy, I was covered in sweat and in terrible pain. When I finally finished I ran into the bathroom and threw up. I was just burning up. It's that back-brace. I put a barber jacket over it so it didn't get covered in hair and I was just sweating terribly! I think

I'll be able to go back for half days soon. I really want to get back to work ASAP."

Staying positive and taking small steps to avoid daily frustration with his pain and inability to do the things he wanted to do was a constant internal battle. If Dave wasn't feeling well, he wanted a quick return to feeling better, and now he didn't have heroin to help him with that. Even though we had established a productive and agreeable daily routine to accomplish his needs, to slow down and focus only on that day was not something that came easy for David.

As with every morning since his emergency room visit in August, September 23 started with a text prior to my picking him up. He was moody and not feeling well. Later in the day, he texted that he felt better and wrote:

"If overcoming suffering builds character then I should be able to overcome anything else that comes at me. I just have to be strong. That's what I keep telling myself. I also need to get my butt back in school when all of this is over. I can do more with my life. I truly believe that . . . but in ten minutes I will tell you that I can't do any of it."

CASE DISMISSED!

In mid-October, David was back in Fairfax County Court. Attorney TK laid out his case perfectly and made the judge sympathetic to David's illness. With me there to support him, along with letters from me and his employer, the judge released David and told him, "Given your history, young man, I would be inclined to lock you back up, but your attorney has presented too many good reasons not to. I'm optimistic that, with the support I see for you in this courtroom, you are on a good path. I'm going to let you go, but I better not ever see you in my courtroom again. CASE DISMISSED!"

HOOORRRAAAYYY!!!

We stayed for a while after court, talking with and thanking TK, who was pleased with the outcome and congratulated David on the progress he was making. David beamed . . . I beamed . . . life was good!

WEASELING OUT

The next Monday morning was a dark, rainy, and miserable start to the week. David texted, "Hey, Mom. It's a nasty morning out there. I want to take today off from CATS. I am tired this morning and just want to take the day off."

I wrote back, "Not a good idea."

Dave persisted, "It will be fine. People in my group take off all the time."

I was adamant, "That doesn't mean you do."

Dave continued to argue his reasons for wanting to skip CATS. My disappointment about his weaseling out turned to determination as I insisted, "I'm two minutes away."

David gave in, "OK, I'm getting ready. I'm sorry I was being so lazy. Did you bring coffee?"

David was still under the care of Dr. M, the Fairfax doctor who diagnosed and treated him for osteomyelitis at the hospital. Aside from a few setbacks, the infection was clearing up. Dr. M scheduled him for a follow-up MRI. David was working well with Dr. P, his infectious disease doctor, to manage his medications. In addition to pain, David was treated for nausea. Getting a new, better fitting back brace helped with both pain and nausea. Healing was a slow process, but as I reminded David when he got frustrated, it took many years to get to this place. Fixing the damage would take time and patience.

David had established a good rapport with his Fairfax doctors, and there was good coordination between the two doctors. Also, having his doctors, medical facilities, and CATS just a few miles from his house was a real plus. Even though making daily trips from my house in Alexandria to Fairfax was time consuming, once I got out there, getting around was easy, and David liked being in "his hood." However, Circe thought the Fairfax doctors weren't rated highly enough to manage David's care. She insisted he get a second opinion from Johns Hopkins and scheduled him for a second opinion with Dr. D for October 3, at Johns Hopkins in Baltimore. Not surprising,

Circe couldn't get away to drive him, so I drove and attended the appointment with David.

GLITCH IN HEALING

On Friday, November 1, David and I met with Dr. M to review the most recent MRI. David was still having pain but doing well, so we were shocked when Dr. M gave us the news that, based on the second MRI, David should have back surgery immediately. In fact, he wanted David to enter the hospital that afternoon. We were stunned. Dr. M explained that based on the second MRI, David's bones were not fusing properly, increasing the danger that he could become a paraplegic.

From the time David's vertebral osteomyelitis was diagnosed, Circe had been determined David should have surgery. And she had already decided that, if there was to be a surgery, it would be at Johns Hopkins. After David saw Dr. D at Johns Hopkins in October, he and his team reviewed the first MRI and recommended waiting to see how the infection cleared up before deciding on surgery. With Dr. M's new recommendation that David have immediate back surgery, it was imperative that the Johns Hopkins doctors review the second MRI as soon as possible.

After the appointment with Dr. M, I dropped David at his house, and immediately drove from Fairfax to Baltimore to deliver the second MRI CD. I called ahead to alert them I was coming for fear that I would not make it before office hours ended. I arrived in time to hand deliver the CD to Dr. D's assistant. Dave emailed later that evening:

> "Hi, Mom. Not a great day for me. That was some awful news today. I really didn't like the way the Fairfax doctor was acting. At least I now know why my pain has been worse. Lately Circe has been goin nuts! If you let her tell it, she has been pushing for (whatever turns out to be correct) the whole time. Thank you so much for taking that CD up there. I just wonder what the Johns Hopkins doctor will say and how long it will be until we see him. I am very nervous about this. Honestly, I do not want to

do this surgery if you are not here. I don't want to be stranded up in Baltimore all alone."

My husband and I were due to leave the following Monday, November 4—in three days—for a three-week trip to India that was planned a year ago to celebrate my husband's retirement. My husband had lived in India when he was a child, and he talked often about going back. He had been looking forward to this trip for years. This put me in a very difficult spot. David's years of addiction and current medical condition had demanded so much of my time and emotional energy, I was mentally exhausted. On the other hand, I had to be so careful not to do anything to disrupt what was medically necessary to repair David's spine. However, I didn't want to let my husband down, either. The India trip complicated everything.

After hearing Dr. M's recommendation that David should have immediate surgery, Circe spun into full drama mode. She was negative about any options to avoid surgery. She also declared that because she paid for his health insurance, she would decide what was best for his care. She had no substantive basis for her hysterical rantings and demands that David have surgery at Johns Hopkins immediately, especially since the JH team had not looked at the second MRI and given an opinion. We tried to reason with her that these were serious decisions that required careful thought, not useless drama. Circe finally acknowledged that she had overreacted and needed to calm down and stop succumbing to raw emotion.

I was concerned about why Circe was hell bent on David having such a painful and complicated surgery unless he absolutely had to. Having surgery did not equate to full recovery. The surgery itself could possibly leave David in a wheelchair for the rest of his life. Another big worry was that David was going to require massive amounts of opioids for pain, and how he would deal with that. None of the doctors had addressed the opioid problem. When I brought up my concerns about the amount of opioids David would need if surgery was required, Dr. D shrugged and said, "That's not my field, but, yes, David will absolutely need opioids for pain following the surgery. He will need to find a doctor for pain management."

To top off this chaos, David got drunk with his roommates on Halloween, the night before the appointment with Dr. M. David was hung over and looked like crap. I was furious with him. His relapses often began with alcohol. He sent me a text to justify getting drunk:

> "Mom, I am not partying. That is the bad part of having roommates. What should I do? I want to wait for you to come back [from India]. Circe thinks I need to get in there and do it right away. I guess I need to wait to hear from the JH Dr. It kind of seemed like Dr. M was blaming me. But I wore that brace religiously for almost the whole time."

Over the weekend, there was much discussion and texting with David about my taking the trip, how we would communicate while I was in India, and whether he should get another MRI. I also encouraged him to get another opinion from the Virginia Spine Center. On the Sunday morning before I left, I texted David and commiserated that the timing for this trip was terrible and it was very difficult for me to leave.

David wrote back, "Well, just have fun. I will be fine and I will keep you posted. Circe is coming over, and we are going out for breakfast. We could come out that way if you want to get breakfast with us." I replied, "I would like that, when?"

Dave answered, "I just talked to Circe and we are going out toward Winchester to look at a couple houses she wants me to see. I asked you about breakfast, not realizing that Alexandria is the opposite way as Winchester so that won't work."

I wrote back, "Ok, enjoy your day!" and Dave said, "I just thought it would be nice to see you before you left but that's ok. I really am looking forward to a ride in the country. Such a beautiful day."

With mixed feelings and a heavy heart, I left for India on Monday as planned. While I was in India, communication with David had to be via email. After Dave met again with Dr. D, he sent an email describing the proposed surgery:

> "In that surgery, they will permanently remove part of one of my

ribs. They also will pull a lung out of the way and then put it back. I don't like the way that sounds. Yikes :-/ Regarding your questions: I will get another MRI in Fairfax, then take the disc to JH. We are not gonna go to the VA Spine Center. Am I ok with this? No, I am not! I am scared as hell, but I am glad to know that there is not a change as severe as Dr. M thought. Dr. M gave me a prescription for a different back brace that hopefully won't be so uncomfortable and for pain medicine to use if the back brace is hurting me. Instead of taking the brace off if it becomes painful, I can take a pill to ease the pain. I think that is a good idea.

"... I think it [Dr. M's urgency for surgery] was a call from the radiologist. Dr. D, however, was able to look at [the MRI] more objectively. He showed us the overhead view and you can clearly see spinal fluid all the way around so there really is very little change [in my bones]. He mainly said that there is a very slight change but it is really a different angle. The bones are what he looks at and there is very little change. So we will put it [surgery] off till you get back. Get another MRI in 4 weeks and then decide."

When I returned from India three weeks later, David's mood was no longer upbeat and positive. In mid-November, Dr. D and his team re-reviewed the second MRI and agreed that without surgery, David's back would continue to deteriorate. They agreed with Dr. M that the bones in David's spine were not properly fusing. David complained that his pain was much worse and that he could not walk without using the walker. I asked if he'd contacted Dr. D about the possibility of moving up the surgery; he said he had but Dr. D was on vacation.

On November 26, Circe sent an email to Dr. D's assistant:

"We need your help to push up David's surgery that is now scheduled for December 11. David's condition has been deteriorating rapidly since last Friday. He can no longer walk without a walker, and his pain level is at a 9. I am very concerned. I don't believe we can wait until the 11th. David has been leaving messages since last Friday, but no one has returned his calls. Can you please call or have the appropriate person call me as soon as possible? I am even considering bringing him to JH's emergency room, but I don't want to handle this the wrong way, especially since this is Thanksgiving week."

Since David moved to the basement apartment, most of our conversations had to be by text because his cell phone did not work well from the basement. I grew concerned because he was not responding to emails or would claim he didn't get them. When he did respond, his answers were short and tart. I asked him about plans for Thanksgiving, but he said he didn't think he could make it—too much pain. Old worries started to surface. The telltale signs of relapse were there; Dave was anxious, isolating, and depressed.

On the morning of the day before Thanksgiving, I sent Dave a text but didn't hear back for several hours. I texted again and said, "Pack an overnight bag, I am coming now to get you."

He immediately responded with: "No. I'm not leaving."

"Yes, you are. Tomorrow is family time and you are part of this family."

Dave insisted, "No, I'm not leaving right now. You can come get me tomorrow. End of story."

I gave in, "Be ready at noon tomorrow."

"OK."

LAST THANKSGIVING

On November 28, 2013, I left my house with enough time to pick David up at noon and sent a text when I was a couple of minutes away. Dave texted back, "I need you to pick me up at the Vienna metro."

David knew I was coming to pick him up at noon. What the hell was he doing at Vienna Metro if he could barely walk? I drove over to the Vienna Metro Station. David was sitting alone on a bench; no one else was around.

He hobbled over and got into the car. I asked him what the hell he was doing at Vienna Metro, and he said, "I was trying to get to your house on my own so that you wouldn't have to come get me."

I was immediately angry and fired back, "That's a lie! You knew I was coming at noon and would be on my way. If you really wanted to save me a trip, why didn't you call a couple of hours ago and let me know that you were taking the Metro? I bet you were in D.C. yesterday when I texted. That's why I didn't hear back from you for hours. Admit it! I knew I should have driven out to your house yesterday even though you said not to. But *noooo*, David's a big boy. I don't need to question everything he tells me! I am so pissed at you right now! I'm taking you back to your house. Fuck Thanksgiving! After all you've—we've—been through, especially these last few months and you still can't live without your good little buddy heroin!"

David didn't look at me and didn't respond with denials or arguments. He just sat there in the passenger seat, looking straight ahead through the windshield. He didn't appear stoned or numbed out or on the verge of dope sickness, just pathetic and obviously in pain. His reticence scared me. I sat in the driver's seat, glaring at him, tense, and unable to move, waiting for an argument. But none came. I didn't know what to do. Stress and sorrow filled the void between us. I let it go.

Without another word, I started the car and drove to my house in silence. David let it go, too. We had a decent Thanksgiving, not knowing it would be our last. Anxiety and worry overshadowed the day, but we made it through without argument. Instead of giving David a foundation of support to stay on a good track while I was in India, the progress of the previous few months had fallen apart. I should not have gone on the India trip. My guilt was unbearable.

David emailed about work the next day:

> "It worked out good. I just handled overflow and there wasn't too much of that because the busy day is the day before Thanksgiving, not the day after and I am feeling much better than I was for about 4 days when I really thought I was dying. I

wish I understood why I have these fluctuations. Good and bad days. The real challenge is tomorrow. I have to work because the new girl works every other Saturday, and tomorrow is her off Saturday. I will be expected to really work tomorrow. I will give it my best. It's the last day that I will actually be needed so I just gotta suck it up. After that, I can continue to just do what I can. The annual barber shop Christmas party is on Sunday night. I'm gonna try to attend if I can. After work, if I am feeling good, I am gonna get this place cleaned up and do some laundry. I need to make the most of my 'good days.' I really want to get this surgery taken care of. It's been such a long wait.

". . . Times are tough again. I just gotta be strong. Someday I will be in a position where I don't have to be so strong all the time. But if I make it through all of this, I will truly have an abundance of inner strength. Then, with no more drugs and an inner strength that knows no bounds, I will be hugely successful and will truly appreciate every good thing that comes my way."

I responded that I was glad to see his positive attitude had returned and it sounded like he was getting back on track. After the Thanksgiving episode, I was pretty sure he had relapsed. All the typical signs were there. I imagined his brain was shouting at him, "Nothing's better than a little shot of heroin to ease your pain and anxiety, Dave, if only temporarily!" I didn't want to think that way. I also worried he might be so desperate for drugs, he would go through with the surgery for what he hoped would be an endless supply of opioids. Could even an addict get that desperate?

On December 2, Circe copied me on an email she sent to Dr. D's assistant at Johns Hopkins. Until I read this email, I had no idea there would be two surgeries. Sounds like David and Circe didn't know either.

"Good morning, I hope that you had a nice holiday. David received a voicemail last week that his surgery is moved to the 13th. Is that correct? The person didn't leave her name but left a phone number. David called it and is expecting a call back. The person also said that David will have two surgeries. Can you please clarify that for us, because Dr. D didn't mention anything about two surgeries? Why would he have two surgeries three days apart? Also, the call that David was expecting last week was not from your office but from the office that schedules the pre-op testing. We are trying to schedule the tests for this Thursday since he is coming there for his appointment with Dr D. Is there any way you can please help us with that or give us direction in case he is leaving messages with the wrong office? He used the phone number listed in the surgery notification package."

Circe heard back from Johns Hopkins the next day, confirming David's December 5 appointment with the surgeon and providing a telephone number for the contact person at the Johns Hopkins campus where David's surgery would take place. Circe wanted all of David's pre-tests and exams done at Johns Hopkins, but nothing was mentioned about setting up a pre-op physical or medical tests. Luckily, David arranged for a back-up pre-op appointment with Dr. K, his primary care doctor, who was well aware of David's medical history and addiction. His MRI was scheduled earlier the same morning in Fairfax. I drove David to both appointments.

Dr. K expressed grave concern about the extent of damage to David's spine, but he cleared David for surgery and explained some of what he thought David would need for aftercare, including coming back to him for a post-operation exam.

Four days before David's surgery, Circe sent David and me an email about downgrading her health insurance coverage and choosing options for vision and dental. She specifically asked me to compare the plans and help her decide what to do. I reviewed the plans and sent back an email with my comments and recommendations. I should have known better than to respond. Another round of Circe's infamous email chains ensued among the three of us, regurgitating all the things she had done for David. She then explained in painful detail why none of my suggestions were viable.

When David told Circe to drop him from her vision and dental coverage because he never used it and agreed downgrading her health insurance was a good move, she insisted he needed dental insurance and would keep him on. I encouraged Circe to get the health insurance that was best for her financial and health needs. I suggested she sell the car she bought for Dave, which could be used for other expenses she was complaining about. She said she wouldn't get enough for it to make it worth selling, and it wasn't up to David or me to decide how she spent her money.

Circe's emails continued—about paying his December rent and saying she would look for a disability lawyer because both his surgery and Hepatitis C made him eligible for disability benefits. She was determined he would not go back to work for at least a year even though the doctor told us most people who have this surgery return to work in two to three months. David may have been an addict, but he loved his work. More importantly, he needed his work. Late in the evening, David emailed both of us, ending another useless email rant.

The next morning I took David for his pre-op appointment with Dr. K. It was snowing. We had fun maneuvering our way through the snow to run errands and have lunch at a small deli near the doctor's office. Circe was supposed to join us for lunch, but she declined at the last minute.

SPINE SURGERIES

David's first surgery for vertebral osteomyelitis took place on Friday morning, December 13, 2013, at 7:00 a.m., at the Johns Hopkins Hospital's main campus in Baltimore. There was back and forth between David and Circe about driving him, but she wouldn't commit. Plan B was for me to drive him.

David was packed and ready to go when I picked him up from his house on Thursday afternoon to stay the night at my house since we would need to leave by 5:00 a.m. We had dinner, and though David was understandably apprehensive and anxious about the following day's surgery, he was settled, and we had a nice evening. It was not surprising when later in the evening Circe called and said she had worked it out and wanted to drive David to JH in the morning. Circe arrived at my house around 5:00 a.m., and they headed to Baltimore. I waited a little while and drove over on my own.

I had discussed David's operations with the surgeon and his primary care doctor, read and reviewed the paperwork, and David and I communicated regularly via email while I was in India. Still, it was difficult to absorb the magnitude and scope of the proposed surgeries. Then there was the surprise that he would need *two* operations. When David and I met with Dr. D, he wasn't very specific. I also didn't know until the day of the surgery that Dr. D would not be the lead surgeon. JH brought in a bigwig specialist, which was why David's surgery was delayed for two days. David's first operation took 11 hours. It was designed to prepare his body and insert the "tools" for the second operation.

Circe and I waited together in a large surgical waiting area for families. We were assigned a number by the surgical information desk that identified David's surgery, and we were told to go to the front of the waiting room when our number appeared on the board where the surgeons would meet with us for post-surgery results. After a few hours when our number didn't appear on the board, we inquired at the information desk about how David was doing. We were told the surgery was on track and going well and to please wait until our number appeared on the board. The lady at the information desk assured us the surgeons would let us know if there were complications.

We waited and watched as the huge waiting room of about 200 people earlier in the day dwindled down to just us two. Our number never appeared on the board. We returned to the information desk just as the lady was preparing to leave and asked about David. The information lady said David's doctors had to go immediately into another procedure and would not be coming out to talk to us. It was almost 7:00 p.m.

The large surgical waiting area was shut down, and we were directed to a smaller waiting area and told we would be able to see David once he was settled in the critical care unit. By this time Circe was a basket case. She was supposedly on a business trip, and her boyfriend expected her home by 6:00 p.m. She had repeated all afternoon that she had to leave by 4:00 to be home by 6:00, but when 4:00 came, she didn't leave. About an hour later, we were finally allowed to see David in the critical care unit. He was awake, out of control, cringing in severe pain, crying, and terribly afraid. Circe said she couldn't stand seeing him like that and left after a few minutes. I cannot put on paper how badly my heart hurt to see my son in such pain. I cradled him as best I could and stayed until he calmed down and drifted back to sleep. The nurses could not give me any information about the actual operation, but assured me that, with the drugs David was taking, he would be out until morning. They promised to call me if he woke up. I reluctantly left and drove home.

I returned to Johns Hopkins early the next morning. As expected, David had slept through the night, and his pain was better controlled Saturday morning. I sought out Dr. D, who said the operation went as planned and briefly explained what he would be doing during Tuesday's operation, where he would be the lead surgeon, and it shouldn't take as long. Without saying why, Dr. D kind of apologized for not talking to us after the previous day's 11-hour operation. He seemed pleased with the results but devoid of compassion for a heroin addict who had shot the hell out of his veins.

I stayed most of the day while Dave drifted in and out of sleep. Early Sunday morning David was much more alert but had little memory of the past two days. He sent me a text, letting me know he was doing fine and Dr. D had stopped by and explained the results of the MRI from the previous night. He was good to go for Tuesday's surgery.

I arrived at Johns Hopkins early Tuesday morning for David's second operation. Circe could not make arrangements to be there. A rod the full length of David's spine was inserted and bolted down on each side with screws. A cage was placed in the area of the damaged vertebrae to support and guide the growth of new bone. Tuesday's operation took about six hours. I waited in the same large waiting room, but this time my number appeared on the board, and Dr. D met with me following the operation. He said the procedure was a complete success and David would be fine. David's spine was straight and bolted down.

Again, when David came to, he was scared and cried out in severe pain. I gathered him in my arms and held his head against my chest, rocking him gently until he calmed down. On Wednesday, I arrived early with his requested coffee and stayed with him until he fell asleep. We took a short walk, and he moved around much better. He was having the usual complications post-surgery but, given the severity of his operation, doing well. When he texted in the evening, he said he slept well and was looking forward to a good night's sleep.

When I talked to David early Thursday morning, they had already given him a chest X-ray, and Dr. D's team had stopped in to examine him and to answer questions. David was sounding more and more like himself. Slowly, all the tubes and wires were disconnected, except for the chest tube, which took a while longer, causing complications and increasing the length of his stay. On Thursday evening, David was moved out of critical care into a regular room to begin healing. On Saturday, the chest tube was removed. Otherwise, David's post-operation process went well, and his spirits were, for the most part, good. His biggest disappointment was he couldn't get the Washington Redskins game on TV in Baltimore.

David was antsy and ready to leave Johns Hopkins. His release was now set for Tuesday, December 24, Christmas Eve.

LEAVING JOHNS HOPKINS

December 24, 2013, was a cold, rainy, gray day. David was to call me when his release papers were ready. From early morning and throughout the day, there was much telephoning and texting back and forth while we waited. He was told his release was delayed because the staff doctors couldn't figure out what pain medications to send home with him. I gave up waiting at home and arrived at Johns Hopkins in the afternoon amid much confusion. David was frustrated, sitting in a wheelchair, dressed, and ready to go; all we needed were the release papers, final instructions for home care, and his medications. Nurses and doctors scurried around. Limited staff and a holiday atmosphere didn't help. Finally, the paperwork was done, and David's prescriptions were ordered. We were thankfully able to fill prescriptions for gabapentin (seizures), cyclobenzaprine (muscle spasms), fentanyl (opioid; pain), dilaudid (pain), and lidocaine (pain) at the Johns Hopkins pharmacy before we headed out on the dark and wet road home. I didn't know then that David told a friend in 2013, "Dilaudid is a beautiful thing. One of my favorites."

We arrived at my house around 7:30 p.m. David was worn out but immediately walked up the 42 steps to the guest room—an amazing feat considering what he had endured the past couple of weeks. After a bowl of soup, he was asleep the minute his head hit the pillow. When I was sure David was settled for the night, I did what I have done every Christmas Eve since he was a child . . . I prepared Monkey Bread for Christmas morning.

We woke to a beautiful sunny Christmas morning, which turned into a wonderful day. I was so glad to have Dave home! My husband and mother came, and so did David's brother and wife and her mother, for brunch and to exchange gifts. When I went upstairs to help David come down and to see everyone, he said he wasn't going downstairs. He felt bad because he didn't have anything for anyone. I gave him a stack of old Christmas greeting cards and suggested he write a note to each of us as his gift. He started to write, and now his words are priceless to all of us. To his grandmother Millie, he wrote:

> "December 25, 2013. Mama, I haven't spoken to you in quite some time. I was ashamed of my situation and couldn't bear to face you. I think of you often, there in that house without my grandfather. I hope you are not hurting. I should be there to come visit and help you with things. If I have learned nothing else from this, I have learned that life is precious and short. We must live it while we have this fight. I cannot be there to wish you a Merry Christmas in person but know that I will always love my grandmother and I have never forgotten about you. Please smile and be happy!!"

After David wrote the cards, I persuaded him to come downstairs. He handed out his cards, and we all had brunch. David was a crooked mass of skin and bones as he curled up in the corner of the couch, but his eyes sparkled and he was smiling. The following days weren't all smooth sailing, but after the stress of the operations and driving back and forth to Baltimore, Christmas morning was a sweet reprieve.

I was beyond delighted to have David at my home to recover. He stayed with us for two weeks after leaving Johns Hopkins. We quickly settled into a routine where we watched movies, played games and cards, took a couple of day trips, and had lots of talks. Circe and David communicated mostly by phone and text; she came once for a short visit. The guest room was on the fourth floor, and within days, he was going up and down the stairs to take outside walks. His stamina and progress amazed me.

Once he felt better, David began reaching out through social media. He rejoined the Drug Forum online with the following introduction:

> "I am a 39-year-old guy from the D.C. area. I have been a heroin addict for 15 years on and off. I know everything there is to know about heroin and Suboxone. I have been to four different rehabs and to jail many times. You would never know these things by looking at me. I am currently in an outpatient treatment program. Recently, I have gotten an infection in my spine. It's a staph infection, and it has eaten away the T11 & T12 vertebrae, and I can barely stand up. What I have is discitis and osteomyelitis. I can talk at length about these things and anything else relating to heroin. Unfortunately, I am an expert. Hobbies and interests: I play chess, cards, read, watch documentaries and movies."

I cried the first time I helped David prepare his back for a shower and then reapply the giant patch of fentanyl. I had never heard of fentanyl and had no idea of fentanyl's potency. Although David was healing well, his body was punctured, scarred, and raw, with long red cuts from the top to the bottom of his spine where the rod was inserted. Twelve inflamed crosses indented his skin on each side of his spine where the screws held down the rod. I could see where the chest tube had been inserted, just above his abdomen where a rib had been removed to make room for the doctors to do the surgical repairs. David was alarmingly thin.

On the first day home, I gave David a couple of those 7-day pill boxes, and we sorted his daily medications into doses, which were mostly opioids for pain but included anti-seizure and muscle spasm medications. Leftover pills were kept in the bottles on the dresser, ready to refill the weekly boxes. I was determined not to be a hovering mother or nagging nursemaid and left David to administer his own medications from the pill boxes. David was well enough to go up and down the stairs and to walk around the block. He had a good attitude and a healthy appetite. In that first week, we talked a lot about his addiction and what it had done to him. He adamantly promised that the infection and destruction to his spine were his bottom. He would never use heroin again. I felt that trusting him with his medications for healing was a good first step for him to take responsibility and to keep that promise. I was wrong.

In early January 2014, David described in his journal what would happen to him if he started using heroin again:

1) I can't stop once I start.

2) I will keep going until everything is gone.

3) I will get arrested.

4) I will isolate.

5) I will ruin relationships.

6) I will become desperate.

7) I will stop paying bills.

8) I will steal.

9) It makes me sick in many different ways.

10) I lose all will power and will relapse if I'm not diligent.

Things went well with David's recovery for about 10 days. Then I noticed he was sleeping a lot more and eating a lot less. I kept an eye on the pill boxes, which he used as he should have, but when I checked his pill bottles, the opioids were depleted. David had dived into his drugs, consuming three times what he was prescribed. When I confronted David, he argued he had to take more than prescribed because the pain was so bad and his tolerance was so high.

CHAPTER 12: 2014—LAST DAYS

GOOD-BYE

After two weeks, in early January 2014, our happy days of healing and my hopes for David's recovery from addiction were gone. David had become morose. He did not leave his room, not even to smoke. When I checked on him, he would not talk to me and avoided eye contact. His iPad sat idle on his bedside table while he slept all day and all night. He refused to eat and drank little. I realized David had gone into some type of withdrawal or depression; things were quickly going downhill.

One morning, David refused to get out of bed when I urged him to shower while I changed his sheets. I tried to reason with him, but he was not receptive. David lay in bed, staring blindly through me. I told myself not to think what I was thinking. What else could be done if this terrible infection didn't put him on a solid road to recovery from addiction? I feared that David was using his situation to justify an endless supply of opioids. I asked him, "Do you just want to lay in this room all day and take pills? Is that all you want from life?"

David turned his head, looked at me with an empty stare, and nodded, "Yes."

I went numb. I thought for sure my heart was going to pop out of my chest. Fifteen years, and I still didn't know what to say or do. I stood there in silence, staring back at him while memories swirled in my head—heroin, addiction, treatments, relapses, lies, jail, infection, the wasted words of love and encouragement. I berated myself for not more closely monitoring his medications. But I couldn't give up and wasn't going to allow him to just lie there either. I said, "It's time for you to go home."

David did not respond or get up.

It was early and neither of us had showered, so I said I was going to get showered and he should too. What I really wanted was time to figure out a way to walk back my words about going home. Maybe he just needed more time. But by the time I had dressed and returned to his room, he was gone and so was his stuff. I found him sitting in the passenger seat of my car, still in his PJs and robe, not saying a word, staring straight ahead, an empty and eerie look masking his face. His stuff had been packed into the back of the car. David's demeanor scared me. I worried that I had crossed some mental barrier from which there was no return. The only other time I had seen him this way was when I picked him up at the Metro on Thanksgiving.

I opened the driver's door, leaned in, and tried to get David to come back into the house so we could talk through whatever was happening with him. He didn't move or speak. It was like he had taken himself a million miles away and I didn't exist. Nothing changed during the drive to his house; he didn't speak and continued to stare blankly through the windshield. In silence, we carried his stuff into the house.

When I was about halfway home, David called me, "Hey Ma, I left my phone at your house. I'm using my roommate's phone. I need you to bring my phone back to me."

"I will bring your phone when I pick you up for your post-op with Dr. D on Thursday. That is, if you want me to take you for your post-op."

"Mom! I need a phone!!"

"David, there is no way I'm going home to pick up your phone, turning around, and making another trip out to Fairfax today. You can manage a couple days." I hung up.

During my drive home, Circe called me because she was concerned that David wasn't answering his phone. I told her what had happened and that David left his phone at my house. The next day, I got an email from David:

> "You are wrong when you say that I don't care about you and that I don't want to do the right thing. I have thoroughly enjoyed

the time we have spent recently. You really painted me as a selfish jerk. That is not true."

The problem, as I explained in an email back to Dave, was that I no longer knew who he was. I knew there was a David inside who was interesting, loving, and fun to be around. Where did that David go? He had spent most of his adult life trying to finagle the system, and the people who loved him, with lies, denial, and manipulation. If only he put a tenth of that effort into managing his life without dope, he could do everything he said he wanted to do and more.

The physical harm he had done to himself had overwhelmed our lives for so many years, I simply didn't have the strength to fight him any longer. I loved him just as much on that January day when I took him home as I did that first day he tested me sitting in his highchair, but I was no longer that young mother. David's addiction and bad behaviors had taken a tremendous toll on everyone who cared about him. He needed to step up and be the man he kept saying he wanted to be. I needed to return to where we were before his infection was discovered.

POST-OP / PAIN MANAGEMENT

The next morning at David's post-op appointment at Johns Hopkins, Dr. D said David was doing great and moving around remarkably well. I said to Dr. D, "I'm very concerned about all of the drugs David has been prescribed. He has been abusing the dosage. I know he has pain, but his addiction is the bigger problem. There has to be another way to manage his pain, or he is going to go back into active addiction."

Dr. D gave me a "you've got to be kidding lady" look and responded, "No, there isn't another way to manage this kind of pain. David's pain receptors are essentially frayed from drug use, and the medications can't get in to do their job, which is why he may need a higher dose."

David got upset with me, "Shut up, Mom! You don't understand, I have a high tolerance and need the drugs. The pain is terrible!"

I wouldn't let it go. David and I started to scream at each other.

I had never challenged a doctor or had a screaming battle in a doctor's office. I was ashamed of myself, but I was desperate. Dr. D just sat there, looking down at his shoes, obviously uncomfortable and wishing we would leave. I shut up. The room went quiet. Dr. D wrote a prescription for dilaudid, gave it to David and said, "This will be the last prescription I can give to you. You need to find a pain management doctor in Virginia to help you manage your pain."

Dr. D's job was done. He did not need to, and would not, see David again. I asked about physical therapy, and that, too, would need to be sought out in Virginia. Good-bye, Johns Hopkins.

On the drive back from Baltimore, David continued trying to convince me that he needed the large amounts of pain medications he had been taking. He pushed aside my voiced concern to Dr. D that when the pain prescriptions ran out, he would go back to using heroin. He kept talking and talking, gesturing with his hands and face about how much he needed another fentanyl patch before the prescription was valid.

I was numb with emptiness. All my optimism and confidence disappeared. I stared straight through the windshield as I calmly and silently drove. I imagined that stupid addiction train headed back to the depot to pick us up. But this time, I wasn't getting on. I dropped David at CVS to get the Dilaudid prescription filled; he said he would find his own way home, which was fine with me.

Not long after I got home, Dave texted:

> "Just for informational purposes, those medications don't get me all doped up anyway. They only dull the pain. It is nothing like heroin. So all of this is wrong. You act like he is prescribing me heroin. That is so wrong. But you don't believe that. Just like you don't believe I'm in pain in the first place. Everything I say is just assumed to be a lie."

I responded:

> "I know you have pain, but you need to suck it up and only take what drugs you absolutely need. You must begin weaning yourself off pain meds instead of focusing on getting more. I only want for you to be happy and healthy. We just don't agree on how you get there. I have to let go and accept your decisions—so that's what I'm doing."

I didn't hear from David for a couple days until I sent a text asking, "Would you like for me to drive you to the pain management appointments on Monday morning?" Dave responded, "Yes. I would like that."

I resolved to myself that there would be no more arguments about pain meds . . . or anything else. David's illness had returned me to caretaker, and I needed to return to loving without enabling.

I picked David up early on Monday morning, January 13, and took him to two pain management clinics in Fairfax. At the first clinic, David was told they didn't prescribe pain meds; they only did epidurals and cortisone shots and couldn't help him. At the second clinic, they told him they weren't equipped to handle someone like him with an opiate addiction. David was frustrated when we got back in the car. "David," I suggested, "how about Dr. K? You need to go back to him anyway for your post-op checkup since he did your pre-op, and Dr. K knows your history. I bet he can help you."

"That's right!" David exclaimed, "I'll call Dr. K right now."

David called Dr. K from the car, and Dr. K said he could see David around 3:00 that afternoon, which meant I either had to wait around in Fairfax for several hours or go home and drive back to take him. David said he was fine with taking a cab. Although I would have liked to talk to Dr. K again, I reminded myself this was all part of letting David take charge of his life and recovery. I had to let him go.

I reached into my wallet and gave David a $20 bill for the cab. I can still so perfectly remember handing David that $20 bill—the magic number for an addict. I see a slow motion version of watching myself reach into my wallet . . .

take out the $20 bill . . . his hand reaching out . . . his eyes focused on the bill . . . the bill floating from my hand to his . . . all the while thinking . . . I know better.

I dropped David off at his house, and while I was driving home, I couldn't stop thinking about that $20 bill and what he could buy with it. I hadn't given him cash in years. Until he could get back to work, I was paying his bills directly and buying him what he needed, but I never gave him cash. I called and told David I would be back by 2:30. However, before I could get home, I got a call from my mother.

My mother, who was 89, needed help. While she was taking out the trash, the can rolled over and fell on her. A guy stopped his car and helped her get up, but she was shaken up, bleeding, and bruised. I had to go and check on her, which wouldn't give me enough time to get back to David's house in time for his 3:00 appointment.

I texted Dave to let him know I couldn't come after all and he wrote back:

> "I have a friend who had an accident a few years back and had to use a pain management doctor. He says the guy was real good. Handled the pain, then tapered him off and also did physical therapy. It sounds real good. You go help Millie. I'll be ok. Calling the cab now. I'm gonna make the best of this situation."

After his appointment with Dr. K, Dave texted:

> "Hey Mom, Dr. K said that the Dr. I told you about is a good man and I should go with him. So that's what we decided to do. I came home and called his office to set up an appointment, but the receptionist said I cannot get an appointment with them because of my history and I've used Suboxone. I will call Dr. K tomorrow to see if he has any other suggestions. I am very frustrated, but I will keep working on it."

David went on to say that Dr. K did not give him any prescriptions, and that he was putting together his tax papers. He sounded good and seemed fine. He said he was taking Tylenol as directed by Dr. D, wearing his brace, doing laundry, changing sheets, and tackling other housekeeping chores like dusting and vacuuming. It was amazing how well he could function when he wanted to . . . or, I wondered, was he just saying what he thought I wanted to hear? He emailed and phoned the Braner Pain Clinic, but his email was sent back undeliverable. I don't know if he ever talked to them.

On January 16, Thursday afternoon, David texted:

> "Check your email. I cc'd you on an email I sent to Dr. D's assistant. I basically said I can't find a pain management doctor and could Dr. D give me a referral. Read the email and tell me what you think. How is Millie? Is everything ok with her?"

Dave also said in his email that he was going to need a refill on his medications soon. He got a response from the spine center's clinical research coordinator a couple hours later, which said they could not help him but sent the telephone number of someone who might be able to help.

I let David know that Millie was fine; she just needed help getting cleaned up and time to calm down. David sent another text later—his last communication to me:

> "Ok, I got your response. Glad Millie is ok. Hopefully they [Johns Hopkins] can help me. I think email is best. That way they can understand my situation. I hate feeling helpless. I went for a walk around the block with my brace on. Swung my arms. Trying to get some strength back. It's a really beautiful day!"

Later, I emailed Dave and suggested that he check YouTube for exercise and physical therapy videos for back pain and post-spine surgery. As an avid walker, I encouraged him to get out and walk because walking is good for the body and the mind. The next morning, Friday, January 17, when I hadn't heard back overnight, I sent him another email with links to YouTube videos.

By this time, David was probably gone and never saw my email with the YouTube links for physical therapy exercises. That Friday morning, I had a 10:00 a.m. eye doctor appointment in D.C., just a few blocks from where I used to work. I also had plans to have lunch after my appointment with a friend from work. I emailed David again, asking him to please check in with me. I kept checking for a text or an email response. When I didn't hear back from him, I panicked and texted Circe during my subway ride into town, asking if she had talked to or heard from David since yesterday. I knew they still talked and emailed daily. She had resumed sending realtor emails in December.

Circe texted back that she hadn't heard from David, but that she would call him at noon. A little while later, Circe let me know she'd called David several times with no answer. She was worried but busy with work and could not drive over to check on him. I was a nervous wreck, trying to be normal at lunch. Finally, I told my friend that I had to leave because I had not been able to reach David all morning. I ran from the restaurant to the subway. After I got on the train and before I could text Circe to see if she had heard from David, she texted me, "Anything yet?"

I texted back, "Noooooo!!!"

My eyes were dilated by the eye doctor and I still couldn't see very well. I didn't care. I ran the five blocks home from the subway stop and was about to leave for David's house when Circe called and screamed into the phone, "I JUST FOUND DAVID IN HIS BATHROOM! HE IS STONE COLD DEAD!! I THINK HE'S DEAD!!! HIS HEAD IS DOWN ON THE FLOOR IN A POOL OF VOMIT!! CALL 911!!!"

In total panic, I screamed back, "ARE YOU SURE???!!! YOU'RE WITH DAVID AND YOU THINK HE'S DEAD AND YOU HAVEN'T CALLED 911?! WHAT THE HELL IS WRONG WITH YOU?!"

Circe exclaimed, "I CAN'T CALL! MY NAME MIGHT BE PRINTED IN THE NEWSPAPER!"

I couldn't believe my ears! I hung up, called 911, and shouted into the phone, "I NEED AN AMBULANCE IMMEDIATELY!!! I THINK MY SON MIGHT BE DEAD!!"

"What's the address?"

"The address?? Oh my God, I know the street name, but not the number! I've been there a hundred times!!"

I began shuffling through the drawers of my desk. Where would the address be? Holy shit!!

I shouted into the phone, "I'M LOOKING!!! The street is --- in Fairfax!"

"I'm sorry, this is 911 Alexandria. You need to call 911 Fairfax."

I couldn't think. My mind deserted me as I screamed at this poor 911 operator, "YOU HAVE GOT TO BE KIDDING ME!!! I'M TELLING YOU THAT I THINK MY SON MIGHT BE DEAD ON HIS BATHROOM FLOOR AND YOU'RE TELLING ME I NEED TO CALL ANOTHER NUMBER!! HOW DO I CALL 911 FAIRFAX?!! I CAN'T THINK. YOU HAVE TO CONNECT ME!!!! PLEASE HURRY!!!!!!"

I finally got through and continued my insane tirade, screaming through my sobs as I gave the 911 Fairfax operator the street information. I called and left my husband a hysterical voicemail. I was terrified to call David's brother... I needed to see for myself... I could not do this to him... this is too awful... *Oh my God, please let this just be another one of Circe's overreacting moments! Please let David still be alive! Oh... Please... Please... Please! I cannot tell Bill his brother is gone!*

I immediately got in my car and drove like a maniac out to David's house. I was an unhinged woman speeding as fast as I could on the beltway. The busy Friday afternoon rush home had started, and I was driving out of control, like a train off its tracks. I was barely able to see through my tears, swerving in and out of the lanes while taking out my anger on the steering wheel, clutching it tightly when I wasn't slamming it with my fists. I was a total hazard on the road. To this day, I'm amazed and grateful that I didn't crash into anyone.

When I got to David's house, emergency vehicles had already lined the street. The police had taped off the house and yard because it was considered a crime scene. Circe was roaming around the yard. A detective approached me and introduced himself as Detective B and asked who I was. I told him and his first question was, "Do you think your son was suicidal?"

I answered, "Suicidal?! No! Heavens, no! He has been recovering from two brutal surgeries but doing well. Why do you ask that? Are you sure my son is dead? May I please see my son?!"

"Did your son use drugs?"

These questions! How the fuck did this man think I could stand there and answer his questions? I needed to see my son and to know what the hell happened to him!

"Yes," I said. "He used heroin, but he has been in recovery since he became ill. Although, he has been taking prescribed pain medications. I want to see my son, *PLEASE!*"

"No, I'm sorry, I can't let you go in until we've completed our investigation. I'll let you know more when I can." Detective B turned and walked into the house.

I sank onto the lawn, pressed my forehead to my knees, and cried. This couldn't be happening. How many fucking times had I said this was going to happen?! *But it just can't be . . . it just can't be.* I finally stood and went over to Circe, who was crying but keeping control. She did not want to bring attention to herself. I gave her a hug.

I asked Circe, "Do you know what's going on in there? What do you think happened? The detective asked me if Dave was suicidal."

Circe responded, "When I went into the bathroom, it looked like David had been sitting on the side of the tub, threw up, fell forward and his head landed in his vomit. There were three syringes of different sizes on the vanity top."

"Oh my God! Could you tell what was in them? Was there evidence of heroin?"

"No. He was stone cold, I think he has been dead for a while. David was hanging out with a woman and dating her daughter. I think one of them must have come to his house last night and brought him the syringes and maybe drugs. He was wearing a fentanyl patch and was able to get new patches yesterday."

My husband and Bill arrived, and the worst nightmare of my life played out. It wasn't too much later when David was rolled out of his house on a gurney in a black body bag. Detective B said that an autopsy would be done on David in the morning to give them a better idea of what caused his death. He asked a few more questions and expressed his interest and concern about why David had fentanyl. He explained that up and down the east coast, fentanyl was being mixed with heroin, causing a higher rate of drug overdoses. The detective gave me his card and said that he would be in touch when he had more information.

When David's basement apartment was finally released from the police investigation and after his funeral, Bill, my husband, a couple friends, and I went in to clean out his stuff. One of his roommates was waiting to move into the space. Circe had already been there, gotten what she wanted, and didn't want to go back.

Even though I had been to David's place several times, I was nervous as I stepped through the doorway. It was a surprise to find everything neat and tidy, and it confirmed what David told me the day before he died—he had been busy cleaning and doing laundry. His bed was made and had not been slept in, which made us think that he probably died the night before or in the early morning. We discovered an unfinished area under the house, attached to his living space, where David stored a lot of items. It was here that we found his laptop, iPad, journal, photos, and other papers, which are the basis for this book. We went through and cleaned out everything. His brother and I kept a few articles of his clothing. The rest of his clothes that were not riddled with cigarette burns were donated to a local drug treatment center. My friend found a syringe in one of David's jackets hanging in his closet. Luckily, she was not harmed. That was the only syringe found. We did find quite a few empty baggies in various drawers of his bureau and bedside table but no heroin or other drugs.

David had made a nice little home for himself.

If only . . .

THE LAST LIE

After David's funeral, I called David's Fairfax probation officer and court appointed attorney, TK, to let them know about David's death. I had briefly met David's probation officer one day when I dropped David off, but I hadn't had the opportunity to interact with him. He was surprised about David's death. He expressed his condolences and thanked me for calling .

I especially wanted to talk to attorney TK to thank him. He had shown a genuine interest in helping David. He expressed surprise and sadness about David's death and said again that he had hoped David would recover to do all the things they had talked about.

I also called Dr. K. I wanted to ask him how he thought David was doing mentally and physically at his post-op appointment the previous Monday. The suicide question still bothered me; maybe Dr. K picked up on something.

Dr. K's voice was sad and quiet when he said, "I'm so sorry. David was a great guy with great potential if he could've just stopped using heroin. I wondered how he was doing and when I would see him for his post-op."

I didn't think I heard him right and said, "I don't understand. David told me he'd made an appointment and saw you last Monday for his post-op checkup and pain management."

"No," responded Dr. K. "I haven't seen David since you brought him in for his pre-op checkup a few days before his surgery."

I was stunned and told Dr. K about the operations and the difficulties David was having finding a pain management doctor. I said I was confused because I was in the car when David called and made the appointment with him for Monday afternoon, January 13.

Dr. K said, "I don't remember talking to David … hold on." I heard the phone drop.

Dr. K returned to the line and said, "I just checked the appointment book and call records for Monday—there was no appointment for or call from David. Are you sure he called me?"

"I was in the car with him when he called. I was concerned that the pain meds would drive him back into active addiction and wanted him to find a way to deal with the pain without opioids. I was hoping you could help him with that."

"Yes, I definitely would have helped him. Based on your description of the surgeries, he would have been in great pain and needed relief that only opioids could give. I too would have prescribed pain medications, which would have been okay while David was recovering. He justifiably needed the pain medications, but he needed them carefully prescribed and slowly weaned off."

I responded, "Yes, that's exactly what he needed."

Haunting images of that $20 bill seeped into my mind.

Dr. K and I talked for a while longer. He told me how much he liked David and enjoyed his company and that David had cut his hair every now and then.

Why did David construct this grandiose lie about going to see Dr. K? Who the hell did he call from the car? The weather? I was skeptical when David eagerly agreed with my suggestion to see Dr. K, but he was desperate. I should have known when David added the "I know a guy . . . and Dr. K says he's a good guy too . . . " The red flag was exposed and after all my experience with David's lies, I'd missed it.

After the call with Dr. K, I sat in my chair in a daze. I was sure that the music for the *Twilight Zone* would come on at any second. Did David use the $20 for heroin? Had David decided that the best option to alleviate his pain could only be found with his best buddy, heroin? Was there credibility to Circe's assertion that some woman and her daughter brought David syringes and drugs?

On January 19, I sent email notification of David's death to Johns Hopkins and included a copy of his last email to them. No response from Johns Hopkins was ever received by me or David.

THE MEDICAL EXAMINER'S REPORT

Because Circe was still legally David's wife, the Medical Examiner's office would only give her access to his autopsy report. After the autopsy and after David was embalmed, I finally got to see him . . . lying in a coffin wearing the clothes I'd selected for him. I noticed a nasty bruise running across the width of David's forehead. I followed up with Detective B about the bruise, asking if he could please help me get a copy of the autopsy report results.

In February, I received an email from Detective B:

> "The bruise on David's forehead is what we refer to as a blanched area. David's forehead was resting on his arm when found. As blood settles after death, any contact (impression) with a body part or object will cause a white area to appear where no blood settles. I assume after a few days it could appear to be a bruise. I will mention it to the Medical Examiner. There is no foul play involved in David's death. His death is not a homicide or suicide. It appears to be an accidental death. Keep in mind, there have been a lot of news reports recently regarding 'Bad Heroin' on the east coast. There have been at least eighty reported deaths after people have injected heroin laced with fentanyl, a powerful synthetic opiate. There have been several cases reported in Fairfax County. I hope that fentanyl is not involved in this case, but we will have to wait for the toxicology report. Even if fentanyl is involved, it is still not a homicide case. I will also speak with the ME [Medical Examiner] Office about you obtaining a copy of the autopsy report."

I continued to periodically email Detective B about getting a copy of the toxicology report but received no response.

Finally, in July, Detective B sent me another email:

> "David's case is still under investigation. I have not officially closed the case yet. I am checking into a few more things. The Medical Examiner has closed their investigation. The Medical Examiner identified the cause of death as 'Adverse effects of Fentanyl, Cyclobenzaprine and Lidocaine.' The manner of death

was identified as an 'Accident.' Our narcotics detective investigated the circumstances regarding possible drugs but did not find anything of importance. I will update you after I complete my investigation. Thanks for your assistance."

The three drugs noted in Detective B's email were three of the five drugs prescribed when David came home from Johns Hopkins. Fentanyl and lidocaine were patches and cyclobenzaprine was a 10 mg tablet. He was wearing a new fentanyl patch. His 10-day supply of the lidocaine patch had run out, but he probably still had cyclobenzaprine. There was no evidence of heroin in his system. I don't know if the syringes that Circe said were on the vanity were tested. I don't even know for sure if there were three syringes. David must have gotten lidocaine from somewhere, but as far as I know, he had not been able to find a pain management doctor. So many questions and only speculation to go on. I called and emailed Detective B a couple more times but never heard back again. I assume he closed the case and had nothing more to add. Another addict . . . another death.

FUNERAL

On a brutally cold, windy, and dreary January day, friends and family gathered to lay David to rest next to his grandfather. Snow covered the ground. Reaching closure on the funeral arrangements did not come easy. Circe's emails, calls, and texts started coming immediately after David's death, demanding what should be done, who should say and do what, on and on and on. This is the same Circe who couldn't dial 911 on the day she found him because her name might be linked to his death in the newspaper. We tried to keep her calm and to do everything she wanted, but nothing was ever right or good enough. It got so bad during the week prior to his burial, I had to stop interacting with Circe. My husband and Bill took over and dealt with her emails and rants.

On the Sunday following David's death, Circe and a friend, Bill and his wife, my husband, and I met at the funeral home to discuss final arrangements for David's burial. Due to a misfortune of timing, David's dad, who had retired many years ago to the Florida Keys, could not be part of the planning. He was scheduled to remarry the day after we found David, but he and his new wife attended the funeral the next Saturday.

Planning my son's burial was difficult enough without Circe being emotionally distraught. At one point during the funeral home meeting, her crying turned into uncontrollable hysteria. I took her out of the room, and through her tears, she explained to me that she was so upset because the funeral home had refused her request when she called and demanded that they stop the embalming process.

Why did Circe want them to stop the embalming process?

Circe wanted David's sperm.

The funeral home had not mentioned any of this to me. When I asked later, they said, "Yes, Circe called numerous times, soon after David's body arrived at the funeral home. She had several requests but mainly wanted embalming delayed until after his sperm could be removed. We explained to her that by the time of her call, we had already started the embalming process and any sperm was already destroyed. We did not want to add to your grief by telling you about Circe's request."

To dress David, I took them a new long sleeve plaid shirt that he got for Christmas, a pair of jeans, his belt, warm socks, underwear, and an A-shirt. His high school sports jacket hung behind his casket, two of his old baseballs still in the pockets. Notes, pictures, trinkets, and a small stuffed animal surrounded him. Circe chose a beautiful casket for David and topped it off with a large spray of red roses.

During the funeral service, several people stood and shared stories about Dave. His boss from the barbershop, who trained him when he was an apprentice, spoke about David and lightened the mood. He shared memories of a cantankerous Dave and a fun-loving, creative guy working at the shop. He knew David well. He didn't judge and always had a barber chair waiting for David when he returned from jail or treatment or an unannounced prolonged drug binge. I commend the patience and support that he and the other barbers gave Dave, and I thank them from the bottom of my heart for caring about my son.

Dave's brother gave the eulogy. For so many years, I'd leaned on Bill, and once again he stood tall and strong, and he helped get me through the worst day of my life. He ended his eulogy with a revision to a poem David wrote many years before. When David wrote the poem, there was no title. Maybe that was foresight. The same foresight David had in leaving me with the wonderful gift of his thoughts and writings, so that his ideas and words would be available for me to share in this memoir.

Bill's farewell poem to Dave:

LITTLE BROTHER

This week was the same
As I looked to the sky

Nothing had changed
I had to ask why.

The sky looks the same
As before you were lost

We can't go back
Someday, our paths will cross.

Until then, you're in my heart
You will forever stay the same

As I look to the sky
Now you are free.

The only difference
Is poor ole me.

I miss you, little brother.

My farewell poem to all the moms who have lost a child. I wrote this poem for another mother's son who died many years before David. His was not an addict's death, but it doesn't matter.

THIS WISH OF MINE

Life cut short
For one so young,
Taken away
From a Mother's son,
A heavy heart
You're left to bear,
For one you thought
Would always be there.

I hope this poem
Will ease your pain,
And memories soon
To shine again,
Of a dear, dear son
You loved so fine,
God grant you peace
This wish of mine.

EPILOGUE

As I write today, I feel sure David would never have been capable of living life without heroin, and a medically-assisted treatment such as Suboxone would not be his cure. I believe his addiction morphed into a disease that for some has no cure. However, there's ongoing controversy about whether addiction is a "choice" or a "disease."

When I stood next to my son's coffin and rubbed my hand across his creased forehead that hit the bathroom floor on the night he died, I didn't care whether his addiction was a choice or caused by a disease. Either reason left him dead. But these questions persisted. Did that first shot of morphine when he was 15 put him on the addiction train? He said multiple times how he remembered that feeling and never found it again until he tried heroin. Is that when he no longer had a choice?

Early in David's addiction, I attended a Smithsonian talk on the brain and the role of dopamine. They showed slides of dopamine in healthy brains and in the brains of addicts. There was a distinct difference. The addict brain had much less dopamine. Is this what happened to Dave after so many years of using heroin?

There's a school of thought that believes addiction is a choice and a myth, and it disputes the notion that addiction is a disease. *The Oxford English Dictionary* defines disease as, "A disorder of structure or function in a human, animal, or plant, especially one that produces specific signs or symptoms or that affects a specific location and is not simply a direct result of physical injury."

In 2000, Jeffrey A. Schaler, PhD, wrote the book, *Addiction Is a Choice*, which focuses on whether addiction is a choice or a disease. Whether it be gaming, sex, smoking, eating, music, or using drugs such as heroin, Dr.

Schaler lumps addictions into one big pile, each representing a particular set of behaviors and values. He writes, "... I maintain that 'addiction' is a myth. I deny that there is any such thing as 'addiction,' in the sense of a deliberate and conscious course of action, which the person literally cannot stop doing. According to my view of the world, the heroin addict can stop injecting himself with heroin ..."

Dr. Schaler goes on to say addiction is not a disease because there must be "signs." He writes, "A simple test of a true physical disease is whether it can be shown to exist in a corpse. There are no bodily signs of addiction itself (as opposed to its effects) that can be identified in a dead body. Addiction is therefore not listed in standard pathology textbooks." However, he says, "It's quite irrelevant what the drug does after it's in the body. I certainly don't for a moment doubt that the taking of many drugs causes disease."

Dr. Schaler asserts that there are good and bad addictions. He calls approved addictions (music, books) "virtues" and disapproved addictions (drugs) "vices," and such choices reflect the person's values. He goes on to say that people choose their addiction, because he or she finds meaning in doing so, finds it enjoyable, or finds it helpful when they are sad and depressed.

Schaler supports the notions that maintaining recovery from heroin addiction does not require abstention and that drug treatment programs are generally misguided and ineffective. Because heroin users can and do go in and out of using heroin, Schaler theorizes that addiction is voluntary. In other words, heroin users have the ability to "moderate" their use if they choose to. He says further, "There simply is no empirical research corroborating the existence of 'loss of control' in alcoholics or any other addicts."

His reasoning follows that if addiction were to be designated as a disease, then addiction would give the alcoholic or drug addict—those with disapproved addictions—an excuse to keep doing what they want to do regardless of the harm they do to themselves and their loved ones.

In the February 2021 issue of *Northern Virginia* magazine, the article, "Addicted," by Dr. Ash B. Diwan, Piedmont Family Practice in Warrenton,

VA, writes, "Opioid addiction is physiological, the brain's outer core is decision making, morality, choices; the inner part, the limbic system, is survival, feeling good. When the dopamine rises 20 times, you feel good; it reinforces behaviors. Drugs bind to the same reward center and opioids increase dopamine by 1,000. The inner system supersedes the conscious human outer core. Rewired, the brain is hijacked, changing circuitry, nothing in the natural world can beat that, but now you need higher doses to feel normal. It takes years to go back to normal."

Dr. Diwan has 14 years of experience treating opioid addictions. He advocates for a multi-pronged approach for recovery from addiction, including awareness and screening, abolishing stigma, understanding treatment, and increasing access to care.

Sam Louie, a psychotherapist and addiction specialist wrote the article, "The Contradiction of Addiction: Is addiction a disease, a choice, or a form of powerlessness?"[31] In the article, Louie writes, "In the 1950s, the disease model of addiction sprouted and took root to help explain alcoholism as a medical condition of the brain as a means to destigmatize a person with addiction …. Since then, we have learned it's not about a person's inherent character or lack of integrity that leads to addiction, nor is it simply being born with a 'bad' brain. Instead, we have learned there is a complex array of biological, social, and psychological factors that can predispose someone to addictions (i.e. trauma, family history, neglect, etc.)."

"So," Louie asks, "do people with addiction have a choice or are they simply controlled by their drug of choice?" Louie concludes:

> The answer is both. It's nuanced in the sense that before a person becomes addicted they did have a choice and 'chose' to consume or engage in behavior they found pleasure and/or relief in. But the choice is stripped over time with continual usage. They become enslaved to their addiction to the point that their brains and bodies have become dependent on their drug of choice to make them feel better.
>
> In addiction recovery, it's important to let clients know they have

> control to break out of their addiction but to also validate how they have lost control through the years and their brains and bodies have been hijacked, hence the seeming paradox and contradiction of addiction that one is both powerless and has control over it.

What have I learned after losing my son to 15 years of heroin addiction? Addiction starts with a choice and may well cause disease and death. Addiction takes time and follows a predictive process. Addiction causes loss of control after continual usage. An addict will not stop using their drug of choice until the reward for not using becomes greater than the reward for using. The quicker addiction is recognized and addressed, the better the chance of preventing what Dave called "full on addiction."

If I could turn back time . . . I would immediately get better educated about opiates and opioids . . . I would learn to identify addict behaviors and how to best react to those behaviors . . . I would put into practice much sooner the steps to avoid enabling . . . I would put aside my shame and confront my son when he lied and manipulated me even if it meant revealing to the world that my son was a heroin addict . . . I would detach with love sooner . . . I would acknowledge sooner when my son was beyond achieving recovery . . . I would accept that living drug-free for my son was never going to be an option.

LOVING AN ADDICT

It wasn't until after David passed away that I found the Nar-Anon Family Groups Forum online,[32] a website forum for families and friends of people coping with addiction. The following post by the parent of an addict best describes the dilemma of loving an addict:

> No one else I know has an addicted child, so they draw upon all the wisdom they have acquired through a pamphlet or magazine

> article they read once. They do not understand the searing pain of watching their child turn into someone they barely recognize, nor do they understand that quite often my child will spend wonderful hours with me being the caring, funny, and sensitive person he used to be and then I fall in love with him all over again. This is the saddest and most torturous love relationship possible.

Accepting the reality of your child's addiction and loving them is tricky. Having an addicted child can be isolating for the parent. The shame and guilt is overwhelming. Yet, you love this person that you created and want more than anything to help him. Then the shame of feeling shame about the person you love, who has become an addict, becomes a double whammy betrayal, adding to further emotional turmoil. I, too, didn't know anyone else with an addicted child and was ignorant of the destructive behaviors that accompany addiction. I needed to get educated, quickly, but didn't have a clue where to start. The Internet had yet to become prevalent in our daily lives. Ideas, answers, and a community of resources and support are now a click away.

I encourage everyone to take advantage of online resources to help maneuver through the addiction battle. If I had found Nar-Anon online when my son's addiction first surfaced, maybe I could have stopped enabling sooner; it certainly would have helped me to not feel so alone, stupid, incompetent, and useless. It was the only place I could fully lay out my love for my addict son, express my grief, possibly help someone else, and build courage to tell his addiction story.

REALITY VS. FANTASY

The following was written by a mom and posted on the Nar-Anon Family Forum. When I first read it, I went back and read it many more times. She perfectly writes what I felt and thought during my own experience with my son's addiction.

> When I came to these rooms, I wanted to figure out what I could do to return my son to 'himself.' One of the things I struggled

with for quite a while was my own fantasy of 'himself' and the reality of it.

I recently read this from a long time heroin addict: 'Without these fellowships, I would take drugs. Because, even now, the condition persists. Drugs and alcohol are not my problem, reality is my problem, drugs and alcohol are my solution.'

I think this struck me hard because I could say the same thing. *Reality* was my problem, *fantasy* was my solution.

I didn't want to face that reality of what my son became. I loved him, but what was it that I loved? Innately, I loved him because he was my son. But take that away and what did I love?

The lying, the self-centered ego, the disrespect, the illegalities, the manipulation, the stealing, the disregard for consequences for himself and those who love him, the pain and heartache he caused his children, his family, abandonment of his children. Need I go on? Not much to like here. Not much to love.

Okay, I know this is a powerful illness and the choice to pick up [drugs] was his, the choice to become an addict was not.

But that isn't about him, it is about me and my feelings. It was hard to love him as he had evolved as an addict. Little by little he no longer even resembled the son I believed I knew.

So I had to ask myself over and over: What was it I loved? What was it I missed?

It was the fantasy of what I believed could be. It was a mixture of that little boy I so adored and what I thought he should have become. He was so bright, he should have gone to college. He has such a personality, he could have gone far in business. He was so tenacious, he could have succeeded at anything he put his mind to.

Could have. Should have. Would have. *Fantasies.* The *reality* was that this did not happen. He became an addict. He couldn't face the reality, and his solution was drugs, more and more drugs.

I couldn't face the reality so my solution was to fix, rescue and save; to force the fantasy to exist. I needed it to believe he would return as the 'himself' I created in my mind.

I loved and missed the fantasy. Not the addict. (Yes, I love my son—a different kind of love.)

I went through this same thing years ago with my first marriage. After four years and two children, my ex decided he couldn't face his reality. He chose to have multiple partners. I was devastated. Crushed. I was pregnant with son number two and he was cheating on me.

Once again, I believed I loved him and could fix this. Separated, I missed him so much. It broke my heart. But what did I miss? Not the liar, the cheat, the super self-centered ego, the betrayal, the emotional abuse, nope . . . I didn't miss that. I missed the *fantasy* of what I thought should have been the perfect marriage, the perfect family.

The *fantasy* of what *should be* is powerful. But it is not the *reality*. Facing the reality allowed me to begin to heal those character defects that kept me in denial and in fantasy.

Are you chasing the fantasy? Are you missing the fantasy? Are you in love with the fantasy? What is the reality?

If the problem is reality, is your solution fantasy and denial of what is?

My son did return from addiction, for today. He is clean. He is not the fantasy I thought he would be. The darkness of addiction has left an indelible imprint on his soul. He is different. That is OK. It is the reality. He went through hell to learn many lessons. Some very hard ones. I find many things in this reality to like, to love. I find many other things I stay out of. They are his to deal with. I don't pick them up.

In reality, I can find my peace and serenity. In fantasy I was always reaching for something just out of my grasp.

When I reached out to this mom for permission to include her post in this book, I sadly learned that her son passed away last year. Like Dave, he was older and used drugs for many years. Unlike Dave, he found recovery for 10+ years prior to his death, but his years of drug use still did their damage, causing the complications and disease that led to his demise.

ENABLING

An integral part of surviving addict madness is learning to recognize oneself or others as enablers. The theory is that the longer an addict is enabled to use (drugs and people), the longer the addict will use. Enabling is doing for the addict what he no longer does for himself because his priority has become getting and using his drug. An addict will not pay his rent. An enabler doesn't want the addict to sleep on the street, so begins paying the addict's rent. An addict will not buy food. An enabler doesn't want their loved one to starve, so buys the addict's food. An addict defaults on a car loan. An enabler wants the addict to have transportation, so loans a car. Thus, a vicious cycle is born. Addicts are experts at using lies and manipulations to establish enablers. When the enabler is established, addiction begins to control the addict and the enabler.

At some point in our loved ones' addiction, we are all enablers, especially in the early stages. It's a natural response to want to help our loved ones when they are sick or hurt or when they need assistance to get through a rough patch. It takes time to become an addict, and even when the signs of addiction cannot be ignored, enablers continue to make excuses for the addict, and to hide in denial. We don't want to know. We are afraid. If we know, we, as parents, have to fix it. And, chances are, we don't have the tools or a clue about where to begin.

In David's memoir I compare our two ski trips in the early stages of his addiction. I doubted that David and his girlfriend had the flu, but I didn't challenge them or do anything about it. I was afraid to. I simply hoped I was wrong. Rather than confronting them and risking having everyone angry and upset with me, I let them stay holed up in the cabin and told myself that there was the possibility they could have the flu. Looking back makes me sad to realize that David and Circe were probably using right under my nose in that sweet little cabin.

An enabler needs time to recognize the fine line between *helping* and *enabling*. Addicts are very clever at convincing their enablers that all the problems that inevitably come up are someone else's fault. There's always a good reason their money ran out, they wrecked the car again, or that sore on their neck just won't heal. Addicts are masters of the excuse and *I didn't mean to!* But we enablers, especially parents, are blinded by the need to help and to fix the addict.

The dilemma: When enablers finally recognize how they are being manipulated by the addict and stop the money, stop loaning or buying cars, or throw the addict out of the house, a major dilemma arises for both the addict and the enabler. When the addict has "real" needs and may genuinely be receptive to family support for recovery, the enablers have become exhausted and frustrated by all the addict's lies and broken promises. The enabler may not be there for the addict anymore, leaving the addict alone when he needs them most. The addict becomes isolated and, yes, you guessed it, returns to using their drug. It's all part of the complex and brutal addiction cycle.

As mothers, it's intuitive for us to want to care for and protect our children. It doesn't matter if they are all grown up. It's beyond comprehension that this little person we've given life to, loved, and cared for would lie and manipulate us. Then the lies, manipulations, thefts, arrests, incarcerations, overdosing, rehab, recovery, and relapsing all piles up. We get caught in the web of our child's vicious cycle of addiction. Addict chaos overcomes us. We feel like failures because loving and caring has turned into enabling a lethal lifestyle. The only way to stop it is counter-intuitive and emotionally challenging, and it has to be learned.

Addicts are intuitive, too. They know the right thing to say and how to say it to get their way. The disease of addiction must come with an unwritten manual—for what to say and how to manipulate, deceive, and spew empty promises—because addict behavior seems to follow a similar course. In the early years of David's addiction, time and time again I would fall right back into his addiction trap and then beat myself up when I realized he had once again used me. I know how Charlie Brown feels when time and time again he thinks he can trust Lucy, yet she pulls that football away as he swings his foot to kick it. She takes it to the very edge every time. That's what addicts do. They push loved ones to the edge with guilt and empty promises, while we are grasping for anything that will spark recovery and bring our child back. Learning to recognize *addict speak, addict manipulation,* and *addict denial,* and to *detach with love* early in our loved one's addiction, is the first line of defense.

Whenever David came out of jail or treatment or when he managed through dope sickness to be clean of drugs, I would have high hopes and believe his promises of never using again. I wanted to believe every word. I would do whatever I could to help him stay on the road to recovery. I wanted "normal" David back and talking to me, but every time he would disappear again, just when I thought *we* had a great plan for curing his addiction. Inevitably, once David had the resources, he would relapse right back into using heroin.

At the time osteomyelitis was diagnosed, David had violated his parole, had multiple court cases pending, and was possibly facing another lengthy jail term. He didn't have a dime to his name, he was in excruciating pain, and he couldn't work or physically take care of himself. I was back in court with him, writing letters to the judge, driving him to treatment and doctors' appointments and shopping with him for food. I began to pay his rent and other expenses—two major operations on his spine and large doses of opioids for pain—I relapsed into enabling.

I could see that my son was physically destroying himself. He was a shadow of the man he'd been 15 years earlier. After the operations, David's back looked like someone had beaten him with a whip. His neck was full of nicks and scars, his veins were collapsed, and his swollen and red hands would never recover. He had Hepatitis C. David was telling the truth when he said he couldn't take it anymore. It took me much too long to understand that his saying that he couldn't take it anymore in no way meant he could or would stop using heroin.

On that day in January 2014, when I told David it was time for him to go home, I was determined not to enable him to lay in bed all day sucking down opioids, which I believed would ultimately lead back to daily trips to D.C. for heroin. I wanted to believe that developing vertebral osteomyelitis was David's "bottom" and his turning point to full recovery from addiction. I now feel sure that, for David, there would be no bottom. Ever. Based on his own theory, David's reward for using heroin was never outweighed by a reward for not using heroin. I had to return the responsibility for his addiction to him. Chasing his high and landing on the puffy cloud was David's curse for life. Does knowing this bring solace? No.

GRIEVING

"DEATH DOES NOT TAKE THE DEAD AWAY; IT ONLY MAKES THEM GROW MORE DEEPLY INTO YOU."*

The crazy drug train speeds down the track, swerves, rattles, goes off the track, and sometimes slows down just long enough for a brief reprieve. However, the ride may be far from over, and there may be many stops before the last stop.

Grieving a death is a process and different for everyone. Pushing the feelings of sadness, hurt, and guilt away doesn't work. Those feelings come right back from where they were left hiding, waiting to emerge, and they are no less

---

* I cannot remember where I read this quote that touched me deeply and exemplifies my grief.

painful. Grieving an addict's death is two-fold because you've already lost your loved one to addiction. I found that I couldn't grieve David's death until I grieved his addiction.

All deaths have their own tragedy, but addiction greatly complicates death for those left behind. David's physical death from addiction was a second death. I *lost* David several times as he cycled through active addiction and recovery. There would be those few times when I felt like I got my "real" son back. With physical death, there's no getting back, even for a second. Then, there are the resulting effects of addiction that don't go to the grave and have to be dealt with. Some families are wiped out financially from either being stolen from, paying for endless treatments and medical expenses, or the addict's piled up debt that collectors continue to call about. There may be irreparable family and personal relationship damage, not to mention the mental anguish that comes by realizing our failure to protect and save our child.

So many things, mostly little things, remind me of David. During those first few months following his death when the valleys of grief closed in on me, all I wanted to do was go and find him. When he was on a drug binge and would disappear for days, I worried about getting the call that he had overdosed, fatally crashed his car, or gotten shot on the streets of Southeast D.C., but I never let myself admit the reality that I might not see him alive again. His death brought home that harsh reality. Never would I see Dave again. I couldn't just drive over to his shop and watch him work through the window. He was gone.

About a month after David's burial, I went to a face-to-face grieving group, but it didn't work for me. Most of the people there had lost an elderly parent or spouse after many years of marriage. No one had lost a child, let alone an addicted son or daughter. I still felt shame and guilt over his addiction, which prevented me from opening up and sharing my grief. I needed a two-stage grieving process for people who had lost a child to addiction.

I periodically attended face-to-face Nar-Anon support groups during David's addiction, so I gave that a try. The people in the group were mostly parents like me; a few were spouses and siblings of addicts. I was the only one attending who was grieving a son's death from addiction. The leader and the group were welcoming, kind, and sympathetic. They gave me much needed support without judgment or blame, which was a huge relief and gave me an opening to express my grief. I continued going weekly for a couple months, but the group's focus, as it should be, was on recovery from addiction. I began to feel like I represented the dreaded destiny of what they were there to avoid, so I stopped going.

Then I met one-on-one with a grief counselor for a couple of months, and he gave me a helpful list of what to expect during the grieving process. There were several surprises on the list that I hadn't thought about. One big item hit me hard and stuck with me. I had to deal with the pain of losing David's future. I had to accept that David would never achieve his dreams of writing a book, publishing a magazine, or opening his one-chair barber shop. We would never again talk through a thunderstorm or sing happy birthday or play tennis. We would never make new memories. I needed to make peace with myself that his death shattered his future and my hopes for him.

Then I found the Nar-Anon Family Forum online. I spent hours each day reading and contributing to the posts. Sharing my experiences and heartache with other parents struggling with their loved one's addiction was invaluable. Posting my experiences on the recovery forum and the grieving form to support others trying to get through a tough day was how I got through my own tough days. Posts would often end with "just for today." I sometimes still have to tell myself "just for today" when grief overcomes me.

Nar-Anon's little blue book addresses regrets for the past and fears for the future:

> Exhaustion is the result when we use energy in mulling over the past with regret, or in trying to figure ways to escape a future that hasn't even come yet. Likewise, setting up an image of the future and anxiously hovering over it for fear that it will or won't come true, uses all of our energy and leaves us unable to live today. Yet living this day is the only way to have a life.

I had to learn to detach with love during David's addiction. I had to do the same with his death. There wasn't a damn thing I could do about his death but I could still love him and keep his memory alive. I just had to figure out how to do that.

We memorialized the one-year anniversary of David's death with a bronze plaque for his gravesite. Designing the plaque was emotionally difficult, but it gave us the opportunity to begin preserving our memories and love for David. Anyone passing by his resting place and seeing the plaque will get an idea of who Dave was and know that he was loved.

"If we free our minds, we can free ourselves," was the premise for David's unfinished book, *Constructs of a Feeble Human Intellect.*[*] David was an avid reader, consumed with finding *truth* and freeing his mind. Those words inscribed in bronze will not only honor David's love of philosophy but also memorialize his need to let go of the noise and confusion and *Just Be.*

David loved his work as a barber. He spoke often of wanting to open his own shop and wrote about starting a men's quarterly magazine, *The Barber Shop.* The barber pole on the plaque not only symbolizes his professional work, but also the importance of his personal connections with his fellow barbers and clients. I didn't know until after his death the depth of connection and the many allowances made for him to continue working throughout his addiction. I was deeply moved and appreciative of those kindnesses, as well as personal and professional sacrifices, which enabled David to continue doing what he loved.

David excelled at sports and loved playing football and baseball throughout his childhood and high school years. Wearing shades and a tough guy stance in his football uniform was so David as he impatiently waited to grow up. In his letter jacket, I found two old beat-up baseballs. He wrote about his batting ritual and how he was able to slow down the ball. Those memories are now and forever represented on the plaque.

---

[*] Excerpts from David's unfinished collection of writings are added, following the Epilogue.

Looking back on the pictures taken the day we laid David to rest, my heart aches not only for David but also for his brother, Bill. He bravely endured pain and sorrow as he gave the eulogy and lifted David's coffin for the final ride. Once again, after many years of depending on him, he selflessly carried the weight of his family and performed the difficult task of saying good-bye to his brother. *"Brothers Forever"* on the plaque symbolizes their love for each other and the enduring deep bond that lives on.

I would be lost if I didn't have Bill to talk to about David. The good and the bad memories. The mistakes and the guilt. The *if onlys*. We were fortunate that, when David passed, our family and many of our friends were there to help and to give us loving support. Bill gets a lot of support from his friends when he posts on Facebook about his memories and thoughts about his brother. On the sixth anniversary of David's death—the first anniversary that landed on a Friday, the day of the week we found David—Bill expressed his thoughts on Facebook and wrote:

> After every day there is another day but not every day is the same as other days . . . every day we think of you and every day we miss you, but today is THE day our hearts feel the heaviest . . . today is the day I received the call and dropped everything and rushed to your house. Today is the day I saw our mom sitting on your front lawn. Her face showed a pain and loss that no parent should ever experience. Today is the day I realized the call I received was true. Today is the day, David, we lost you. So, today is the day every year my heart and our hearts are the heaviest. Today is just one day, but this is the day that changed all of my days for the rest of my days. Miss you, Buddy.

A friend of mine, who had lost her husband a few years before, wrote to me: "Grief goes in waves, and just when you think perhaps the worst is behind you, a thought, a word, a phrase, a forgotten memory surfaces and you are back under water. Give it time. That is the only thing that will ease your sorrow and your pain. Not eliminate it, but ease it."

I soon learned just what she meant. While David was recovering from the staph infection, he began preparing more of his meals, and we often went to the grocery store together. One day not long after David died, I was grocery shopping. I reached the cheese section in search of a bag of shredded cheddar cheese. Hanging on the rack in front of me were bags of string cheese. I stood in a trance looking at those bags of string cheese and broke down with uncontrollable sobbing. I stood in the grocery store aisle for several minutes and bawled like a baby until I could contain myself and finish shopping. String cheese was always on David's grocery list. He loved it.

Not long after David died, I was walking in town. I spotted a guy a couple of blocks away and was absolutely sure that that guy was David reincarnated, but he disappeared in a blink. I know it's crazy . . . I immediately ran to the spot where I saw him and searched several streets where I thought he might have gone but no luck. In my mind, I knew it wasn't David, just a guy with a similar build, but in my heart that glimmer of hope had to be followed.

A friend of David's says that he "nudges" her. Bill says that David often turns on the laundry room light for him. Occasionally the light on my desk will be on when I'm sure I turned it off. The most eerie "sighting" was just a couple of years ago when a small shadowy cartoon-like figure wearing a square hat appeared next to my bed during the night. My husband and I were camping in our RV on a dark and spooky inlet in Nova Scotia. The wind was howling, and the sound of the fog horn at the nearby lighthouse periodically pierced the quiet. The shadowy little figure was gone in a split second . . . he seemed so very real.

Two-and-a-half years after David's death, I happened to look out the window to see a young man walking by. He reminded me so much of David by the way he walked and held his head that the words for the following poem poured out of me.

DREAMIN'

He strode by with that lanky
Confident swagger,
Head and chin tilted high
Half a smile, almost a smirk,
Ego springing from him
Like the puff of dirt
That follows Pig Pen.

What caught my eye?
The A-shirt,
Only his was black
Not a white one, like
He once wore.

Tears formed quickly
As I hurried to the window,
Just to watch him
And to dream.

To allow a fantasy . . .
It would be so grand, if
He found his way back,
And the nightmare
Turned to a dream come true.

And then reality . . .
What would I do, if
The old nightmare
Returned with him?
The one that didn't end
With a dream come true.

A-shirts, 7-11s
String cheese and a prickly beard,
Some of the things
That bring him back to me,
Along with sad reminders
That sometimes nightmares come true,
And dreams are only for dreamers.

I had to say good-bye to my beautiful son at the last stop of that rickety old drug train, but David lives on in our hearts and memories, and now, through his stories, poetry, and essays.

LAST WORDS: When I was reviewing the last edits for this memoir, I needed to confirm an edit, which meant digging back into the large expanding file where I kept some of David's hand written documents. As I sorted through the papers, I found in the bottom of the file a loose crinkled up piece of torn notebook paper that I had somehow missed throughout the process of preparing this memoir. There was no date on the paper. Chills ran through me as I read his words. I leave you with David's closing thoughts.

"YOU SAY THE WORDS YOU WROTE ARE BEAUTIFUL,

BUT BEAUTY MUST MEAN NOTHING,

BECAUSE THE WORDS COME FROM
THE DESPAIR INSIDE ME,

AND WHAT YOU WRITE HAS NOTHING TO DO WITH
THE DESPAIR FINALLY,

BECAUSE DESPAIR ISN'T BEAUTIFUL,

SO BEAUTY THEN IS A HORRID IRONY."

~ DAVID MATTHEW TREFRY

ACKNOWLEDGMENTS

Without knowing it, I started writing this memoir seven years ago. I didn't know how to recover from the nightmare of addiction that led my son to his death. So, I dug into his laptop, iPad, phone, and notebooks with no idea of what I would find. A couple of years passed, and I had produced a timeline of events from all of our journals, calendars, letters, messages, and crinkled up scraps of paper . . . You probably noticed in the memoir that ellipses are used quite a lot. David loved his ellipses.

My handy computer file tells me the first draft of this memoir was completed late in 2019. After two more years of drafts, here I am, finalizing the "master" that will morph into a real book. The few people I've told about the book inevitably respond that I must be so excited, but I'm not. I'm still hesitant about telling our story. This is a sad story. Who wants to read a sad story of despair and loss? Then I remind myself: David's words and thoughts will be published as he wanted, and maybe—hopefully—another mom like me will be helped through the terrible nightmare of drug addiction.

My thanks begin with my former colleagues and good friends Pat and Sheri, the best nonjudgmental listeners in the world; Randy and Kristie at The Barber Shop for never giving up on Dave; all the people who work day and night to help detoxify and provide treatment and hope for our addicts; Scott, Mike, Jason, Brice, and David for carrying their old friend on that brutally cold winter's day; my nieces, Dawn and Lori, and other family members who helped get me through those terrible first days; my forever friends Helen and Ken for shielding me against the cold wind and managing the sad task of clearing out Dave's stuff; Mark and the Nar-Anon Family Support group for taking me in and helping pave the way to begin grieving; members of the Nar-Anon Family Group Online Forum who share their daily struggles and hope with an open heart; DianeB at the Forum for her insight and wisdom; Deri for sharing her grief and childhood memories; Nita for compassion, inspiration, clarification, and for sharing her "nudges"; Chris and aspiring writers at The Writer's Center; Bobby for sharing his personal struggle and expertise on coping with addiction; DianeM for excellent editing and moral support; Donna, Patty, and Liz for reading, encouraging, and giving valuable suggestions; Sherrill for guidance navigating the publishing world and introducing Acorn; Acorn Publishing for helping me tell David's story; Liz for giving us new life to enrich the future; my husband for having to endure far too many of my solitary and distracted days; my son, Bill, my rock; and David, for guiding my hand to ease the despair and restore the beauty.

PART TWO

CONSTRUCTS OF A FEEBLE HUMAN INTELLECT

AS TOLD THROUGH A COLLECTION OF SHORT STORIES, ESSAYS, AND POETRY TO REVEAL THE THOUGHTS AND IDEAS OF SOCRATES H. DILLINGER

Published Posthumously

I WILL WRITE A WHOLE BOOK ABOUT THIS IDEA:

LOOKING AT HUMANITY FROM A DIFFERENT PERSPECTIVE.
THINK OF HUMANITY IN TERMS OF ONE HUMAN LIFE.
WE HAVE BEEN JUVENILES BURNING CARBON.
BUT NOW IT HAS BEGUN—THE AGE OF INFORMATION.
WE NOW ARE GOING TO BECOME OUR POTENTIAL.

ENLIGHTENED BEINGS.

~ SOCRATES H. DILLINGER

INTRODUCTION

On January 17, 2014, Socrates H. Dillinger, 39, was found dead on his bathroom floor, his head on his arm in a pool of vomit. He lived a short life beginning sometime in 2011. He only appeared periodically. The rest of the time he was a son, brother, grandson, barber, husband, friend, lover, and heroin addict. His real name was David, most often called Dave. He was also a writer who wanted to be a serious author and publish a book.

I discovered David's draft book, *Constructs of a Feeble Human Intellect*, on his laptop after he passed away. Freddy, the protagonist in most of David's fictional stories, is his alias. He chose the pseudonym, Socrates H. Dillinger, for his book and his blog. I can only suppose he chose this pseudonym as a way to incorporate his interest in philosophy and what he liked to think of as his "gangsta" ways. David was a big fan of gangster movies. I'm not sure what the "H" stands for, but I can guess.

Included here is Dave's writing ideas list, five fictional short stories, poetry, and essays. His writings reflect events and stages of his life, dreams, nightmares, philosophies, and using heroin.

His earliest story, "A Brief Moment of Clarity," was written during his 2005 fall semester at Northern Virginia Community College (NOVA) and was submitted to NOVA's Calliope Literary Journal. It's a fictional story written in the first person about a college student who comes upon people lying all over the ground and in the street, but no one seems to know why. Is it a cult? Are they drugged? Are they being hypnotized?

Dave's story, "Through the Void Travels a Momentary Exchange of Perspective: Freddy All Star Story," written in 2011, contrasts the sparkling days of spring with the darkness of heroin addiction. Dave started playing T-ball when he was four and played every season after through high school. The story centers on young Friedrich Huxley, aka Freddy, playing baseball and dreaming about an electronic drug machine. Ike, the other main character in the story, dreams of once again finding youth and confidence but is stifled by the ugly reality of his heroin addiction. Ike describes in detail the process for using heroin. Freddy's batting "ritual" in the story describes Dave's real life batting ritual. Author Beverly Conyers wrote the following about the psychological basis of addiction, obsessive-compulsive disorders, and rituals:

> To begin understanding the psychological basis of addiction, we must first recognize that addiction is fundamentally obsessive-compulsive in nature. Obsessive-compulsive disorder in the general population is a mental condition that causes persistent unwelcome thoughts and images accompanied by the irresistible urge to perform repetitive actions or rituals. It is an anxiety disorder thought to originate in unresolved internal conflict. In addicts, powerful obsessive-compulsive urges center on obtaining, preparing, and using alcohol or other drugs. Like others afflicted with this condition, addicts are unable to control their thoughts, and they feel compelled to use again and again, despite severe consequences that often result from their actions. (*Addict in the Family*)

David's longest story, "The Certain Eventuality: A Memory of a Time Yet to Come," is a coming-of-age story about a fight and reflects the real life 1991 incident described in the memoir when David was a senior in high school. In the story, Freddy instigates a fight to satisfy his need to feel "real," experiences young love and sex, struggles with the legal system, and brings out his "now" and "time" theories. Mr. Coleman, Freddy's English teacher in the story, is based on David's favorite high school English teacher. Though David was a gifted student who liked to read, and English was his favorite class, he avoided and fought his academic potential.

In his mid-20s, David was trained and became a licensed barber, which was his profession for the rest of his life and inspired his story, "The Man Who Played by the Rules." Written under his pseudonym in 2011, this story is about working at the barber shop, an overbearing wife, and sexual fantasies.

The story "When a Man Must Face the World Alone" was written in 2012 after David was released from a difficult nine-month jail term. In the story, Freddy has problems with a wife who is exhausted by his drug use and his womanizing. The story also addresses difficulties returning to society and staying sober after being in jail and losing everything because of addiction to heroin.

Reflected in his stories and poetry, David often questioned who he was. Was he two people in one body? Did he have a split personality from the beginning, or did his drug use and heroin addiction split him in half? Was he a madman? Why was he obsessed with truth, illusions, and delusions when he told so many lies, numbed himself from reality with heroin, and tried to live a double life? Why would David allow drugs to fog his brain if he were truly searching for clarity? Would he ever be able to practice what he preached and free his mind?

CREATIVE WRITING CAREER IDEAS

David was born on the 27th of May. He often used the number 27
for other things, like his football jersey and passwords.
I was deep into writing this memoir when I realized that
Dave's "path" for writing consisted of 27 ideas.

THE PATH

1. I need to find out how to start a magazine; Google it. Also think of several magazine titles, find out who started them and their story on the Internet. If I can figure out how other people started a magazine, then maybe I can figure it out for myself. Title: *The Barber Shop*. It will be a quarterly (to start) men's magazine. It will be funny but not as raunchy as *Maxim*. Plus, no half naked girls on the cover. Although that does attract men, you can't really go around in the real world carrying that. People will think you have a porno magazine. (Note that time I was on the plane with *Maxim*. Lots of dirty looks and even an inquiry by the plane steward. He tried to tell me I couldn't read porno on the plane.) Readers of *The Barber Shop* won't have to worry about that. I also noticed on my recent flight that there are no good men's magazines anymore. My magazine will talk about sports, movies, music, cars, and any other men's topics. Every issue, I will write an interesting and attention-grabbing editorial.

2. Stop using heroin completely and forever! If I can do that, I can do anything.

3. Start writing my book!!!!!! Go ahead and start to tell my story. Not as a biography though. Just begin to do it and as I know, my writing will begin to take on a life of its own. This is how I am lucky. It is my skill; it can be difficult for me to access the ultra-creative part of my mind on my own, but the beauty of my skill is that all I have to do is start writing. It's amazing how

it works. All I have to do is start!! I could be done in a month or two. This could be the most important thing I have ever done. Once I get this legal stuff taken care of, I will begin! If I go to jail, then I will write it there.

4. Begin to write the short story entitled 2 Dreams <Details> <Young baseball player / stealin' bases / dream of electronic drug machine> <older dope fiend dreams of youth, skill, power, strength, and freedom>.

5. You'll only find me in my ragged company. Send me dead flowers—stones—this will inspire a creative mindset.

6. An explanation of why my perspective is so unique. Many people are naturally introspective. Everyone has these different perspectives.

7. Overwhelmed, I chose to run.

8. No one plans to take the path that takes you lower.

9. Start work on the book, which will be an objective explanation of what it is like to be a heroin addict.

10. As confusion once again overwhelms the light, I must step away in hope that I may find passage.

11. So seldom my thoughts ring true.

12. I know for a fact that I cannot trust my thoughts.

13. I do not believe in good or evil, just confusion and enlightenment.

14. I sit here alone on this couch that is my bed, trying to decipher these thoughts in my head.

15. No sad piano violin combo plays when I am down. No camera is following me to document my life.

16. Two philosophers lie on their deathbeds in a hospital room. Both chose different paths. Compare their conclusions.

17. Confusion: It's like I make it through the labyrinth only to find a more confusing dangerous labyrinth at the end.

18. Story of a wimpy guy with an overbearing wife and kids: Goes to the barbershop. Doesn't drink (not allowed). Bad kids. They take all his money. His dreams and wishes.

19. A line for a wimpy guy: "Everyone around me is crazy. I fear I may be the craziest of them all."

20. I will put together a book of basic thoughts and ideas. Some short stories, poetry, etc. Self-publish it and hope the world will want more.

21. When you become so profoundly aware of the illusion that grips your life and the life of everyone you know, what do you do then?

22. Beware the Righteous—write a series of short stories depicting supposedly "righteous" people for their true ruthless selves. Show at the end of each one how they sleep well every night because they ignore what they are really doing.

23. How can I trust my own thoughts if I am so affected by morning/night spinning or the earth day/night cycle sleep process? Concept: Punk rock in the morning, Bob Dylan at night.

24. Try to articulate the K experience, the clouded vision, inability to hold onto a thought, the waking dream-like state—Ketamine.[33]

25. Write a book about a character who is a great man, or a man of great potential, but has more than great potential. He displays his attributes throughout his life, but circumstances are always such that he never actually becomes the great man he could have become under the right circumstances. Think Churchill, Roosevelt, and other people who are great men but maybe wouldn't have achieved so much if it had not been for World War II. A great thinker who just never really gets recognized. A man of courage, wisdom, and perseverance. Go deep into developing the characters and then their surroundings. "A great man surrounded by nothingness and in a time of very little occurrence." Working title: *The Man of Consequence*.

26. If I can ever finish this book, I look forward to trying to sell it. This could be a "DREAMS COME TRUE" kind of thing so I should be working on it constantly. It is very difficult though. Writing a book is HARD, VERY HARD. I HAVE TO GO OVER IT AND OVER IT TO GET ALL OF THE WORDS RIGHT. THEN KEEP WRITING. IT COULD TAKE A YEAR IF I'M NOT DILIGENT!

27. Write a series of books called, *A Glimpse Beyond This Illusion*. Each volume will represent the identification of and solution to a different, commonly accepted illusion.

THROUGH THE VOID TRAVELS A MOMENTARY EXCHANGE OF PERSPECTIVE

FREDDY ALL STAR STORY

"ALL THAT WE SEE OR SEEM IS
BUT A DREAM WITHIN A DREAM"

~ EDGAR ALLAN POE

SPARKLING DIAMOND DAYS

It is the finals for the All Star little league baseball tournament and young Friedrich Huxley is at the plate for the Cubs; bottom of the ninth and the score is 2-1. Freddy's team is losing and there is a man on first base.

The pitcher, who Freddy got two base hits and a walk against earlier, has been relieved. The new pitcher is someone Freddy has never faced but has heard of because he has the fastest fast ball in the county. Freddy feels no nerves as he walks to the plate. He loves pitchers who throw fast. As his batting ritual dictates, Freddy swings the bat twice while walking to the plate. In the batter's box, he completes his ritual of movements and kicks the dirt backwards with each cleat. Two more swings, then he points the bat toward the fence. Just as the pitcher starts his windup, Freddy looks away twice. Freddy doesn't know why he goes through this same batting ritual each and every time at bat; it's automatic.

On the first look back he sees his mother's long blonde hair. On the second look back he sees her smile and her elbow held high. She always gives him the elbow up sign, which is part of his silent ritual because the first time she did it, he hit a home run. Freddy also realizes that if he has his elbow up, he will get more power on the ball.

Looking back during the windup started at batting practice when Freddy realized how well he could see the ball. No matter how fast the ball comes at him, he has the ability to slow it down and plan his swing. Looking back also is Freddy's added challenge to push himself to be better than the guy who had just connected with the ball. Other guys may hit home runs and win games, but do they look away from the pitcher twice when the windup starts?

The first pitch comes in fast and low. Freddy follows it with his eyes and leans in to give his swing all his power, but he lets the ball spin by.

The ump calls, "Ball One!"

Freddy thinks to himself that the Bears' coach hasn't done his homework or he would have put in a pitcher with a nice curveball or slider. Instead, he put in a guy who throws heat, and that is Freddy's bread and butter on the ballfield. The second windup begins and Freddy looks away twice. The pitch is perfect. Freddy swings level and hard, hitting a line drive straight over second base. Freddy takes off for first base, watching the center fielder as he scoops up the ball. The runner who had been on first is now approaching third base as the third base coach signals him to go home. The center fielder's throw is short, cut off by the pitcher, preventing Freddy from getting a double. The runner slides into home and ties the game. The Cubs' fans are on their feet, waving and cheering. Freddy is hyped and his confidence soars.

The next batter on the plate is Mickey Thibidoe. Mickey is the Cubs' pitcher and the worst batter on the team. There are two outs. Freddy gives his coach a look of reassurance across the field as his coach signals the steal sign, although any Cubs fan already knows there will be no question whether Freddy will steal. Freddy takes a huge lead off of first as the pitcher looks over, mean and wide-eyed. The pitcher makes his move to put Freddy out at first, but Freddy starts running to second. The throw is high and by the time the first baseman jumps to catch the ball, Freddy is safely on second base.

The pitcher goes into his windup for the first pitch to Mickey. Freddy takes off as another fast and low ball speeds toward the catcher's glove. Mickey swings hard but misses the pitch. The catcher jumps up and throws the ball to the third baseman. The throw is perfect as Freddy dives for the outside of the bag.

"Safe!" calls the ump.

Freddy stands up and brushes dirt from his uniform as the crowd roars. While staring at Freddy, the pitcher sets up for his next pitch. Freddy takes his lead and looks directly into the pitcher's eyes. The pitcher throws to third but Freddy makes it back in time. Another wind up and another low fastball flies past Mickey and through the legs of the catcher. Freddy jumps immediately and breaks for home. The pitcher stumbles and also runs for home plate. The catcher retrieves the ball and throws it chest-high to the pitcher just as Freddy slides head-first toward the outside of the plate. The pitcher makes the catch but swings his arm down too late to make the tag.

"Safe!" yells the ump.

The crowd thunders with applause, whistles, and screams of wahoos as Freddy's team rushes the field to claim their victory. They pick Freddy up to once again celebrate young Freddy's success stealing bases. Freddy's mother runs to him and gives him a hug, and tells him that she loves him. In that moment, Freddy knows he is a winner, smart, powerful and confident, and that the world is his to do whatever he wants.

After the dust clears and the Cubs finish celebrating winning the All Star tournament, Freddy and his mother walk off the field and head to their '84 Toyota Camry. Freddy's coach runs up to the car. "Good job, son, you played great! Now, can I talk to your mom for a minute?"

Freddy, still high on his cloud nine win, says, "Sure, Coach Don."

They walk into the darkness and Freddy's coach says to his Mother, "Ms. Huxley . . . "

"Please, call me Samantha."

"Samantha, I want to tell you how proud we all are of Freddy. That boy is a great ball player."

Freddy's mother replies, "Thank You."

"Listen though, I have never met a young person who is so bold and fearless, which is great on the baseball field, but sometimes I worry about him because he could hurt himself if there isn't someone there to guide him. I know you are a good mom. I just wish his father was around to guide him. I want you to know, Samantha, I can be there for the boy if you need me."

"Wow, that is quite an offer, Don." Freddy's Mom replies. "Sure, I would like that."

"OK, good. You guys have a good night now."

ON THE OTHER SIDE OF TOWN

Ike Jackson lies on his couch in the basement, watching *Leave It to Beaver* on TV Land. His wife and kids live upstairs. He can hear them talking loudly even though the door to the basement stays closed to keep Ike out of his family's world and to keep them out of his. Ike tightly grips his 40 oz. Malt Liquor and takes a chug. He knows that the beer won't kill his pain, but he hopes he can get drunk enough to forget about it. Sweat drips from his brow as he tries to pay attention to his TV show.

Finally, Ike hears footsteps and the front door closes as he runs to the small basement window. He can just see the feet of his family walking to the Dodge minivan that Ike never gets to drive. As soon as the engine starts, Ike heads for the stairs. He grabs a Heineken from the refrigerator and pries it open with his lighter. He makes his way to his wife's bedroom. He searches every drawer but comes up empty. Then he goes into the closet, turns on the light and stops. He closes his eyes as a drop of sweat drips down his cheek. He says out loud to himself, "Where the fuck is she hiding the cash now?"

Ike digs into the back of the closet and sees the large North Face coat his wife wears during the winter. A feeling of relief rushes through his body as he slides his hand into the inside pocket and pulls out two twenty dollar bills. He pushes the coat back where it was, checks to make sure everything is as he found it and turns off the light. Elated, Ike stumbles down the stairs and out the front door, running to the path that will lead him to the liquor store while thinking to himself, "Man I hope he's there." He slows to a walk but can't contain himself and begins to run again.

Ike emerges from the path and can see the liquor store with several people standing in front. Even though the sun is setting, there's just enough light to see their silhouettes. He recognizes his buddies but searches for one specific person. He gets close enough to see, and there he is! Smiley is there and that can only mean one thing. Ike feels the same rush as finding those two twenty dollar bills and heads toward Smiley with a look of assurance. Smiley spots Ike and returns the look with a telltale smile. Ike's heart is pounding with excitement, and suddenly feels a cramp in his anus.

"Oh, shit!"

Ike knows well the pain of an impending attack of diarrhea causing him to scowl when he needed to be cool. He slows his walk and clenches his ass until the cramp subsides. Staying cool, he saunters over to Smiley and calmly says, "Can I get five for forty?"

"Come on man, you know I want $45 for five," Smiley tells Ike.

"I know, man, but that's all I got, and I really need five."

"Of course you do, but I'm telling you that I need $45. I've got some good shit. It's on fire and worth every penny."

Ike loses his cool and starts to beg, "Let me get five bags this time, man, and I will owe you $5. You know I'm good for it!"

Smiley grins, enjoying the power he has over Ike. "OK, man." The exchange is made. Ike turns and walks back toward the path. Once Smiley is out of sight, Ike breaks into a run home.

As Ike approaches the end of the path and the clearing where he can see his house, he slows to a jog hoping to see his wife and kids aren't back. The van isn't there, although his nosy neighbor is taking out his trash. Ike jogs fast trying to look cool, just a guy out taking a run. He cruises by saying "Hi" to his neighbor but never breaks stride. There is no way that Ike is going to stop and chat.

Through the front door, Ike runs down the basement stairs. Another cramp comes on. Ike squeezes his ass and runs to the bathroom, drops his pants, and diarrhea shoots out of him as he holds onto the sink. As soon as it is over, Ike cleans himself and hurries out of the bathroom to the unfinished part of the basement.

Ike closes the door and turns on the light. Reaching behind the work bench, he pulls out an old coffee can. He opens it up and pulls out a large folded up rag. Ike unrolls the rag to reveal his tool kit, which contains several needles of different sizes and colors, and empty Ziploc baggies with various colors and designs on them. He takes a second to stare at the blue baggies, remembering their quality. He hopes that what he just bought will be just as good.

Ike grabs his cooker, which is the bottom of a soda can cut off with the sharp edges bent over, and pulls off the tar-stained cotton ball. He reaches into his pocket for his pack of Newport 100s and takes out a cigarette. With his teeth, Ike pulls a piece of cotton from the filter and places it on the cooker. Then he reaches into the small watch pocket of his jeans and pulls out the five bags that are tied up with a black rubber band. He empties two bags of tan powder onto the cooker and considers his selection of needles. He chooses the medium gauge needle so he can inject into his jugular vein. Next, he sucks some water from a glass into the syringe and sprays it onto the powder. Then he pulls out his lighter, lights the flame, and holds it under the cooker to heat up the powder and water. The powder melts into the water and creates a dark colored liquid. Ike's heart sinks. He can see that the quality is indeed very good, and it wouldn't be long.

Completely lost in the moment of completing his favorite task, Ike grabs another bag and empties a quarter of it on the liquid and heats it again. Finally drawing the liquid up into his syringe, Ike is careful to get the air bubble out without losing a single drop of the precious liquid. Savoring the moment to come, Ike slowly and carefully puts the top on the syringe and places everything back in the coffee can.

In the bathroom mirror, Ike studies his neck as he put his finger on a small purple dot where he had success before. He feels for his pulse with his fingertips. His heart sinks once again as he finds it and puts the needle straight into the same spot on his neck, pushing it in all the way. Then he pulls the plunger back and dark red blood shoots onto the brown liquid. Once again his heart sinks; he knows he has tapped the best vein in his body for a perfect injection, the jugular vein. Slowly, he pushes the plunger down and watches the dark liquid disappear. He pulls the syringe out, grabs a piece of toilet paper to cover the wound and sits on the toilet. Relief washes over him.

BACK ON FREDDY'S SIDE OF TOWN

The night after the game, Freddy dreams that he is a grown-up with a grown-up mind, but his body hasn't aged. Walking through a post-apocalyptic setting, he sees his friends, who stand in a shanty town looking at a makeshift shack with a line of people waiting at the door. The people waiting in line are missing body parts—arms or legs—while other people just have chunks of their abdomen missing, or a nose or ear, although there is no blood, bones, or tissue exposed. The missing parts just look as if they had disappeared. A bright light flashes and an electric-type of sound buzzes when a person goes into the shack. Freddy notices that the area where the body part is missing is slightly larger when they come back out of the shack. Freddy is scared and wants to run away but can't make his legs move.

Freddy's friends start getting into the line and he says to them, "No, No, don't go! Your body parts will start to disappear like these other people."

They ignore him and move along with the line. Freddy asks a man coming out of the shack, "What is happening in there?"

Looking through Freddy, the man answers, "It is the only thing that matters."

"But won't you lose part of your body?" asks Freddy.

The man doesn't answer and walks to the back of the line. Freddy waits, terrified as his friends near the door. As one of his friends goes in, Freddy watches closely and sees the light flash through the cracks of the shack. When his friend comes out, Freddy cannot see any body part missing. Freddy runs to him and begs him to explain, "What is it, what is it? What happens in there?"

His friend quietly replies, "You must find out for yourself."

Freddy's mind is screaming at him to leave but he continues to watch as people enter and return from the shack, always getting back in line, patiently waiting for another turn to enter. He can see that the areas of missing body parts increases slightly every time they return from the shack. Freddy becomes obsessed and decides that he has to go through just once. As Freddy stands in line, he realizes he is scared but at the same time eager and excited to find out what this thing is. He no longer notices the people or their missing body parts. He is completely focused on this new and mysterious experience.

As Freddy passes through the door, two filthy and disgusting creatures lead him to a small X-ray-like machine and without hesitation, Freddy gets into it. A bright light flashes and suddenly he feels the most wonderful sensation wash over him. The sensation gets more and more wonderful as each moment passes. Freddy feels completely calm, confident, and unafraid. His earlier fears dissolve and his perspective changes. All he cares about is holding on to this blissful feeling for as long as he can. He forgets about missing body parts and everything else. As the feeling becomes more and more intense, he abruptly wakes from the dream. Freddy jumps up, disoriented as he shakes himself awake. It takes him several moments to realize that none of it had been real. *Just a dream*, he thinks.

Freddy lay down with an overwhelming desire to go back into the dream and drifts slowly back to sleep.

BACK ON IKE'S SIDE OF TOWN

Ike, too, is having a dream. Only he is a young boy with a clear mind but the same worn out body. He is on a basketball court, invisible to the players surrounding him. He sees his friends in the stands, walks over and sits with them. No one speaks to him because they are absorbed by what seems to be a very important basketball game. Ike looks at one of his friends and asks, "What game is this?"

Without looking at Ike, his friend gives no response. His eyes remain fixed on one specific player.

Ike turns to watch the player and sees that the player is completely dominating the game. Every time the defense gets the ball, this player steals it and dunks on anyone who is in the lane and then makes three-point shots with ease. He is unstoppable as he dribbles the ball straight down the middle and dunks the ball into the basket. His confidence is so apparent and contagious that Ike becomes drunk with it, making him feel strong, potent, and important. Confidence pulses through his veins, and no other sensation exists. The crowd reacts with yells of praise and exhilaration over everything this guy does. Ike, too, becomes enamored as he watches the player, admiring the way he moves and his ability to play the game, but what really catches Ike's attention is the player's complete and unshakeable confidence on the court.

Suddenly, the stands go silent. Ike looks around. He is standing alone back out on the court, and the stands are empty. "Where did everyone go?" Ike says out loud.

Ike remembers feeling confident, being in control of the game, reveling in the praise and attention from the crowd.

Ike wakes from his dream, trying to grab back the powerful feeling of confidence flowing from the player in his dream, but the more he becomes aware that it had been a dream, the faster it fades. Ike nods back into sleep, hoping to drift back into the dream.

THE CERTAIN EVENTUALITY: A MEMORY OF A TIME YET TO COME

The image would haunt Freddy for years to come. The feeling, too. When everyone had abandoned him in his darkest hour, the image stained upon his mind of the rejection and pain he caused someone beautiful was going to solidify the mistaken notion that he deserved to be alone.

THE FIGHT

The sound that hard-soled dress shoes make on a tile floor by a person moving quickly down a narrow hallway is the sound Freddy is making as he walks. The sound of important people with meaning to their lives. This is the moment Freddy has been waiting for. For the first time in a long time, Freddy feels like a real person.

Freddy isn't an important person headed to an important meeting. In fact, he's a deviant kid headed to a court date. Freddy got himself in trouble, big trouble. It wasn't the first time and surely would not be the last, but this time, he is potentially in serious trouble. He could possibly go to jail for the first time. Freddy's mother is scared and worried about him. He isn't in a place where he wants to be, but Freddy feels real, and to Freddy, that is all that matters.

It had been a standoff like the one in the movie, *The Outsiders*. He loved that movie and wanted to feel like an outsider. Some people called Freddy Hux although he never asked them to. His close friends called him Freddy. If someone called Freddy Hux, he immediately knew their perspective and that they were more familiar with his reputation than they were with him, the person, and he didn't like that. They would expect a persona that wasn't Freddy. He was a popular, friendly, and caring guy. He liked to read, play sports, and party a little too much. Hux established him as a tough guy with a reputation that he could do nothing about. Truth be told, he didn't want to do anything about it. Freddy enjoyed having an alter ego that he didn't necessarily have to take responsibility for.

It wasn't Freddy's style to be part of a specific gang. He'd rather be part of all of them. Freddy wanted action, comradery, and respect from everyone. He didn't dislike anyone. He wanted to be fearless and correctly known by people before he walked through the door.

For whatever reason, his friends wanted to instigate a fight. A fight was a big deal for Freddy, too. He envisioned a fight as an opportunity to etch his name into everlasting teenage lore, a myth-making moment he could ride until he discovered his purpose in this confusing world.

The fight was planned and consisted of about 30 guys ready for battle. Two guys took the lead to instigate the fight and walked into a backyard where a party crammed with teenagers was taking place. Darkness shrouded the backyard except for a small area where the drinks and food were set up. Light beams streamed through the small wooded area between the party and where Freddy and the rest of the guys waited. Even though he wasn't sure if anything would happen, Freddy was armed with a billy club. If a fight did break out, he was going to be up front and get as much action in as he could.

The music coming from the party was loud. The talking and laughing of the partiers was even louder. Suddenly, screaming blasted from the instigators' Freddy couldn't understand what they were yelling, but there was no mistaking the sound of bricks going through the windows of the house. *That'll do it*, Freddy thought to himself.

As Freddy hoped, the knowledge that the fight was real infected him. He longed for moments when daily life no longer mattered, and he was left with only the now pressing down on him with a force that could not be ignored. He felt weakness in his strong, young knees. Freddy gripped tight to the billy club as if it were the last branch on the side of a steep cliff.

Freddy's excitement grew as he thought to himself, *It's happening now. There's probably a hundred people at that party, and I am part of the gang who just threatened them and threw bricks through the window. Now it is real.*

This was the feeling Freddy was looking for—scared but very alive. Suddenly, the two instigators came running into the dark clearing where the gang was waiting. A party goer was yelling that he saw which way the instigators ran.

"They know where we are. It won't be long now," Freddy quietly said to his comrades.

Freddy's fear was consuming, and adrenaline pulsed through his veins. He wanted to run away. Instead, he stepped to the front of the group but not because he was brave. He wanted to find purpose in the fear, to know that the fear was unjustified and not real—just like everything else in life.

Six or seven silhouetted figures came through the trees and stopped about 30 feet in front of Freddy. He couldn't see their faces although he didn't care who they were. For this moment, they were the enemy instead of Freddy himself. Freddy held his ground. Everyone held their ground. For the moment, no one on either side advanced. Freddy was intoxicated by the feel of collective fear; as a feeling of power overwhelmed him, his fears evaporated.

Knowing they were outnumbered, the party group began halfheartedly yelling profanities and threats. Freddy gave out a yell and advanced with several of his gang following. He drove straight for and focused on one guy, the largest guy at the party. As Freddy approached, the guy froze and his friends scrambled to abandon him. Shadowy figures scattered back toward the trees and just for a second, Freddy hoped his guy would follow, but he didn't run. Freddy was committed to him.

Quickly and without a word, Freddy swung the club at the head of the faceless shadow and was surprised when the swing connected. The sound of the connection filled him with dread. *It doesn't make a sound like that in the movies*, Freddy thought.

The sound and the force he felt in his hand as he delivered the blow scared Freddy to his core. As the big guy dropped fast and hard, a snoring sound came out of him. Stunned and standing over the guy, Freddy couldn't believe what he had just done. With one swing of the wooden billy club, Freddy had done something he didn't realize he was capable of. Momentum drove him to once again lift the club and slam it down on one of the guy's legs, but the guy just lay there and gasped for air. Freddy took another swing, hitting the curb and splitting the billy club in half. *Thank God, I can retreat!* Freddy thought.

Freddy was disappointed—this wasn't a real fight. The guy didn't hit back. He couldn't even get up off the ground. Freddy was there to fight and to feel something that was real. There was no pleasure in hurting a guy who didn't fight back, and he didn't want to kill the guy. He looked down at the dark crumpled figure and wanted to take back what he had done and to help him. The guy was crouched in pain. His friends had abandoned him when he had been so brave not to run.

God, I wish he had run, too, Freddy thought.

Freddy felt bad, but it was done. He had to get out of there, fast!

It was only when Freddy was running back to the cars that he realized no one else had fought. Except for that one guy, everyone else at the party ran away. Freddy's group didn't fight either. They just stood and watched as Freddy put on a gruesome display. Freddy felt sick. *What have I done?*

Freddy was left standing alone and had really fucked up. "Where were the two guys who got this started? After all the gangster talk about fucking these guys up, no one did nothin' but me!"

Everyone began scrambling to get away. A caravan of about 10 cars raced out of the dark suburban street before the sounds of sirens could track them down. The people in Freddy's car were frantic, screaming and chanting as if the victory of a lifetime had been achieved. Forgetting thoughts of regret, Freddy held the broken club out the window of his mother's '84 Camry and shouted, "I am the King!" while his friends cheered him on.

CONFUSION

Freddy spent the next day in a state of confusion, replaying the fight over and over to fully comprehend what had happened. Before the fight, he hadn't given much thought to the concept of physically hurting anyone. If that isn't what fighting is all about, then why did he carry a billy club?

All he thought about was being the tough guy that brought fear—like in the movies. Where were his values? He struck an innocent guy with a billy club, hurting him badly, and he couldn't take it back. Freddy went into deep contemplative thought about whether this was something he regretted.

In his place of contemplation, Freddy began to break down the event. He visualized how he enjoyed the moment he heard the windows shatter. He reveled in having the real experience of fear coming. He wanted to understand why his whole body came alive at the moment of anticipating the fight. It was a beautiful feeling when nothing else existed except being completely consumed and driven by fear. Seeing the silhouettes come through the trees was a rush through his heart even though he had immediately had a powerful desire to run away. Deep down, Freddy knew he was a coward. The great Friedrich Huxley had wanted to run away. Freddy hated himself, and his mind went blank.

MIRANDA

Freddy turned his thoughts to his beautiful girlfriend, Miranda, and how sweet she was to him. No matter what he did or what foul things he said to her, she continued to adore him. Being with Miranda made Freddy feel powerful and confident, validating his existence when he felt unsure. Miranda was a simple girl and happy most of the time. She loved to laugh and play and would do anything he wanted her to do. He thought about how awful he treated her at times and about his willingness to have sex with any other girl who would let him, and he didn't feel bad about it. Freddy took and took from Miranda, giving very little in return. This was not the kind of relationship Freddy wanted, but he would never willingly let go of the steady sex she provided. Plus, she let him get away with it. He wasn't going to stop seeing her, but she didn't deserve to be mistreated.

Freddy visualized Miranda's smile, her long strawberry blonde hair, and her big blue eyes. Her perfectly shaped breasts were so soft and her big pink nipples had no defined borders; they just tapered off into her pale skin. He thought about what he was going to do to her beautiful body the next time he had the pleasure of being next to it. Instead of just fucking, he wanted to learn how to enjoy her whole body and her company. He knew that he was lucky that a girl like Miranda let him be with her.

Freddy remembered a night when he and his friend, Jeff, went to a party at Amy's house. Everyone was playing around and cracking jokes when Freddy sat down next to the gorgeous Lorraine. Freddy had talked to Lorraine a couple of times, but he had never caught a sexual vibe from her. But on this night, when he sat next to her, she looked at him differently. Freddy remembered exactly what she said to him: "My God, you smell so good. What is that cologne you're wearing?"

Freddy looked her in the eye and said without thinking, "It's something special I put on just for you."

Freddy never forgot her reaction. It was almost as if she lost her entire being to him. It all happened so quickly. Freddy's cool turned to fear, and he wanted to run away. Instead, he stood up, looked into her eyes, and said, "Come on."

Freddy led Lorraine into a bedroom next to the party room. He kissed her deep and hard, not soft like he normally would when he was trying to seduce a girl. He didn't have to put his hand up her shirt or stick it down her pants. They both knew what they wanted; he didn't have to play games. This was not the way he seduced other girls. This was grown up sex, and Freddy was in heaven.

After they finished having sex, he kissed Lorraine and fell to the bed to catch his breath. Lorraine stood up, cleaned herself with a towel, got dressed, and left the room while he reveled in what had just happened. Freddy dressed, opened the door, and discovered the secret of women.

Everyone at the party, including the girls, had heard what happened on his side of the door, and they made no attempt to pretend they hadn't heard or to hide their stares. Freddy swaggered outside to the patio and lit a cigarette. He was trying his damnedest to be cool and not show the energy and esteem flowing through him.

Freddy jolted back from his trip down memory lane. He thought of that night often. It came to mind now because on that special night he learned a life changing lesson about women. All he needed to do was convince a woman that everything he does, he is doing for her, and they will melt in his arms and beg to be fucked. Then he would leave them, and they would never know how weak and what a coward he really was. That was the secret . . . and he was pretty damn sure that Obsession cologne was magic. Freddy made a mental note to buy a large bottle the next time he went to Macy's.

CLARITY

As Freddy tied the Lorraine sexual experience with the fight's fear experience, he began finding clarity about his cowardice. As the fight approached and fear set in, Freddy was exhilarated but his instinct was to run away; however, he stood his ground. It was the same with Lorraine. Anyone watching would never guess he had such thoughts. His mind wandered to a quote from Shakespeare's *Julius Caesar*: "A coward dies a thousand deaths, but the valiant taste death but once." Freddy had only read one Shakespeare play—he loved to say, "Et tu, Brute, Beware the Ides of March."

These new thoughts sent Freddy back into contemplation and fantasy. He envisioned having a best friend with whom he could share his thoughts. A friend who liked to read the same interesting things he did and enjoyed seeing the same movies. They could have deep discussions to critique and break down the true meanings of what they learned. "If I had a friend like that, we could integrate books and movies into our lives and communications. We would only have to say a couple of words to convey complex and dynamic ideas to each other. I could tell this type of friend when I was feeling guilty about my fears and my friend could quote Shakespeare and I would have any problem licked."

Freddy let the friend fantasy pass and moved on to his Julius Caesar revelation. *Mainly, there is no difference between the feelings of a brave man and the feelings of a coward. The difference is how they respond to those feelings. It's that simple. Based on this theory, his behavior falls into the brave category.*

Being a coward was not his main concern. His main concern was the possibility that his mind created a delusion to confuse him. *Delusions must be eliminated.*

Freddy liked to be seen as brave and admired by his friends. What he didn't like and what ate him up inside, was remembering the horrible feeling in his hand when the club hit that guy's head. He couldn't hide from the fact that he had seriously hurt someone for no reason other than to appear brave for his friends and to prove to himself that he wasn't a coward. He had to accept responsibility for committing a disgusting act. The fact was that he was not defending anything or anyone. He had not been noble. It was juvenile to care whether his friends admired his bullshit legend or how many girls he got to fuck because of it. Freddy knew in reality that he was just a punk and he needed to change.

Now, he felt shitty . . . good, but shitty.

WHAT DO YOU BELIEVE IN?

The next morning Freddy arrived at school late, as usual. He always set his alarm but always turned it off. He loved the snooze button. Sleeping in those nine-minute increments was his favorite sleep of the night. It was like he could be aware of his sleep and thereby enjoy it more. There had been times when he hit the button all the way till noon.

Second period was already in session, so he went directly to English class. Mr. Coleman, his English teacher, said nothing when he walked in but looked at him in an unusual way. He usually ignored Freddy's tardiness because he and Freddy had a good teacher-student relationship and Freddy always enthusiastically participated in class. He admired Mr. Coleman and found him to be very interesting. Mr. Coleman recognized Freddy's academic potential; however, he also saw his lack of ambition. Freddy's classmates gave Freddy an odd look, too, but that was not unusual. Most of them didn't care about literature. They were more annoyed that Freddy got to come and go as he pleased. Freddy settled into his desk and tuned in to the conversation.

The class was discussing the novel *1984,* by George Orwell. Freddy enjoyed reading *1984* and was looking forward to hearing his teacher's insight on the book. It frustrated Freddy that he didn't always catch a book's meaning as he read it, but through class discussions, the ideas and characters became clear. He loved the transition to clarity. His only solution was to read every book twice even though that made him feel dumb, and he didn't like to feel dumb.

Geneva was sitting next to Freddy and passed him a folded note. Freddy looked at her curiously, and she smiled. They sat next to each other in every class they had together, which must have been her doing because Freddy didn't pay attention to where he sat but he enjoyed her company so it worked out for him. Geneva was a cute, sweet, and shy girl. She didn't hang out with any of his friends. Freddy pretty much only talked to her in class.

Freddy unfolded and read the note, "I have to talk to you after class—VERY IMPORTANT & CONFIDENTIAL." Geneva drew a heart next to her signed name.

Freddy nodded that he would talk to her after class. He had never flirted with Geneva but sensed something different about the way she was looking at him and felt warmth fill his jeans. Geneva was turning him on, which had never happened with her, but he wanted to fuck every girl he met, so why would Geneva be any different?

Mr. Coleman continued to dazzle Freddy with his insight on *1984,* and class came to an end. Mr. Coleman released the class but asked Freddy to stay behind. After the class cleared, Freddy approached Mr. Coleman, who sat at his desk and gazed out the window. "What's up, Mr. Coleman?"

Still looking out the window, his teacher asked, "Mr. Huxley, what do you believe in?"

Freddy, confused by the question, answered, "I don't know, Mr. Coleman. Why?"

"Come on, Mr. Huxley," Mr. Coleman said, now peering directly into Freddy's eyes. "Take a moment and think about it. Then give me a thoughtful answer. I know you've thought about it because we've talked about it, but your actions don't reflect it. Or maybe they do, which is why I'm asking."

Freddy was floored because he had given a lot of thought to what he believed in and wanted to answer, but he was caught off guard and drawing a blank. Freddy turned to sit at a desk, and as he did, he saw Geneva standing outside the door waiting for him.

For a second his thoughts returned to the note, then back to his teacher and the question.

Freddy began, "Well, I suppose I could answer in many ways. I can answer what I think you want to hear or what I think sounds smart, but the truth is I don't know. You are right when you say that I have invested a lot of thought on what I believe in, but it seems that the more I think about it, the more confused I get. I wish you would just tell me what I should believe in."

"I wish I could do that, but we both know that you would never accept being told what to believe. I cannot give you the answer, but I can tell you that sitting before me is a special young man." Mr. Coleman continued, "Freddy, you have an inquisitive mind, you're a good looking kid, you project unflinching confidence, and you light up when we talk about literature. You have the tools to choose what path to follow as you learn and grow, but instead, you seem to choose to play a role that I don't think is you."

"What am I to do?" Freddy asked.

"Listen to your gut and utilize the energy inside of you. What you do and the beliefs you form today are what will set the mold for you as a man tomorrow. Tapping into your energy to build confidence in your beliefs is not easy at your stage of life and is often misdirected. Some guys find power through domination over women, talking down to people, or denying accountability when their misdeeds harm others. Other guys share energy through entering into what I'll call lifelong energy exchange contracts—they give and they take and call it a relationship. You have the ability to decide what to do with the energy you develop into power based on who you are inside. This time of learning and growth is short but it will last a lifetime. Do you understand what I'm telling you, and why I'm concerned that you may have lost your way?"

Freddy understood what his teacher was saying, but he didn't understand why he was saying it now. Mr. Coleman, who was usually more like a peer than a teacher when they talked, was kind of creeping Freddy out. This was a much more serious Mr. Coleman than Freddy was used to, and he wasn't sure he could trust his motivation for speaking to him in such a solemn tone.

"That's it, Mr. Huxley. Just remember that everything you need to establish your beliefs is already inside of you and that you don't need to take anything from anyone else to be who you want to be, not ever, not under any circumstances. You don't need to take the energy of another human being to find your energy."

"Ok, well, thank you for giving me a lot to think about. See you later."

"Good day, Mr. Huxley."

SNAPSHOT IN TIME

Freddy walked out of the classroom, intrigued and a little mesmerized by Mr. Coleman's surprise conversation. Geneva still waited and nervously stepped toward him.

Geneva looked up at him. "You know, Freddy, I like sitting next to you in class. You are smart, make me laugh, and don't seem to care that I am not as popular as your other friends."

Freddy smiled. "Of course, I don't care. You are a beautiful girl, and I like sitting next to you in class."

Geneva hugged Freddy and blurted out, "I love you, Friedrich Huxley! I love you!"

Freddy's jeans tightened as he felt her soft breasts press against his chest. He returned her hug and kissed her neck, and Geneva pulled away to look into his eyes. Freddy touched her cheek. His mind was racing, knowing what the consequences would be if he full-on kissed her, which was what he very much wanted to do. She was so cute and more importantly, willing. Freddy imagined her naked and without thinking put his hand on her butt. They stared at each other as Freddy debated whether he should kiss her. Then thoughts of Miranda crept into his mind.

Freddy didn't care about cheating on Miranda. All he cared about was getting caught, and the hallway was not safe from prying eyes. Plus, he liked and respected Geneva, and he did not want to lead her on. Then, out of the corner of his eye, he saw Mr. Coleman at his desk, looking right at them. He also saw his buddies, Steve and Derek, coming toward them, giggling to each other. Freddy's jeans immediately loosened.

He looked at Geneva and abruptly said, "Look, you know I have a girlfriend. You have put me in a bad position. Why are you telling me this now?"

A single tear welled up in her eye, spilled over her eyelash, and slowly ran down her cheek. Freddy's heart sank. He wanted to cry, too. He became fixated on her tear as he put his thumb on her cheek to stop it. It hurt to make her or any girl cry, especially when her only crime was expressing innocent love for him. Freddy turned and walked away without saying another word. He walked fast, hoping to get away from the ache he felt. He heard a voice yell from the end of the hallway, "You the Man, Hux!"

Freddy didn't look back. He knew it was Steve or Derek and raced to his next class to get a 50-minute reprieve from the drama. Freddy arrived at science class just as the bell rang. Again, everyone stared at him as he walked to his seat even though he was on time. Without making eye contact with anyone, Freddy sat down and looked through the window of the classroom door to see Miranda looking at him, smiling and waving. His heart sank, but he put on a smile and waved back to her. She blew him a kiss, and he pretended to catch it.

He couldn't get Geneva off his mind and thought about how small, unexpected occurrences stay with a person. Years later, Freddy would recall the image of Geneva's tearstained cheek and how sad it made him feel, especially during his darkest hour when he felt abandoned. This snapshot in time was a reminder of the rejection and hurt he caused someone beautiful, and it somehow solidified his mistaken notion that he deserved to be alone.

Freddy closed his eyes and made an inventory of the morning's events.

Geneva weighs heavily on his mind. He imagines leaving his class, going to her classroom, and watching her through the door, then catching her eye and waving for her to come out. When she immediately rises and leaves the classroom, he tells her to follow him, leading her to a book room where he has fucked Miranda many times. He begins to kiss Geneva in the way he had wanted to in the hallway. He can almost feel her breasts perk up as he puts his hand up her sweater and unbuttons her bra to caress her naked breast.

"Everyone! Please hand in your homework," Freddy's teacher loudly demanded, pulling him out of his sweet fantasy just in time to notice that his dick was full and throbbing, leaving a wet feeling in his jeans. Fumbling through his backpack, Freddy finds his homework and passes it forward. His thoughts returned to Geneva briefly, but he did not return to his fantasy. He needed to be thinking about something else, but he couldn't focus. Then it hit him. His heart sank in his chest as he remembered beating someone with a billy club two nights before. Now, Freddy felt angry with himself for remembering. He would rather think about Geneva and his fantasy in the book room.

WHEN IT ALL COMES DOWN

Without knocking, a large black man in a dark suit walked into the classroom followed by another, smaller white man, also wearing a dark suit. The large black man went to the teacher and whispered in her ear. The teacher looked up and pointed at Freddy. Both men walked toward Freddy, confirmed his name, and asked him to stand up and put his hands on the top of his head. Shocked, Freddy felt himself go numb, and he did not move.

"My name is Inspector Lanier, and this is my partner, Detective Ramsey," the black man said.

As he stared at the two men, Freddy felt like he was having an out-of-body experience. He was also confused and scared shitless.

"I'm asking you again, Mr. Huxley. Stand up and put your hands on your head."

Freddy complied and whimpered, "What did I do?"

"You are under arrest for the malicious wounding of one Marcus Sampson."

Freddy felt relief that it wasn't something worse and caught his breath as they put handcuffs on him. His fear subsided as he looked around at the astonished faces in his classroom. Everyone would be talking about this after he left the classroom, which made him feel important and alive.

Freddy grinned and boldly proclaimed, "I ain't sayin' shit till I see a lawyer."

As the police led Freddy out of the classroom and directed him toward the head principal's office, he considered his options. He was still 17 and a juvenile, which was good. Not so good was that his mother was surely on her way, and she had the ability to make him really miserable. He wasn't too worried, though, because he was going into total denial.

Then the name Marcus Sampson slid into Freddy's mind. He didn't know him but was pretty sure Miranda had dated a guy named Marcus Sampson. This was probably the reason Freddy was a suspect and being taken into custody for questioning. The police may think they have a motive, but because of the darkness, there couldn't possibly be any witnesses. Freddy would proclaim his arrest was a witch hunt and then keep his mouth shut. They wouldn't be able to prove his guilt. He didn't even know who he had hit! The only problem was that they didn't know that he didn't know whom he had hit. He couldn't believe his bad luck—he beat up a guy who he could have had a motive to beat up! The hell with it. Total denial was the way to go. Deny and shut up.

After a long wait in the principal's office, Freddy's mother appeared. She didn't say a word, but she looked at him with disgust. Then she gave him her annoyed "what have you gotten into this time" look. This hurt Freddy, but he wasn't going to let her intimidate him. He held to his plan: Deny and shut up. Inspector Lanier called everyone into the principal's office except for Freddy. How could he implement his plan if they didn't include him?

When everyone emerged from the principal's office, Freddy's mother made a beeline to him and quietly said, "How could you?"

Freddy whispered back, "I didn't do anything, Mom."

She looked at him and said through a clenched jaw, "You are going to ride with the police to the police station. I am going to follow and meet you there. Tell them the truth!"

Freddy was disappointed that she didn't give him any benefit of the doubt. He nodded without emotion. They had gotten to his mother, and she couldn't be trusted. He should have been afraid, but he wasn't. He felt empowered, alive, and confident.

THE ALIBI

Freddy needed an alibi. He would have to tell the police where he supposedly was that night if he hadn't been at the party. He couldn't say he was at home with his mother—a good mother would protect her son. Maybe Miranda would cover for him and say they were out together. He thought about a recent night they spent together . . . they went to the movies, had dinner at Bennigan's, then parked the car by a golf course and fucked in the car. It just might work to replace that event with the night of the fight. Surely Miranda would do whatever he told her to do. The problem was getting to Miranda and telling her what to say. Fuck it! Nothing was safe and no one could be trusted. Deny and shut up, he repeated to himself—just don't say shit!

The detectives ignored Freddy and talked trash between themselves the whole ride to the police station. The gross things they were saying made him angry, but he kept his mouth shut. When they got to the police station, they put Freddy in an interrogation room.

Freddy's mother came in first and asked, "Did you beat up Marcus Sampson?"

"I didn't do anything, Mom, and I need you on my side. I am being accused of something I didn't do, and they are trying to turn you against me. This is the time I need you to stand by me. I didn't do it, Mom. Whose side are you gonna take, Mom? This is the moment, Mom. This is the moment when I need you here for me. Are you with me or are you with them?"

"The pictures, Friedrich, are horrible. Someone smashed that boy's head in, and they think you did it because Miranda used to date him. Tell me, is it true?"

"No! Mom. Maybe the pictures are bad, but I didn't do it. You can't turn on me just because of grotesque pictures."

She got up close to his face, stared him in the eye, and pointed her finger. "Are you sure you didn't do it, Freddy?"

Before Freddy could answer, Inspector Lanier walked in.

"We know all about you, Mr. Huxley. We know it was you who beat up Mr. Sampson, so you might as well admit it."

Freddy looked at his horrified mother and knew that they were using her to weaken him, so he turned his full attention to Inspector Lanier to avoid looking at his mother.

"We also know why you did it. Being in a gang is tough when someone from another gang is fucking your little lady. Isn't it, Freddy?"

Freddy recoiled. "What? What gang? I'm not in any gang."

Freddy's mother started to cry.

"Look, Mom, these fuckin' cops are trying to turn us against each other. Do not listen to them, and please do not cry!"

Detective Ramsey walked in. "Here's the deal, Freddy. We want to help you and we want to get the right guy. We know you aren't the leader of your gang. We will go easy on you if you will just tell us what you know about the night of the party and the fight."

Here it comes, thought Freddy, *the ole good cop-bad cop routine,* which he considered an advantage. Freddy just sat there and focused on Inspector Lanier, who was obviously irritated but said nothing. A slight blushing appeared on the pale cheeks of Detective Ramsey. Freddy knew they were frustrated with him and that's just where he wanted them. Although it might mean they would come back harder at him, he wasn't going to let them trick him into saying something he didn't want to say. The quiet in the room gave

Freddy a feeling of calm and confidence. His mother's eyes were swollen and red, but her manner encouraged him to stay calm and think. To the detectives, he was just another cocky punk taking up too much of their time.

"Oh, smart guy, huh?" Inspector Lanier said as he got up close into Freddy's face.

Not to be intimidated, Freddy shot back, "That's right, Inspector Black, I mean, uh, whatever your name is."

Inspector Lanier's frustration turned to ire as he pulled out the gun from his shoulder holster and placed it on the table. Freddy's mother freaked out and screamed, "No!"

Lanier looked at her and angrily said, "Give me a minute. I'm trying to make a point here."

Then he pulled a gun out of his ankle holster and placed it next to the bigger gun on the table. Lanier introduced the bigger gun as Truth and the smaller gun as Justice and began a lecture on righteousness. In later years to commemorate this moment, Freddy had Beware the Righteous tattooed on his chest, arched just below his neck.

"Dude, no one gives a fuck about the little lecture you prepared in your bathroom mirror. Can't you see that you're scaring the shit out of my mother, and she's going to have a nervous breakdown if this goes on much longer? If you have nothing else to ask us or a legitimate reason to hold me here, release us so we can go home and have dinner. Anyway, it's a school night and I have homework."

At this, both detectives began another barrage of questions and accusations. Freddy thought to himself, if you argue with an idiot, then to a third party watching the argument, it won't be clear which one of you is the idiot.

To keep from being the idiot, Freddy looked over at his mother and calmly said, "Don't listen or respond, there's nothing more you or I can give them."

Inspector Lanier loudly threatened, "There isn't much time. We are giving you a last chance to tell us what you know before your gang homies do."

The stupid cops continued with their foolish interrogation. Freddy rolled his eyes at the Inspector but the word "Time" struck him in a profound way and sent him into a tangent of contemplation. He saw the word "Time" with his eyes but not with the letters. Freddy suddenly saw Time itself. Time as a whole new thing. Time was something that could not be experienced with the senses. Yet Time is so important. How could something we can't see, hear, smell, taste, or touch mean so much?

Freddy stared ahead and remained silent, deep in his thoughts. *Time doesn't exist. It's a tool we use so we can understand the mysteries of life. It seems that we need Time to understand Time. All we ever see is The Now—a steady procession of a continuous Now. If we are always in The Now, we can do something Now to affect the future. Yet we cannot do anything to affect the past. In this way,* Freddy concludes, *Time is real.*

Then Time made sense—we are always in The Now, and that can affect the future because the Future Now has not happened yet. But the Past Now is in the past. Nevertheless, we can never escape The Now. Ever. Having an understanding of Time gave Freddy a good feeling because he felt that he had used this Time, this Now, wisely, instead of giving these crazy cops his Time!

Freddy snapped back to reality. He needed to do something now. In his current situation, time was running out. He needed to escape from The Now. Freddy felt better until he looked over at his mother, who he'd forgotten was even in the room, saw her expression of worry and sadness, and felt like a piece of shit.

Having finally reached the conclusion that the interrogation wasn't working, the detectives released Freddy into his mother's custody. When they got to the car, Freddy's mother gave him a hug. "I love you, Freddy. Let's go home and get something to eat."

Freddy grinned. "OK, Ma! I love you, too."

While Freddy's mother fixed dinner, they discussed his options while he set the table. He insisted he hadn't hurt anyone like they claimed. Freddy did admit that he was at the party and that he was drinking, but he assured her that he did not beat up anyone.

"Well then, who did?" Asked his mother. "If you want to get out of this mess, you have to tell me and the detectives."

"Here's the thing, Mom. I don't know who beat up this guy Sampson and even if I did know, I wouldn't tell. It was pitch black dark where the fight happened, away from the party where I was. The cops are just trying to scare out a confession."

Freddy's mother listened and then cautioned, "You know, even though the detectives' tactics didn't work on you today, they could very well work on others, who out of desperation might point the finger at you."

"That's a good point, but I'm not going to worry about it. We'll just have to wait and see. The most important thing is that we show a strong, unfaltering unit. I need you on my side. Please do not let them trick you again," Freddy pleaded.

"OK, I will stand united with you in this, as I always have, just me and you once again against this crazy world. Since we left your father, we have been a team and we can't let that change."

Freddy liked those words and breathed a sigh of relief as he cried out, "Music to my ears! Me and you, Mom! Me and you!"

GOOD ADVICE

The following day was a Tuesday and Freddy was dreading it. He woke up late as usual and got dressed. As he drove to school, his thoughts returned to his concept of Time. If only he could find a way to go back in time and undo the fight. Freddy pulled into the parking lot of Poe Senior High School. *The Poe Ravens*, Freddy thought. Edgar Allan Poe was one of Freddy's favorite poets. He wondered how many of the students made the connection of Poe's poem, "The Raven," to the name of the school mascot who entertained Poe's sports supporters and fans during half time at football and basketball games?

Freddy got to school as second period was letting out and noticed that both of the school security officers were standing out front watching him as he walked from the parking lot. Freddy and Mr. Shifflett, the head security officer, had a good relationship. Freddy always spoke to him and they joked around. But today, Freddy felt uncomfortable and avoided eye contact as he walked by.

"Freddy, I have some bad news for you."

Freddy's heart sank. "What is it, Mr. Shifflett?"

"Come here, son, and walk with me. I want to talk to you."

Mr. Shifflett told the other security officer that he would take care of this and started walking toward the side of the school. Freddy followed.

"Listen, Freddy, I know you're a good kid, so I want to give you a warning. The police have been in the main office all morning interviewing your friends. I was asked to sit in on the interviews and was worried that you would be brought to the office before I could warn you. I was relieved when Principal Plutz sent me outside to wait for you. Freddy, your friends are identifying you for the fight over the weekend. I'm not going to ask if you did it, because I don't care, but I do care about your future, so I am going to give you some advice. You know that I was a police officer for 30 years?"

"Yes, I do," Freddy replied.

"Then you know that I know how these things work. I want to help you, but I won't reveal that when we get inside the office. For now, refuse to answer questions and insist on having an attorney present. They will try to intimidate and convince you that you have to talk, but I promise you that, legally, you have the right to an attorney during questioning. Here's the rub—listen to me carefully—they want to charge you with attempted murder. Freddy, this is not a joke, they are not playing games, and you must be careful not to incriminate yourself."

Freddy pursed his mouth and squeezed up his nose as he flailed both arms in the air.

"Freddy, calm down and listen to me! No matter what the hell they tell you, do not talk to them unless you have an attorney present."

Freddy's face fell and went white as he stood still, staring down at the sidewalk. He felt dizzy as he looked up at Mr. Shifflett and nodded his head.

"Good luck, son. Follow me and don't screw this up."

Freddy followed Mr. Shifflett into Principal Plutz's office to find several familiar faces and a few unknown faces looking at him, all with different levels of intensity. The police and the principal looked at him with anger. Freddy's counselor's look of empathy made him want to cry.

Principal Plutz told Freddy to sit down and said, "The police are here today investigating an attack that took place over the weekend. Several of your friends have already been interviewed. Please tell us your whereabouts on Saturday night."

Freddy stared straight ahead, let out a heavy sigh and said, "I cannot answer your questions today."

Principal Plutz looked at Freddy with shock and shouted, "Did you attack that boy, Freddy?"

"No, I did not!" Freddy shouted back.

Inspector Lanier walked into Principal Plutz's office looking confident, "Hello again, Freddy. We've interviewed several witnesses this morning who have confirmed that it was you who attacked and maliciously beat up Mr. Samson." The inspector threw several pictures on the table in front of Freddy. Freddy did not recognize the guy with a bloodied face and a bandage wrapped around his head.

"Do you know who this is?" Inspector Lanier asked.

Freddy screwed up his face and had an overwhelming desire to try and talk his way out. He really wanted to spin a convincing lie that would clear him. Instead, Freddy forced himself to heed Mr. Shifflett's advice and said nothing.

"Ok, Freddy, you leave me no choice. You are under arrest for the attempted murder of Mr. Samson. Please stand up and put your hands on your head. Freddy's counselor started to cry.

Freddy put his hands on his head, looked at his counselor and said, "Did you know, Mrs. Octavek, time is just an illusion? Time is just something created to understand the universe. There is no past and there is no future. There is no day time and there is no night time. We are just on a spinning ball near another spinning ball made of fire. Time doesn't really exist. Time is a constant state of The Now. It is always Now. When this Now ends, there will be another Now. Mrs. Octavek, this isn't my best Now, but I will be OK."

Mrs. Octavek was spellbound. She tilted her head and gave Freddy a sad smile of understanding. Freddy looked over at Mr. Shifflett and saw a small twitch in his eye squelching the muscle from winking. His silent words rang in Freddy's ear: *You're doing good, son. Remember, don't say a word no matter what.*

THE ARREST

The detectives took Freddy back to the county jail and booked him as an adult for attempted murder. Inspector Lanier stood Freddy in front of a group of officers and announced to them all, "This young man thinks he can go around beating people with billy clubs."

The officers scowled at Freddy as Inspector Lanier continued, "You guys should have seen the size of the guy he beat up. If I was a young punk like him, I would be scared to fight that guy straight up, too."

The officers murmured to each other, calling Freddy a pussy and a little punk. At six foot and 180 pounds, Freddy was not a little guy but compared to the six foot five inch, 250 pounds of Marcus Sampson, not so big. A young, red faced and muscular deputy fingerprinted Freddy and told him that he had dainty wrists. When he took Freddy's mug shot, he said that he had to get the little person lens for the camera. Inspector Lanier stood by, watching with a sneer on his face while making direct eye contact with Freddy.

Freddy could no longer contain himself and gave his best tough guy response to the deputy: "Nice complexion, pimple boy. You're gonna need the bad motherfucker lens." The other officers couldn't help but laugh. Freddy needed to show them that he wasn't intimidated. Inspector Lanier took Freddy by the arm and walked him to a small room with a table and two chairs on each side of it. There was a large window and deputies were positioned on the other side to watch the interrogation. A camera was also in the room. Freddy knew that this was all part of the intimidation process and meant to prime Freddy with fear so that he would slip up and tell them what they wanted to hear.

"Sit down," Inspector Lanier demanded as he walked away leaving Freddy alone.

It wasn't easy being a cool dude while his mind swirled in so many different directions. Attempted murder! *Jesus Christ, how in hell did this get so out of hand? And those damn cops. I hate cops and anyone who acts like one,* Freddy thought to himself. *The truth is, they are professional tattle-tales and act like little old ladies so excited they wet themselves while waiting to spread a nasty rumor. Cops are the quintessential example of the friendly rattlesnake. Shit, my father is a cop. Maybe that little nugget of information could help my case?*

Freddy calmed down, remembered Mr. Shifflett's warning, and realized that they were pushing him to the edge of not handling the situation well and that he needed to act quickly and insist on an attorney. In the meantime, he needed to be smart and not let the deputies' pointing and laughing through the window get to him. He was confused enough and didn't need their added taunting, which would win the mental battle and surely take him over the edge. *The correct path is not always clear, and knowing what to do is hard.* Freddy felt sure that if he could resist revelations of confusion and fear, and use his knowledge competently, a solution could be found.

Ironically, Freddy considered telling the truth a very big deal. Yeah, he was guilty of stretching or avoiding the truth at times, especially when it came to girls, but he believed that the truth sets a person free. It isn't even the great or important things that happen when we accept the truth—truth does not always create greatness—it is more about the terrible things we do to ourselves in the process of avoiding the truth and creating delusions. Then the delusions pile up and result in a worse state of confusion. Freddy couldn't let that happen. He had to find a way to stay cool and alert in this current state of confusion. He had never been so nervous but began to search his mind for ideas to ease the confusion until he could get help. Showing anger toward the detectives and deputies and seeking revenge was not the answer for now.

The truth lies in the details, popped into Freddy's brain and he began scanning the room to find some detail he could use. While avoiding the eyes of the cops, he looked out the window and noticed many signs on the walls. He saw another locked up person being led out of the booking area, but he was not being placed into an interrogation room. This guy was being led to another area marked "Magistrate," where his cuffs were removed. Freddy's buddy, Patrick, got locked up for a DUI and got out on a bail bond, which must be what the Magistrate does because this guy is getting set free! Why hadn't Freddy been taken to get a bail bond? Could they even offer him a bail bond before his eighteenth birthday? This is an adult jail, and I'm a juvenile being held with no offer of a bail bond, no attorney, not even a phone call! Freddy squeezed his eyes almost shut as the detectives returned.

"So you wanna beat people with baseball bats," Lanier started.

Freddy stared straight ahead and did not reply.

Detective Ramsey spoke up, "I want to remind you that we have several witnesses putting you at the scene. Help yourself and tell us what happened. Maybe you were just defending yourself? If it was self-defense, tell us and we can make this whole mess go away."

Freddy knew that they were just trying to get him to confess.

"Wasn't me."

"We have you, Freddy. We know it was you, tell us why you did it. I like you, Freddy. Just tell me it was self-defense, and we will let you go."

The words "let you go" rang in Freddy's ears but he knew it was a trick.

Freddy looked at both detectives and asked, "Why didn't you take me in front of the magistrate or give me a phone call?"

Lanier smirked at Freddy and said, "You won't get zilch until you tell us why you felt the need to bash in Samson's head."

"I didn't do it," Freddy calmly replied.

"Yes, you did, Mr. Huxley, and we are going to sit here until we find out why."

"Why do you call me Freddy sometimes and Mr. Huxley other times?" Freddy asked. The detectives shared a look and shrugged their shoulders.

"So, because you like me and now you're my friend, I should just open up and tell you what you want to hear and you'll let me walk. Is that it? Well, I'm not gonna tell you shit. How's that answer? Still my friend, Inspector Black?"

"I have all day, Mr. Freddy," Lanier calmly replied.

"I have all day, too. You have me at the wrong jail and haven't given me a bond or a phone call. I'm only an ignorant high school kid, but my guess is that several important legal rules are being broken here, Mr. Inspector." Feeling a little more confident, Freddy smiled and quietly said, "I want a fucking lawyer right now, or release me."

Lanier's calm turned to rage "I am going to get you! You little prick!" He stormed out of the room. Freddy felt better and let out a soft, "Thank you, Mr. Shifflett."

Freddy was left alone in the interrogation room through most of the afternoon. He got no information from anyone. He watched as Detective Ramsey put on his jacket and hat, and left the building. Then he saw his mother through the window—he had never been so happy to see her. A deputy came to the door and led Freddy to the front where his mother was standing. He could tell that she was very upset, but she hugged Freddy and asked if he was all right. Freddy said loudly that he was not OK, and that he had once again been mistreated and denied his rights. The deputies ignored

Freddy while his mother signed some papers. "Come on, honey, let's go home."

FREDDY'S DEFENSE

Freddy and his mother went to the car. His mother said, "Two days in a row, Freddy! They kept you there all day and no one even contacted me! Even if you are guilty, you have certain rights and those rights have been withheld. A friend of mine who is a lawyer is on his way to our house and will meet us there. Did you tell them anything?"

"No, Mom, I just told them that I wanted a lawyer, and they got mad."

"You did good then. Let's go!"

A BRIEF MOMENT OF CLARITY

It's almost two o'clock. I have to hurry, or I'll be late for class. Tuesdays are always hectic for me even though my classes don't start until two o'clock. It seems that the more time I have, the more time I will take. I would be running behind even if my class started at three. Unfortunately, though, I must rush, and this busy sidewalk isn't helping me get where I need to go. I am about two blocks away, and I see, way in front of me, the back of my ex-girlfriend. That long blonde hair, I could spot it from anywhere.

I have dreamt of running into her many times and spent so many walks down this same street just hoping I would run into her. Wouldn't you know it, today, late as I am, and there she is. I had better go down a block so I don't run into her. I would hate to have to rush a chance reunion like this. Besides, I'm over her, so there is no need to waste time on her. I cut through an alley where I used to spend my time drinking and getting high with that crowd I used to run with. No time to think about that though, I've got to get to class, besides, I've left that part of my life behind me.

As I walk through the alley, for a moment I notice the pretty trees that almost completely shade the street on both sides. They leave a long crooked line of sunshine going down the middle of the road. Cars are parked on each side of the thin road, and I wonder how many cars get hit by drunk drivers and ladies putting on their makeup. They probably never leave a note when they do it, just a nice sized dent and a smear of paint from their car, which most definitely the police would use in their report as evidence left behind at the scene of the crime. They would say that they were going to do everything they could to find out who did it, but that report was sure to find itself in some filing cabinet in the basement of the police station.

Out of the corner of my eye, I see something. There is a crowd gathered down the street. I take a closer look and see that there are three people lying in the middle of the road, two on the sidewalk, and one in between the cars with his feet poking out into the street. There is a crowd around them, and I can hear a mild commotion among them. I am intrigued but know that I have no time to investigate. I turn to continue my journey taking another look back to see a few more people on the ground. I wonder what is going on. Was it a horrible accident? Maybe a shooting, but I didn't hear gunshots or tires screeching. Anyway, I don't have time to focus on the misfortunes of these people, I need to concentrate on school.

Classes went as they usually do—a barrage of information I am forced to memorize while I continuously remind myself that I will never have to apply any of this stuff in real life. As I come out of school, I stop at the corner market across the street to get some smokes. There is no one in here. The door is wide open, yet no one is around. I yell "hello" but there is no answer. I decide to just grab some smokes and leave the money on the counter. I think for a minute about not paying, but I do because I feel like I'm being set up. I could see my court date now . . . I'd be screaming about entrapment and they would just laugh in my face, fine me excessively, and give me two weeks in jail. They may not think much of two weeks in jail, but it is just enough time to lose my job and have my friends move in on my girlfriend. I leave the money and exit the store.

As I come out of the store, I notice that the streets are very crowded and upon further review, I see the most unbelievable thing I've ever seen in my life. There are people everywhere laying on the ground. They are strewn all over the place. Some in the street, some on the sidewalk, some in the front yards of the townhomes along the street. There are also people walking around, looking at each other in awe. I ask a guy who I know from my freshman year English class but never spoke to until now, "What's going on?"

He says he has no idea, and I can see he is pretty freaked out. We wonder if they're dead but we both agree that they are alive because we can see them breathing. I go to a young girl, tap her with my foot and ask, "Why are you guys laying in the middle of the street?"

She turns and looks at me with the most peaceful looking face and waves me to come closer. She freaks me out so I jump back and get away as quickly as possible. I look back at her as she turns back to her original position. She moves as if our brief encounter had absolutely no effect on her at all.

I look around for my friend from English class. I figured he was probably freakin' out and would want me to help him get out of here. There he is, but he's bending over to talk to one of them. I yell, "No, don't do it," but he doesn't hear me. Then I see the second most unbelievable thing ever. He, without hesitating or contemplating at all, lies on the ground like the rest of them. I don't need him; he was always kind of weird, anyway. I start running as fast as I can to get home. People are on the ground the whole way home. Every time I see someone bending over to talk to one I yell, "No!" but no one listens.

I finally reach my apartment building. I barrel through the community door and up the stairs to my door. I hope my roommate is home. Maybe he'll know what is going on. I fumble for my keys but drop them on the floor. When I finally get into my apartment, I make a beeline for the TV Every channel is talking about it. They say it started in the city and has now spread out to the suburbs. They interviewed analysts of all kinds with different theories of cults, drugs, and hypnotism. But they all agree on one thing—if you speak to one, you will become one.

I turn off the TV to contemplate this on my own. What could be happening? I wonder. I don't think they are slipping people drugs. I would have seen something. I know it can't be a cult, because my friend from English class had no idea what was going on. It is clear to me that they are saying something to people that gets them to do this. But what can it be? I have read my share of profoundly meaningful things, contemplated Nietzsche, and read Huxley with no substantial reaction like this. Especially when it appears they are saying only a few sentences. Maybe someone has discovered the meaning of life? I laugh. No matter what they say, the meaning of life can't be to lie down in the middle of the street. My mind begins spinning in circles, thinking of the possibilities. I can't stop wondering what they are saying. I decide to go outside and have another quick look.

There are many more people lying on the ground now. It's as if they had fallen out of the sky. I see someone lying down who I recognize. Oh, it's that mean old man who lives below me. He might not like noisy neighbors, but he sure isn't going to tell me some craziness like the meaning of life is to lie in the middle of the street. So I tap him with my foot and ask him why he is laying on the ground. He turns his head toward me and waves me to come closer. I pretend to be hesitant, but I can't overcome my eagerness to hear what he has to say. He begins to speak: "Lie down and you will understand." At this point I start to see the world spinning without the dizzying effect. Thoughts become clear. I see my life for the utter foolishness it has been, but I am not ashamed or embarrassed. Nothing is good or bad, right or wrong, happy or sad. It just is.

I wake up to my mother banging on my bedroom door. She is yelling through the door that I had better get my lazy ass up, find a job, and not hang out in some filthy alley all day. I sit up and reach for my wallet; it's empty. Desperation overcomes me. No lying around for me!

THE MAN WHO PLAYED BY THE RULES

Stuart walked into the Barber Shop, looking at the floor. He grabbed a magazine, sat down, and pretended to read it. Freddy waved and smiled at him.

Stuart glanced at Freddy, then quickly looked away.

The other barber, Carly, a pretty blonde with very large breasts, gave Freddy a wink, and then turned to Stuart and asked, "May I help you, sir?"

Stuart smiled, careful to avoid eye contact with Freddy. "Sure you can."

She smiled and turned her chair toward Stuart as he got up and walked toward her. "So, what can I do for you today?"

"Well, my wife said not to cut it too short. I like it short but she doesn't, and she is the boss, so just a trim." Stuart gave himself a laugh hoping to incite a courtesy laugh from Carly, but he did not receive one. It always made Stuart feel uncomfortable when he didn't get a laugh from someone when he had clearly solicited one. Carly started to cut Stuart's hair, and he pretended to watch the football game on TV

When Carly finished, she turned Stuart around to the mirror to show him his haircut. Stuart pretended to look at the haircut. "I think my wife will approve." He gave himself a chuckle but found no courtesy laughter in response.

Carly smiled at Stuart. "I think you look cute with your hair short."

Stuart was amazed at the comment. Carly was looking right at him, so Stuart looked back at her eyes and could tell that she was flirting with him. He held her gaze for a moment, mesmerized by how pretty she was, and could not resist the temptation to look at her cleavage and beautiful breasts. Stuart felt his jeans tighten, and he quickly looked away. Just then, his phone rang. He could see that it was his wife calling and immediately felt an attack of irritable bowel syndrome. He rejected the call and paid Carly, who was still smiling at him. Now, a conflict raged in the jeans of Stuart Mendalson as he clenched his ass while trying to conceal his erection. Stuart focused on the door and got out of the barber shop as quickly as he could.

Stuart's wife, Judy, called again just as he got through the barber shop's door. Stuart quickly answered it. "Hi, Honey!"

"Why did you reject my call, Stuart?"

"I'm sorry, Honey, I was getting a haircut," Stuart responded.

"I hope they didn't cut it too short. My parents will be here tonight, and I can't have them thinking I married a skinhead. When will you be home?"

"I'm on my way now."

"Did you go to the store yet?"

"Oh, I didn't know you wanted me to go to the store. What do you need me to pick up?"

"I told you, Stuart. I'm baking a cake and need milk, eggs, and a green pepper for the casserole."

Stuart, knowing his wife had not mentioned the store before, responded, "Oh, yes. I'm sorry that I forgot. I'll go straight to the store and be home soon."

"Hurry up, Stuart," his wife demanded.

Stuart quickly did the shopping and went straight home. When he opened the front door, he smelled the sweet smell of cooking in the kitchen. He could hear his kids in the living room, playing a video game. Stuart briefly reflected on his own good fortune. "I'm home!"

He waited for a response but received none. He took off his coat, went into the kitchen and was surprised to see that his wife's parents were already there. Judy's mother, Mildred, was telling a story about the incompetence of the current White House administration. She paused very briefly, acknowledged Stuart, and continued her story.

Stuart walked over to shake hands with his half asleep father-in-law. "Hey, Jack. How are you?"

"I am well, Stuart. So, what are you handicapping now?" Jack had only two topics of discussion—golf and fishing. Judy rarely allowed Stuart to play golf, but he always pretended to Jack that he played more than he did.

"Well, Jack, my handicap hasn't changed much since the last time we played." He spoke the truth. It was the last time Stuart had played, although he didn't mention that fact.

"Well, we have to get back out there and play a round together," said Jack.

"I would like that, Jack."

Judy gave her husband an approving look, and Stuart felt good because he had pleased his wife, and life was much easier when she was pleased.

Stuart's mind wandered back to Carly as he joined Jack to watch the golf program. He allowed himself to fantasize. Once upon a time . . . in a land far, far away . . . a time when love spread throughout the lands . . . a profound experience occurred in the life of the great warrior know as STUART and the fairest of maidens in all the land, CARLY.

The epic tale unfolds with Stuart lying on a bed in his apartment . . . he is just hangin' out . . . thinking about having sex with Carly but not expecting anything unusual. Carly comes out of the bathroom without any clothes on . . . normally that would be no big deal . . . but it is . . . he is completely caught off guard and watches in awe as she walks from the bathroom to the bed, as if in slow motion. Stuart has seen naked women before but this time he is really affected . . . more than just, *oh, I have a pretty girl here and I get to fuck her* . . . something chemically triggers his mind. He thinks that she is the most beautiful girl he has ever lain eyes on. Stuart and Carly have sensational sex and lie naked, talking, joking, and having more sex all day.

Days later, Stuart closed his eyes and relived in perfect detail Carly's fantasy walk from the bathroom to the bed . . . and decided he'd better change barber shops!

WHEN A MAN MUST FACE
THE WORLD ALONE

It was a cold but sunny day in January when Freddy was released from prison. From his cell, he stared at the snow on the ground and knew that a cold world awaited him in more ways than one. He was happy to leave although he felt a little sad leaving behind some of the people who had become his friends. He knew that this was one of those times when he had to suck it up and face the outside world . . . and this time, alone. He couldn't take his new friends with him, and no one would be waiting for him at the door.

Freddy felt the love that most inmates feel on the day they leave prison. The man getting released is always the most popular guy, and everyone told him on his way out what a great guy he was. Freddy knew this wasn't true, but it felt good to hear anyway. He finally got his chance to walk out the front door and was surprised to find his beautiful mother waiting for him. He noticed immediately that her face was beginning to show the strain of time. It hurt Freddy to see that.

She smiled at him, gave Freddy a hug, and said, "Come on, honey, I'm taking you home."

Freddy hugged her tight and felt tears fall down his cheek. He hadn't spent a single moment in that place dignifying the thought of tears, but something about a hug from his mother forced it out of him.

They got into her car, which was brand new and expensive—very different from the one she used to drive. She had done well for herself although Freddy knew it had been no thanks to him. They drove to the house Freddy had once called home. As they walked through the door Freddy was overcome with thoughts of his past. It seemed like a lifetime ago when he had called this place home. He was a very different person then. Freddy could still see hints of the home he used to live in but changed with the addition of her new husband, Frank.

Frank was a good guy although very different from Freddy. Freddy often wished he could be a simple, laid back kind of guy with hobbies and a sense of purpose. He thought, *Maybe someday that will be the temperament I can adopt.*

Freddy felt from Frank a bit of jealousy, accompanied by a feeling of a cold welcome. He knew he wouldn't be staying there long, but he also knew his mother wanted to take care of him for a few days. Freddy spent three relaxing days with his mother and Frank, and then she drove him to his condo.

It had been quite some time since Freddy had been to the condo that he owned with his wife, Miranda. The place was almost empty, because Miranda had moved most everything to her new boyfriend's house. His mother helped him set up his few pieces of furniture and put the groceries she bought for him in the kitchen. He hugged her, thanked her for the help, and watched as she walked to her car. Freddy turned around and looked at his empty home. Sadness overcame him as he looked upon a home that used to be full of decorations and life. He thought about this empty shell of what used to be and he realized that he was once again alone. This time, though, he felt like it would be this way for a long time.

Freddy activated his old cell phone and called his old boss. He received the good news that he could start back at his old job immediately. After a few days, Miranda started to come around, and he was starting to see hope shining through. Freddy was working as much as his boss would let him and saving his money. He came up with an idea for making some big money. It was legal too, which was a plus because he still had five years back up time on his parole. Freddy started studying the stock market. He spent all of his spare time studying charts and reading books on how to become successful at trading stocks. He opened up an account with an online brokerage firm, deposited $1,000, and began to trade.

Freddy felt good about what he was doing, and every so often he would fantasize about his possible future. He could see himself eventually quitting his job and trading stocks full time. He was sure that once he had enough investment capital, he could make $5,000 to $10,000 per week. He needed a car but decided a truck was the way to go so he could haul things. He would be making good money, so it should be a luxury truck like a Cadillac Escalade. Freddy adored this idea.

Then he thought about how he would buy a nice house in the country but not too far out—more of a country house with a little land near the city. He knew just the area. Miranda would leave this guy she was with. She and Freddy would move into the house together and be so happy this time. The best part of his plan was that this would all be legal, and he would never have to go back to prison again.

On the first day of trading stocks, Freddy used his new-found knowledge to pick a stock. He was thrilled when it started going up. He watched it closely to be sure he could get out at just the right time. He sold the stock and was thrilled to see that he'd made $300 in just a few minutes. His confidence soared. He watched the stock go back down and saw an indicator in the chart that it was likely to bounce back up. He bought back in, but the stock continued to go down. He waited for the bounce. He knew better than to panic and sell right away. *That would be an amateur move,* he thought. The stock kept going down, more and more. Finally, Freddy panicked and sold the stock, losing all the money he had made and then some.

Freddy continued to use the strategy he had developed, and he found nothing but failure. He put more and more money in the account and lost more and more. Freddy decided that he could not successfully trade until he had more capital to work with. The percentage gains needed to profit on a trade were just too high with so little money invested. Freddy was disappointed and needed to come up with some other way to get the money he needed.

Freddy was seeing Miranda every day now. They were looking at houses to rent after she moved out of her boyfriend's house. She made it clear that it was Freddy she wanted to be with but she said they needed to do it right. Their condo, where Freddy was living, was in foreclosure, so she didn't want to move back in and then have to move out when they found a new house. He didn't like the situation of her continuing to live with another man, but he wanted to believe everything Miranda told him.

One Saturday night, when Miranda's boyfriend was out of town on a fishing trip, Miranda went over to the condo and was very excited. Two of their old friends were coming into town, and they planned to go out and party like they used to. Freddy made a few calls to some other old friends. They were all set to meet up at the restaurant where they used to party when things were very different. Freddy liked the idea but he also worried there might be problems. *Things are very different now, and this party could go bad*, Freddy thought.

When he showed up at the restaurant, everyone was there, and they were drinking heavily. They were all happy to see him and told him how healthy he looked. Freddy was no longer the drug-addled fool he'd once been, and they were impressed. Freddy ordered a beer and sat down to join the party. Things were going well and everyone was having fun. Sara, a good friend of Miranda's, started flirting with Freddy, which he enjoyed but didn't feed into too much. Another friend, Judy, whom Freddy knew to be a little crazy, was dominating the conversation. She started talking about Miranda's relationship with her husband-to-be and how it was such a great relationship. Judy complimented Freddy on how mature he was about Miranda finding a new love and remaining such good friends. In a casual and matter of fact kind of way, everything Judy said completely contradicted what Miranda had been telling Freddy! Freddy began feeling angry, but more than that, he felt stupid and hurt, and he began drinking his beer in gulps.

When Freddy could take no more of Judy's critique of Miranda's great new relationship, he got up and went to the other side of the pub to find Sara, who gave him a pretty smile. Freddy went straight to her, gave her a hug. "God, Sara, you are looking good tonight."

Freddy could feel her large silicone filled breasts pressing against his chest. His jeans got tight, and he gently kissed her neck. He looked into her eyes and could see that she was begging him to kiss her mouth. Without thinking, Freddy reached around, squeezed her soft round ass, and pressed his erection into her small body. He quickly realized what he was doing and tore himself away. He returned to the group's table, hoping the conversation had changed, only to hear Judy still casually tearing Freddy's heart out. Freddy left the table, this time avoiding Sara, and joined a table of drunk guys to have easier conversation, but all he could think about was how good it would feel to fuck Sara. Freddy had not been inside a woman in a long time.

Freddy convinced himself, "Why shouldn't I? Why shouldn't two adults with no commitments do what their bodies are telling them to do? Miranda is so in love with her fucking boyfriend, so fuck it. Sara is staying with me tonight."

The bartender yelled, "Last call!" and the lights went on.

Everyone was drunk and the atmosphere was full of laughter and sorrow that they had to leave. Freddy's group came together to figure out how they would get home. Since Sara was supposed to spend the night at Miranda's, it was decided that Freddy and Sara would ride with Miranda. Freddy was to be dropped off at the condo alone.

On the way to the car, Freddy quietly told Sara, "You are staying at my place tonight. You want to right?"

"I want to very much, Freddy, but how?"

Freddy said, "Just follow my lead," as he kissed her neck.

Freddy's jeans tightened up again. Sara put her hand on Freddy's erection. "I cannot wait to have you inside of me, Freddy."

"Just follow my lead and it won't be long."

Miranda drove to their condo and said, "Good night, Freddy, it was fun to have you with us, honey."

That made Freddy pause, but he had made up his mind.

Freddy said, "Wait a second."

He got out of the car and walked around to Sara's door. He opened the door. "Come on, Sara, you're staying here tonight."

Sara quickly got out of the car and followed Freddy, careful not to look at Miranda. They walked to the condo, and Freddy opened the door.

Just as he was about to close the door, Miranda stopped it with her foot and pushed her way in. "What the hell are you doing, Freddy?"

"I'm doing what single people do, Miranda. Clearly you have a wonderful relationship with your boyfriend. That means that I am free to do what I want to do."

Miranda looked over at Sara, who was pretending to be passed out on the couch.

"Is this what you want, Sara?"

Freddy interrupted, "She wants to stay here. Now go home to your boyfriend's house."

"I was talking to Sara. Is this what you want, Sara?"

Sara murmured to Miranda, "I am just going to sleep on this couch."

Miranda was livid and started yelling obscenities at both of them.

Through a clenched jaw, Freddy said, "Shut up, Miranda! Making a scene won't do you any good. It's late and neither of us wants the neighbors to call the cops."

Freddy knew that the condo was in foreclosure but Miranda's name was still on the title, so he also knew she wouldn't want any trouble. Miranda gave them both her best "I hate you" glare and left.

As soon as the door closed, Sara sat up, looked at Freddy, and smiled. Freddy walked over and gave her a long, sensual kiss. He pulled away, then said, "How about some wine?"

Sara and Freddy drank wine and made love all night. Immersed in the moment, they didn't speak of the possible repercussions. They enjoyed a night neither would ever forget.

Miranda showed up very early the next morning to pick up Sara. Freddy was disappointed because he had hoped they would spend the day together. After Sara left, it occurred to Freddy that Miranda had come so early because her boyfriend was on his way home, and he expected Sara to be there. Miranda wouldn't want to have to explain where Sara was. *More evidence of how deep Miranda's deceit goes,* Freddy thought.

Freddy spent the majority of the day nursing his hangover and thinking about his night with Sara. He heard nothing from Miranda. On the third day, Miranda called Freddy and said, "I cannot believe what you have done. I have put up with your drug use and womanizing for a long time. This is the final straw. I am done with you, Freddy! I am done! Fully and completely! Do not ever call me again!"

Several days went by and he heard nothing from anyone. He felt more and more alone. It had been six months since the day he was released from prison. Freddy counted his money and realized he had managed to save very little. He looked at the condo he lived in and realized how little it had changed since the first day he had gotten there after his release. He knew that this was one of those times in a man's life when he must face the world alone.

I found the following short passage, dated October 2011, on David's laptop:

"The Old Man walked on up his front porch and sat on the porch swing. "Is that you Honey?" He heard his wife Mabel holler from inside the kitchen." "Yea Darlin, I'm home," the Old Man said. "Did you have a good day at work, sweetie? Mabel said as she handed him a glass of iced tea and sat next to him on the swing. "Weren't much different than any other day. 'Cept one strange feller come into the station. Don't know Mabel, this Man just weren't right," the Old Man said as he sat looking . . . "

This passage touched me and needed to be finished in the spirit of how David wrote his stories. David wrote a lot about dreams. I titled and finished "Finding Freddy" to create my dream vision of David's journey from addiction to recovery.

There is no doubt that David was thinking of his maternal

grandparents when he drafted this passage about an Old Man. My
father, Joe, owned and operated a service station for 33 years. My
mother's name was Millie, and she had a sister named Mabel.

FINDING FREDDY

PART 1

The Old Man walked up onto his front porch and sat on the porch swing.

"Is that you, Honey?" his wife Mabel hollered from the kitchen.

"Yeah, Darlin', I'm home."

"Did you have a good day at work, sweetie?" She handed him a glass of iced tea and sat next to him on the swing.

"Weren't much different than any other day, 'cept a strange feller came into the station and I can't seem to get him out of my mind. I don't know, Mabel. This young man just weren't right," the Old Man said as he sat looking down at his worn out shoes.

"Well, what in particular made you think he weren't right?" Mabel asked.

"His eyes . . . his eyes were glazed and sad, like deep pools of misery," replied the Old Man. Misery was not a stranger to Buck and Mabel, but Buck recognized a different kind of misery in the strange feller who came into the station that day.

Buck continued, "He said his name was Freddy, just passing through, hoping to find his destination soon, with no mention of where that destination might be."

The Old Man immediately liked Freddy, which was unusual, but he felt like he knew him before they even spoke, and his antenna went up for the son he'd lost. Buck had to smile at the way Freddy twisted his body when he picked up a bag of Skittles and tossed them deftly behind his back from one hand to the other, then simply dropped them on the counter beside his large coffee laced with enough vanilla creamer and sugar to bake a cake.

Freddy glanced back at Buck and grinned, "How much do I owe ya?"

Mabel studied her husband, who had that faraway look in his eyes that she had seen before. "Did you get to talk to him?" she asked.

"Not much, just enough to check him out at the register."

Mabel and Buck sat quietly on the porch swing, enjoying the summer evening and drinking their cool iced tea, each absorbed in their own thoughts.

Buck wasn't much of a talker, and he regretted that he had let the young man leave without finding out more about him, but what difference would it have made? This guy wasn't staying in town. He was just passing through. Wouldn't make a difference whether he got to know him, and the more he thought about it, the more he was sure that this young feller was not Luke reincarnated. But he did have those strange eyes. Maybe he was a doper . . . yeah, that was it, he was probably a doper. The Old Man couldn't tolerate dopers.

It was not unusual when the sheriff came into the station the next day. Buck liked the sheriff; he had a pretty little wife and two young boys who loved to play baseball. Every once in a while, Buck would wander over to the field to watch them play and wondered if Luke would have ever taken up baseball. Truth is, he secretly liked to pretend that he was their grandpa watching the game. Every once in a while, when they caught a high fly or got a base hit, he caught them checking to see if he was watching—that really made his day! But he was careful not get too close. So, when he saw Sheriff Liming come through the door, he half expected to see one or both of the boys, but the sheriff was by himself and obviously on town business.

"Morning, Buck," said the sheriff. "Seen any strangers lately?"

"None who are hanging around. Being on the main road, I get a lot of passers through," replied Buck.

"Yeah, I know," said the sheriff, "but I got a call from the State guys and they lost the chase to a young feller who they think might be pushing dope out this way. Just keep your eye out and give me a call if a young stranger stops in. This guy will probably just be passing through."

The sheriff got himself a cup of coffee and took his usual seat in the front of the station where there was a breeze. Before long he was joined by Stuart, the barber next door, and Lily, who ran the diner across the street. Buck heard the sheriff telling Stuart and Lily to be on the lookout for the stranger. It wouldn't be long before the lookout for a young stranger would be the talk of the town.

Buck wondered, *Why didn't I tell the sheriff about the young feller who came in yesterday?*

Late in the afternoon, the skies grew dark, and a storm rumbled on the horizon. It had been humid and hot for days and made the oil and gas stick to the old man's skin, which was now like leather. His fingernails got black underneath from spending so much time under the hoods of cars, but each evening he made sure to shower and scrub himself fresh before he sat down for dinner with Mabel.

Mabel was a good country cook and could work wonders with a lima bean. He planted and worked the garden, then reaped the benefits at Mabel's table. It had been just the two of them for 40 years. Not for lack of trying. The good Lord just hadn't seen fit to give them another chance after Luke. Buck knew Mabel suffered the absence of children, but she kept her feelings to herself.

The storm was well past by the time dinner was done and cleared away, so Buck and Mabel sat in the swing as was their routine on summer nights.

Mabel was unusually fidgety this evening, to the point where Buck had to ask her, "Something bothering you?"

She squirmed even more.

Buck could see the sweat droplets that dotted her brow. "Mabel, what in hell is wrong with you tonight?"

She avoided his question and his eyes and attempted to get up from the swing. He held her down, forcing her to look at him. Mabel started to cry, not just a tearful whimper, but a howling, aching cry. Buck instantly pulled back, afraid she would break if he pushed her. He let her go. Mabel stumbled from the swing and disappeared into the darkened house. Buck waited to go in until the moon came around the corner of the porch.

The service station business is an early morning business, and that suited Buck just fine. He liked to be up before the sun so that when he arrived at the diner, ate his two eggs, two strips of bacon, and buttered toast, and finally sat back satisfied to finish the hot cup of coffee that Lily always kept filled, it would be about time to watch the sun rise over the station. *Pure heaven*, Buck often thought. *Pure heaven*. But not this morning.

Mabel had locked the bedroom door last night. Even with his pleadings, she wouldn't let him in and wouldn't say what was wrong with her. Finally, near midnight, he gave up and sacked out in the spare room. This morning he didn't even try to talk to Mabel when he saw the door still closed. It wasn't unusual for Buck to begin his day before Mabel got up, so he just went about his normal routine.

Mabel knew that even though Buck was a fine and gentle man, he wasn't going to tolerate being thrown out of his bedroom two nights in a row, especially without knowing why. She also knew that he was genuinely worried about her, and she couldn't let that go on. But how could she possibly tell Buck that the stranger named Freddy was sleeping in their garage? Like Buck, when she opened the front door and saw the strange young feller standing on the front porch, she felt like she already knew him, and she did . . . kind of.

After Luke passed, Mabel found life unbearable. She could find solace nowhere. Buck was helpless to help her. The Vietnam War lingered, and Buck had orders to report overseas. Buck was scared sick to leave Mabel, but he had to. It was 1968, and the draft lottery gave him a low number. Didn't matter that he had to leave a wife with no family after losing her only child in a bizarre accident. Much of Buck's guilt over the last 40 years was not only about leaving Mabel in such a state but also about feeling relieved to go. As much as he loved Luke and as difficult as his death had been, he'd found a way to grieve and to replace future dreams for Luke with cherished memories of his two-and-a-half years on earth. Mabel couldn't do that and, deep down, held a grudge that Buck could.

Eight and a half months after Buck's departure for Vietnam, Mabel gave birth to another son. Mabel never told Buck about the baby, because she gave him away. She had to. Mabel could not bear the thought of loving another child and then losing him. Mabel was sure that son now stood on the other side of her screened door and his name was Freddy.

Freddy had told Buck the truth—he was in search of a destination. As Buck had described to Mabel, Freddy's eyes were glazed and sad, and his shoulders were weighted down with unknown burdens. Mabel's heart twisted with a powerful ache, and her eyes filled with tears as she looked at Freddy through the screened door.

"Hello, Ma'am. Any chance you need some chores taken care of in exchange for dinner?" Freddy asked.

"Why, no. My husband takes care of the yard and garden," said Mabel.

Looking Freddy over, Mabel noticed his large hands, especially the backs of his hands, which were swollen and red.

Mabel shifted her weight and tilted her head. "On second thought, I've been wanting to clean out the garage. Maybe you could help me with the sweeping and getting some of the clutter boxed up."

Freddy gave Mabel a smile that melted her heart, and they set to work in the garage while Grover, Buck's old hound dog, kept watch.

PART 2

Freddy woke up with a start and had to remind himself where he was. He looked around the small room and thanked the Lord that it wasn't a jail cell. Then he remembered the night before when Buck's truck rolled across the field, puffs of dirt following close behind. Freddy was in the garage leaning against his broom, Grover's paw resting on the top of his foot. The sun was slowly going down on the front side of the house. When Buck got out of the truck, he stood in the shadows, but Freddy recognized him as the service station guy. Grover darted out of the garage to greet Buck.

Mabel came out from the kitchen just in time to make introductions, "Freddy, this is my husband, Buck. Freddy has been helping me get some of the clutter cleaned out of the garage, and he fixed the fence."

Stretching out his hand and looking Buck in the eye, Freddy said, "Nice to meet you . . . again."

Mabel tried to look surprised as she shifted her eyes from Freddy to Buck. "Have you two already met?"

"Yep," Buck answered with a frown. "Remember, I told you about the young stranger in town? Well, this is him."

"Oh, yes . . ." feigned Mabel.

Freddy pulled his hand back and thought to himself, *This isn't going so well, probably wasn't such a good idea to stay around.*

After he'd helped for a couple of hours in the garage the day before, Mabel kept her promise and gave him dinner—Freddy's first home cooked meal in a very long time. As he ate, they talked some, and Mabel explained that her husband would be home soon and she would wait and have dinner with him. Freddy could see that Mabel was a little agitated and nervous—like she was doing something wrong behind her husband's back, which he guessed, she technically was. Freddy had felt an instant comfort level with Mabel and thought she did with him too, so he didn't want to cause her problems.

"I better get going," Freddy said as he stood up from the chair.

"Where are you headed?" asked Mabel.

"I'm not sure." He wished he could tell her what he was running from.

"Well, if you're not sure and don't have to be anywhere anytime soon, maybe you could stay on for a few days and help me with a couple more projects."

Freddy couldn't believe his ears and was about to decline when she continued, "If you don't mind sleeping on a cot, you can sack out in that little room you just swept out. It isn't much, but I'll get you a clean sheet and towel and you can use the laundry tub over in the corner to wash up."

Freddy was tired, not so much physically tired—the afternoon's physical labor had felt good—but too much idle time in jail had messed with his sleep cycle, and when he did sleep, his dreams didn't allow him to rest. What made it worse, was that he could never remember his dreams, and that bothered him. His belly was full and the offer of a quiet room to himself was hard to pass up.

"Ummm, I don't know . . . maybe you should check with your husband first. I don't want him upset with you because of me."

"Oh, best not to mention it to him just yet. Let's get a little more work done, and when he sees what a great job we did, he'll be a little more receptive to my letting you stay and help out."

Freddy didn't know what to do. He wasn't accustomed to being trusted—hell, he wasn't even sure he could trust himself. He could remember a time when it wasn't that way, maybe this time would be different. What he did know was that for some reason this woman trusted him and he didn't want to let her down.

"OK, if you're sure. I could use a good night's rest. I've been sleeping in my car."

"Good. It's settled then. I'll go get your sheets and towels while you get set up."

Freddy couldn't believe his good fortune and didn't want to screw it up. He put the cot by a set of metal shelves where he put a lantern for light so he could read. A real bonus was the small window where he had the pleasure of watching the dark clouds build up and a storm roll in. Thirty minutes later, Freddy was sound asleep.

Buck turned to Freddy and said, "Thought you were just passing through."

Freddy knew he had to be very careful with his answer. "Yeah, I was, but I'm running low on cash. It's just a coincidence that I chose your house to stop at and ask if I could earn a meal. I ain't had nothin' but Skittles and coffee for the past couple of days."

Buck gave Freddy a hard look. "The sheriff tells me that the state guys are on the look-out for a guy suspected of pushing dope out this way. Know anything about that?"

Oh shit! Freddy thought to himself. *Buck is never going to believe that's who I'm trying to avoid. Oh shit, shit, shit . . . Motherfucker!! Can't I get some peace!*

How could Freddy explain to Buck that when he walked out of the D.C. DOC, his old dealer, Eddie, was sitting in his fancy new Cadillac waiting for him. Freddy knew that as much as he wanted to get out of that hell hole of a pig pen, he was walking out to a world that didn't want him back.

During his last heroin binge and before he went to jail the last time, Freddy destroyed just about every one of his relationships—the good ones, that is. While he was inside, he even managed to piss off his mother, and he wouldn't be able to make up with her this time. She'd died two months after he went into the system. Heart attack . . . a Goddamned heart attack!

Freddy had known something must have been terribly wrong when his name was called over the pod's loudspeaker, instructing him to report to the visitor's area. His father was there but it wasn't a visiting day, and his father had *never* come to visit him in jail. A retired cop, his father didn't try to hide his disgust as Freddy approached the glass that separated them. There would be no hug or sad eyes, just "Thought you should know and good-bye."

Freddy was devastated, but he had to hold strong to survive the next eight months in the animal house. He would grieve when he got out. Any sign of weakness now would destroy the reputation he had built since his arrival. No one fucked with him, and he wanted to keep it that way.

Freddy had learned some time ago that he was adopted, which helped him handle his father's lack of feeling for him, but Freddy knew his adoptive mother loved him and he would miss her. She would have been there waiting for him like she had done so many times before. This time, he knew he would have to face the world alone. He also knew that one hit of heroin, just one lousy hit, would put him right back there . . . or eventually kill him.

As Freddy walked out the prison door, Eddie caught his eye and with a sly smile waved a tiny baggie at him. *What to do? What to do? What do I do? I promised myself that, this time, I would not forget the pain and anguish I've put myself through because of what's inside of that baggie!* He had to avoid that puffy cloud!

Freddy looked away from Eddie and ran as fast as he could for as long as he could. When he finally looked back, there was no Eddie.

Buck didn't make a move as he closely watched Freddy. "Well, are you the doper the sheriff is looking for?"

Mabel moved between them. "Buck, leave him alone. He's been a perfect gentleman. He's on the road and needed a meal, which he earned. That's all."

Freddy looked down as Grover nudged his hand, hoping for a scratch behind his ear.

Buck gently took Mabel's elbow and pulled her around behind him.

"I'm asking you again. Are you the doper they are looking for?"

"No."

Buck rubbed the stubble on his cheek and chin. "Then what's your business here? Where's your destination?"

"I don't have business here, and I don't know my destination. As I told you when I came into the station, I'm just passing through."

All the tactics that Freddy had taught himself to adjust to in jail, rehab, and living with roommates deserted him. He could not . . . he didn't want to bullshit his way out of this situation. He wanted these people to like him. *Jesus, like me? Who am I?*

Buck gave out a heavy sigh, turned, and started to steer Mabel toward the door from the garage to the kitchen.

Freddy took a small step but quickly stopped when Buck swung back around. He looked at Buck, speaking quietly. "It could be that the guy they are looking for is looking for me. I owe him money. He may have followed me after I got on the road, but since I don't know where I'm going, neither does he. I don't think he knows I stopped at your station because when I was leaving, I saw his car speed by on the main road. He didn't see me. I'm sure about that because I waited and he didn't turn around. I thought it would be a good idea to let him get a couple days ahead, so I stayed around, or maybe he isn't even looking for me. I don't owe him enough for him to follow me too far. He is a drug dealer. I can give the sheriff information on him and the car if that's what you think I should do."

Buck nodded toward his truck, and he and Freddy left.

Freddy met with the sheriff and gave him all the information he had about Eddie, which wasn't much more than his name, where he lived, the color of Eddie's new Cadillac, and the sad history of their dealer/user relationship. Freddy decided to use the meeting to confess to the sheriff and Buck that he was on the road because he had just gotten out of prison for possession of heroin and that he was indeed running away to escape a cycle of addiction that was going to kill him if he did not find a way to free himself.

Once Freddy started talking, he couldn't stop. He felt a flood of relief overcome him as he bawled like a baby and told his story—his *real story*.

Buck and the sheriff were mesmerized as the words poured uncontrollably out of Freddy.

Freddy had told his patented drug story many times while in jail and rehab, and to NA groups, only to return to numbing himself with heroin and empty boasts that he knew who he was . . . how special he was . . . his ability to perceive the truth . . . how he could *just be* and control the confusion and chaos of any situation. But *now,* by some miracle, the real story dissolved the old story as Freddy freed his mind, bringing peace to replace the pain-versus-pleasure battle that had raged within him for years. Freddy did not understand why or how, but he wasn't going to let the gorilla find him again.

PART 3

"Are you ready, Freddy?"

"Ready for what?"

"To go to heaven . . . "

"Whoa . . . wait . . . let me remember, please let me remember!"

Freddy opened his eyes and saw his wife sleeping soundly beside him. Dawn was just lighting up their bedroom when the voice woke him. *Am I ready . . . to go to heaven?* Freddy thought to himself.

What the fuck?! Is this some kind of an omen? The first dream—if it could be called that—I can remember in forever, and it's asking if I'm ready to go to heaven?! Too strange, too strange . . .

Freddy slipped out of bed without waking Becci and got in the shower. As he reached for the towel, the phone rang. Freddy checked the screen. It was Buck. He smiled—only Buck would have the guts to call him this early.

"Hey, Buck! What's happening so early this Tuesday morning?!"

After a few seconds, Buck said, "Freddy, I have bad news."

Freddy felt chills run down his spine. "What? What's happened?"

"It's Mabel, Freddy. She just passed."

"Oh no, nooooo, no—it can't be! Oh, please, please, noooo!"

Buck waited on the line until Freddy calmed down. Becci took the phone and asked Buck if he was all right. Buck said he would be. Becci promised that Freddy would call him back in a little while.

After Freddy's *true confession* in front of the sheriff, Buck took him back home to Mabel, who nursed him mentally and physically. Within a short time, Freddy's glazed and sad eyes sparkled bright. For the first few weeks, he and Mabel cleaned and fixed everything they could find. Staying busy was Mabel's motto for recovery.

Freddy and Buck pitched the baseball back and forth in the yard, and often walked over to the local baseball field to watch a game. They became a family and added a little friend for Grover, whom they called Mr. Boodle. Freddy continued to sleep in the garage room until he and Buck built a small studio close to the house where Freddy could work, sleep, and *just be.* After a few months, Freddy settled down enough to start the book that he had carried in his head for years.

Freddy, still plagued by insomnia and dreams that he couldn't remember, told himself he was living a dream each day, so it didn't matter what he couldn't remember. Triggers to Freddy's old life surfaced less and less, but he remained alert and motivated to fight the urges because he knew they could creep into his brain and take over at any second. Freddy's revelations in the sheriff's office kept him vigilant, along with his mantra:

IF WE FREE OUR MINDS, WE CAN FREE OURSELVES.

POETRY

David was about 11 when he wrote the untitled poem below.
He and I were sitting on the front step on a late summer evening,
watching the moon rise. "The Match" and "Analogy of a Soldier"
were written while he was in high school.

UNTITLED POEM

The moon's gleaming kalsomined body
Looks like an exquisite sculpture.
When night falls,
It creeps out and turns everything into a silhouette,
Casting its brilliant beams across the land and sky
Creating a beautiful atmosphere.

THE MATCH

Total darkness,
I see no pain, no suffering,
I feel free because I can't
See any obstacles.

Everything seems beautiful
Because darkness hides
The ugly things.

Strike, goes the match,
Providing sight and knowledge,
But as the flame nourishes my eyes,
I feel hatred,
I see dirt and scum everywhere.

I see people killing people
For no reason,
I see people holding me back,
Trying to keep me from myself.

I wish I had never seen through this light.
Everything is so dreadful
When you open your eyes.

God, I wish I had never given life
To this evil fire.
The flame slowly burns out.
Again, I reach total darkness.
Beauty is restored!

ANALOGY OF A SOLDIER

The troops pile on the bus
Going to the big game,
They're backed with many men
And they're ready to fight.

After a long ride,
They arrive on the battlefield,
The game is just starting for them
Although it has been going on for years.

They've practiced long and hard to get ready,
Now, the time has finally arrived
To kick off the first battle,
Sending their fastest and toughest to start,
To run down and put away the opponent,
The enemy.

The crowd cheers them on,
It's a brutal battle,
They are losing men left and right,
I just put out my first man, who cares?
He's the enemy, right?

It's not fun anymore.
The crowd is booing them.
They are losing.

The taste of blood is in my mouth.
I've been hit, it's not so bad though,
A drink to refresh me, a drug to forget.

I wouldn't touch it before I came,
But now it's my escape,
From the hell of this game,
And being here so long,
Could I be addicted to what kept me strong?

Through this experience,
I've met a lot of friends,
Most of them are gone now,
I don't worry about them,
Just hope they made it out alive.

Fourth quarter,
I don't think we're gonna win,
Even so, we continue the game.

Finally we leave to see our families.
It's over, we are going home,
Started with 200 men, now 27.
Amazing
How a human can lose so many friends
And remain sane.
Is that possible?

We arrive home,
Loved ones greet us at the bus,
Such a great feeling to see them,
It's been so long.

We almost forget about the game,
Then peer off in the distance,
Large groups of people
arching toward us,
Yelling and holding up signs.

We can't read the signs,
Can't understand
What's being shouted
But my heart tells me,
These people are upset.

I move my family aside,
To understand
What these people want.
Could it be they are here
To welcome us home?

A short old woman throws something toward us.
All the marchers reach down,
Picking up rocks and throwing them at us,
Why?! I wonder
As I make for cover.

Do they hate us because we lost?
Are they worried?
So many got hurt,
My mind is total confusion.
We went for them, no congratulations?
Aren't we heroes?!

Soon it was all explained to me.
People are mad that we went to the game,
But we had no choice,
We were forced to go.
When I left,
I was a hero.

Now that we're back,
Hippie spiritualists
Proclaiming it all wrong,
God, please explain to me,
I am so confused.

Years have passed,
That hellacious game still with me,
Every day, every hour,
Can't get a job,
Still addicted to what kept me strong.

End of the game,
My life not worth shit,
I feel nothing,
I love nothing,
I hate everything!

EvERytHing iS going In CIrclEs
WhaT aM I? WheRe aM I?

A NOOSE!!!

David's stories, poetry, and letters frame who he was.
What he was thinking. His ideas, dreams, and nightmares.
For a high school poetry assignment, he wrote the following
untitled poem that spelled my name in code.

Pushing me through life is a woman
Who always keeps me out of trouble
And she tries to help me in any way she can.
Although she is the most stubborn person you'll ever
Meet, she can be really sensitive to my needs.
I know that she likes excitement, even though she doesn't
Show it. I sometimes have a fear of her, because she can be
Vicious. Other times I know she'll understand right away.
She is my mom and I love her, you'd love her too.

SPORTS

Any story about David would have to include sports, especially
his love of football and baseball. He started playing T-ball
when he was four and ankle-biter football when he was six.
He played both sports through high school.

Boys
strong, mighty
running, jumping, playing
football, baseball, makeup, clothes
walking, talking, laughing
graceful, cute
girls

Football
fun, exciting
throwing, tackling, kicking
Riggins, Bosworth, Dr. J, Spud Webb
running, jumping, passing
enjoyable, great
Basketball

EXTREMITY

I began as a small baby,
I was a person the rest of my life.
I started to walk,
I ran the rest of my life.
I learned to speak,
I yelled the rest of my life.
I learned to drive,
I crashed the rest of my life.
I started getting older,
I felt old the rest of my life.
I tried drinking,
I was drunk the rest of my life.
I LOVED once,
I HATED the rest of my life.

SO SELDOM MY THOUGHTS RING TRUE

Swimming through my thoughts,
The answers elude my every try.

I escape my attempts,
Just so I can get by.

The rooster crows at dawn,
But I only want to sleep.

I search my mind for something to grasp,
Even if it's a lie.

I shudder at the thought,
Of joining the other sheep.

The lies I tell myself,
Are better than theirs.

I can confuse, and
Push their thoughts down the stairs.

To only assure me,
I remain alone.

PLAGUE OF UNCERTAINTY

I suffer from a sickness, I know this is true
No complete truth ever comes into view
This sickness is my truest burden to bear
I go to the booth and I pay my fare.

Never quite sure how to pick the right show
Never am I certain, never do I know
The plague of uncertainty
Is the condition I have.

For this sickness,
I know of no tonic, no balm, no pill
I am truly not sad, I don't even feel blue
I simply do not know what it is I should do.

FACEBOOK CONFUSION

Tread lightly my friend
Facebook will take your soul
Not like a drug or a woman
Facebook won't TAKE your soul,
It will appear that . . .

Soon the illusion seems to be the truth
Confusion will dominate your thoughts
Without warning, seemingly and tragically
YOUR SOUL YOU WILL GIVE TO IT!!!!!

Tread lightly my friend
"'Tis a dark and narrow path you walk"
Float well my friend.
"'Tis deep and murky waters you sail"

What?
What was I saying?
What is this place?
I am confused . . .

ESSAYS / THOUGHTS / PHILOSOPHIES

*In November 2011, David had a long string of Facebook messages
with a friend about many topics that provides
a window into where his philosophies came from.
Excerpts from David's responses include:*

"I never lock myself into any predetermined political construct, I gotta remain objective . . . capitalism breeds greed for sure, that is why all anyone cares about is money . . . I don't like government; I believe in teaching children how to become enlightened, this is the future . . . objective truth, this is what we must see but our perspectives are skewed by greed and propaganda . . . I still have to function in this world and Buddhism is not often applicable, but the more people who become enlightened the easier it will become; right now ignorance is King but I have faith in mankind . . . I am not a Buddhist, I am just a seeker of truth; I don't go around preaching these things . . . I don't talk about politics because as long as we have this system then I will not partake in it . . . Mercedes makes the best cars, of course I would drive one, but I won't lust to portray an image . . . *Plato's Republic*, some people think that is where Karl Marx got his inspiration, but books are only guides, we must think for ourselves and do that thinking without perspective; free your mind and the rest will follow, that much I know . . . I got high and read Nietzsche . . . I am not defending my heroin use but I wasn't out partying and shit . . . we are all one thing, completely and totally; when one person suffers then a wave of negative energy flows into the world . . . I dislike our system; these people took everything from me; I wasn't stealing or hurting anyone; I did not deserve what I got and am still getting . . . I feel anger inside me when I think about these things. I cannot allow anger to infiltrate my mind. That is a downward spiral and I will not indulge it . . . we all have our struggles, it's what you do about it and how you cope that matters . . . Just do this for me, try to identify when you are coping with suffering, like when you feel lonely, do you seek attention? When you are angry, do you take it out on people? Just try to become aware of your actions, don't try to change them, just try to understand them. Once you understand why you do the things you do, then you can find solutions . . . find your coping mechanisms . . . take back your energy, we have to learn that we have our own energy factories within us, we don't need to put someone down to feel good . . . guard your happiness and sense of freedom with your life . . . just let it all go, then you will be free to be anything."

David wrote "The Snooze Button" in 1994, when he was staying with his brother. He had graduated from high school and attended classes at the local community college, but he had not found direction for his life.

THE SNOOZE BUTTON

Today, the tenth of November, I rose from the couch at 6:45 a.m. I did so with the intention of using the shower before my brother, so I would not cause him to be late. But, as I arose, I heard him entering the shower so I then proceeded to hit the snooze button. Nine minutes later I was again awakened to the sound of my alarm clock. I could hear he was still in the shower so I hit the button again. I can see now that if I persist at this rate of extreme detail, I shall never finish.

We then arrived at the office where my dad was surprised to see me. It was raining and you cannot do termite work in the rain. My beloved father then, with all of his keen knowledge, rerouted his schedule to bring maximum effectiveness to his time. We then proceeded to go to Maryland, near Rosecroft Raceway, to a condo complex. We climbed ladders and scraped shit off of the windowsills. The pizza has just arrived and the dork pizza man just gave us a lot more information than we needed to receive a pizza!

David's essay on aging is a true account of a visit with his maternal grandparents during the fall of 1995. The essay gives insight into his thoughts on the aging process and the pressure of time.

AGING

There comes a time in the life of every living creature when old age sets in and the senses that have always been taken for granted begin to deteriorate. It was my grandmother's birthday, and the whole family was getting together for a cookout. I was standing in the kitchen where my grandmother stood making hamburger patties and my grandfather sat at the kitchen table, sipping his iced tea. My mother and aunt were discussing the new oven my grandmother had gotten and how nice it was. The only problem, my grandmother explained, was her old oven was 36 inches wide and these days, they only make ovens 30 inches wide. This left a three inch gap on each side of the new oven.

I told them that I could move the oven flush to one counter top, put a six inch filler on the cabinet face, and replace the small counter top with one six inches longer. Since the next day was my grandmother's real birthday, I offered to do it for her then. I took some measurements and told her I would go to the hardware store first thing in the morning. I would get to her house around 11:00. She said she wouldn't be home, but my grandfather would be there. He would help me out. My grandfather smiled and nodded.

The next day I showed up and my grandfather seemed especially glad to see me. He looked at the supplies I had and asked me what I was doing there. Apparently, he hadn't heard any of the conversation and had no idea of what we had talked about. At the top of my voice, I explained what I was doing. While I did the work, he went downstairs to watch television. The whole house shook from the sounds of the Channel 4 news. When I finished, my grandfather thanked me, and I headed home.

When I got home, my dog Patches was at the front door to greet me. I petted her and walked into the kitchen. Patches was still sniffing around the front door looking for me. She's 14 years old and blind as a bat. I called, "Come here, girl," and she started running toward the sound of my voice with a big smile on her face. Right as she got to the kitchen, she missed the hallway opening and went face first into the living room wall.

With modern medicine we can keep life going, but we can't stop the aging process. It happens so gradually that we don't realize how bad our senses have become. The body simply cannot handle the pressure of time.

SPINNING, OR THE EARTH DAY/NIGHT CYCLE SLEEP PROCESS

Every morning I have always gotten ready with the sounds of California Punk Rock, but lately, every night I have only wanted to go to sleep to the sounds of Bob Dylan. I was pondering this fact and came to this conclusion:

I think every morning I experience the delusion of hope and every night I experience the realization of truth. There is a definite difference in perspective in these time periods . . . so my real question would be this . . . if the spinning of my planet in relation to a giant fireball, i.e., day/night and the process of sleep having that profound of an impact on my perspective, then how can I trust my own thoughts?

HATE COPS

Posted by Socrates H. Dillinger on Facebook, May 2010

HATE COPS and anyone who acts like one. They are professional tattle-tales. And that is the truth. I know you have probably met some cops that were cool and don't agree. That, my friends, is their fundamental problem. Cops are the quintessential example of the friendly rattlesnake. They act all cool and then they turn on you. They will run and tell on you and do it in the name of righteousness. That is the problem I have with them. Believe me, I know several cops, I cut their hair all the time. I became very friendly with several when I was locked up. Shit, my father is one. It is not because they are not cool. It is because they can't be trusted with anything. ANYTHING. Always keep a cop at arm's distance, if not further. Trust me, if not, don't say I didn't tell you.

CURE FOR CONFUSION

Confusion consumes my mind. I step out of the library to smoke. It is a beautiful day, but I can't seem to appreciate it. I close my eyes and envision myself floating on a raft. The raft is sinking low in the water from my weight. I brush the burdens from my shoulders; they fall into the water and wash up on the nearby shore. The raft now floats with ease. I open my eyes and feel the sun shine warm upon my face. I feel a cool breeze gently blowing my hair. I look down on an intersection in downtown Fairfax and see people going about their day. A car drives by with the windows down, radio blasting "Rambling Man," and I think to myself . . . I like The Allman Brothers.

*Dave's slave/master theory comes from a November 2011
Facebook conversation he was having with an old friend
about loyalty in relationships.*

SLAVE / MASTER THEORY

I have a theory on relationships, whether male-to-male or male-to-female. The theory is that most of them fall into what I call slave/master relationships.

Relationships seldom start off that way. Sometimes both people get a mutual benefit from the relationship that fuels it. Other times there can be just a mutual appreciation for each other. But eventually, somewhere along the line, one person in a relationship will take on the dominant role. Once that happens, the dominant one has a choice to dominate the submissive one in a mutually healthy way, or he can choose to take control of the energy source of the submissive one and drain him of his energy. The dominant one will strip away the submissive's confidence and make him believe that he must have the dominant one to survive. Then the submissive automatically forfeits his energy to the dominant one and the dominant one rations it back to the submissive as he sees fit. Generally, the dominant will give the submissive just enough energy to get by.

A slave gives his master sun-up to sun-down labor, but only gets enough to eat to survive. The thing is, the slave can create much more on his own than he gets from his master, but the slave does not know how to fend for himself. The slave is brainwashed to believe that he needs his master to tell him what to do and to get his energy. The master needs to suck energy from the slave. They become dependent on each other for their self-worth.

You see, our energy—self-confidence, self-worth, feelings of importance—represents these things within us. We are our own energy factories. We don't need to suck the energy from someone else, and we don't need a master to provide energy to us. The problem is that we often forget where to find our energy. We must look deep within ourselves and break the shackles to discover our inner power and learn to be completely good with ourselves. Then we are free to have healthy relationships.

The problem, I discovered when I set myself free about 10 years ago, was that almost every person I have a relationship with will insist in some way on this slave/master dynamic. I discovered that, as much as I disliked the slave/master dynamic, I was not able to avoid it. I decided that the only possible course of action was—outside of being alone—to insist on a dominant role in relationship, but to not suck the energy from the other person and to guide the relationship in a way that allows each person to grow instead of to destroy.

This concept is complex and may not make sense with this brief description. I could write a whole book about it. Nevertheless, I have tried to explain it and hope you have some understanding and see this specific point: Some people need to have people to dominate and don't know how to create their own feelings of self-worth; by having submissive people around them, they feel like they can thrive. Not all of the people around such a person are submissive, but you can be sure that they serve a purpose. This concept goes much further and deeper, but in a nutshell that is it.

ILLUSION OF SECURITY

When I was younger, so many more people were willing to take chances in search of happiness and a true understanding of life. Now, everyone has settled into a life. They have chosen to "settle" for something less and often just choose to give the illusion that they'd found what they were looking for and what they have is what they sought. Well, I never found it. I still don't know.

The problem with the searching and chances is they often don't pay off. They leave us in a bad place, because security is seldom found on that road.

People seem willing to sacrifice everything for security. As long as they can put forth their illusion of attainment, they can live within the constructs of security and delusion and alleviate that feeling of a need for understanding and enlightenment. They become sedate.

In April 2011, David started posting his thoughts and essays on his blog, "Constructs of a Feeble Human Intellect." His first blog post was a paper he wrote for a Philosophy class in 2005, "Truth vs. Illusion: Finding the Correct Path to Happiness." David's interest in Philosophy grew as he immersed himself in the class. He used this paper to introduce his blog because, he said, "It will give people an idea of what my blog is about."

Also posted on his blog is "Truth is God and A Conversation," which is taken from a Facebook exchange in May 2010. Other postings included his "Formula to Change the World (U=ET²)" and the "show cause" letter he wrote for the court hearing in May 2009, which he later titled "The Final Refuge of a Scoundrel" for the blog.

TRUTH VS. ILLUSION: FINDING THE CORRECT PATH TO HAPPINESS

In the world around us we see many different people with many different beliefs. Some people maintain these beliefs simply to comply with some sociological standard, while others are willing to die for them. The happiness, or contentment, these people achieve is entirely subjective; we cannot convince someone they are or are not happy. Can a person be mistaken in attributing happiness to oneself? It would seem that if a person believes he is happy, then he is. According to Socrates, Plato and Jean-Paul

Sartre, this is not the case. Ultimately, true freedom and happiness depend on knowledge of what is real; according to that view, one could have the subjective experience of being free and happy but actually be a slave and unhappy.

In Plato's Allegory of a Cave we see a story where a group of people are bound, forced to watch the shadows on a wall. One of the men is released and led outside. He goes reluctantly and is almost blinded by the light. When he does come to see things clearly, it is quite scary and shocking to him. After a while he comes to understand that what is going on is the truth and what he saw before was just illusion. He goes back to the cave and sees the devices that were being used to make the shadows. He now knows the truth. There is no question to him about this truth; he has seen it.

He decides to tell the others in the cave what he has learned. To his surprise, they are not receptive to this truth at all. They reject it and declare him crazy. This man cannot go back. He cannot become what he once was. He is now the philosopher and unable to deny the truth. Now new challenges will arise for him. He will be forced to deal with this new world alone. This will be difficult as he is not equipped to deal with this new reality. At times he may long for his days in the cave. He knows now that it was just an illusion, but at least he understands it. He was not scared, and he felt a sense of purpose.

Now, every day is filled with uncertainty and fear. This man stands on the threshold of what may be the most important philosophical question in the world. Is the truth really better than the illusion? If so, then why? The truth is much more painful and confusing. Many people live their whole lives within the constructs of this illusion and seem happy. According to Socrates, they are ignorant of their own ignorance. They are so trapped in the realm of artificiality and manipulation, they insist at all costs on the "truth" of their world.

Perhaps a man may successfully complete his life within the constraints of his delusion. Perhaps he is wealthy and powerful. This does not make him successful, though. He has contributed nothing to the enlightenment of society and therefore has contributed nothing to Plato's ideal state. He has simply perpetuated the plague of ignorance and opposed Socrates's affirmation "that the unexamined life is not worth living" (Plato, "Apology," 92). This still has not contested the fact that this man died believing he was happy.

To analyze this we must first ask the question: what is happiness? Happiness is a constant theme in all of our lives but in order to achieve it we must first understand what it is. Webster's Dictionary defines happiness only with the synonyms "gladness" and "contentment." "Gladness" can easily be removed in our pursuit of an understanding of happiness; it is fleeting and cannot last. "Contentment," however, seems to be our closest synonym. The two do have qualities in common, especially in terms of the feelings involved. "Contentment" is defined by being satisfied and free from anxiety. This is not a person plagued by insatiable passions; he has reached equilibrium with his abilities and his passions. This sounds like the correct path; however, it is not.

John Locke said, "For who is contented is happy. But as soon as any new uneasiness comes in, this happiness is disturb'd, and we are set afresh on work in pursuit of happiness." (Locke 273) The contented man becomes tranquilized. For example, consider the figure of the contented slave or the institutionalized prisoner. They are content with their positions in life, but they are not happy with them. Therefore, happiness cannot be contentment.

To define happiness we must look within. To the questions that have plagued mankind since its inception. Who am I? Why am I here? It is within our most primal questions that we can grasp our most elusive endeavor, which is defining and achieving happiness. This is Socrates's idea of an examined life. When a person starts to contemplate these questions, his enlightenment will soon unfold. The answer comes directly from an engraving on the wall of the Oracle at Delphi. It says simply, "Know Thyself."

So now we will look at the insidious lure of the illusion. Sartre said that "man is condemned to be free" (Sartre, Existentialism). Within this statement lies three crucial points: "We did not choose our freedom; we cannot escape from our freedom; and we often wish that we could escape from it." Consequently, Sartre says we are free whether we like it or not. If this is so, then are we not also free to embrace the illusion? Why not? Existence contains so much that we would prefer to deny, such as death, suffering, and meaninglessness. Furthermore, most people are willing to sacrifice a great deal in order to be like other people. Sartre says that people, who don't live authentically, live in denial of their own freedom, resulting in living without a genuine awareness of their own possibility. People who deny their own opportunity to create themselves, instead adopt predetermined identities. Embracing the illusion offers a person some comfort, but it does so at the expense of autonomy.

To contemplate the two we can see that the truth is the better path. It is initially more painful but only as long as we resist it. We must all find this out for ourselves. The most arduous task we will most likely face is to determine the truth. Next we must find some method for differentiating our truths from our delusions. Ultimately, we must accept the suffering that we are doomed to face in order to ease that suffering. Only then are we on the correct path to happiness.[34]

TRUTH IS GOD

The man who exists free with hatred on his mind and anger in his heart is a prisoner. This man creates a wave of negativity that flows through his oneness, creating a ripple of hatred and anger out from him. Pain and suffering result even in the most indirect of places.

Conversely, the prisoner whose mind is free and whose heart is filled with peace also sends a wave of energy into his oneness. This wave of energy results in peace and freedom showing up in the most indirect of places. The free man may look down on the prisoner for being imprisoned. However, the truth is that the prisoner is contributing more to humanity than the free man. The free man is a thief. He wants to steal the energy of the weak. He wants to spread his hate and anger. The prisoner wants to spread his peace.

The truth cares nothing for societal or cultural norms. The truth is pure.

Truth is without malice or sympathy. In this way the truth is divine—Godlike. Therefore, to pursue the truth is an endeavor that is divine or Godlike.

A CONVERSATION

It is interesting that you would say that. Given the fact that upon first look, pleasure seems to be the opposite of pain, but as I'm sure you know, it is not. You see, this brings up one of the most complex and fascinating concepts known to philosophy. Although pleasure and pain do oppose each other, they exist in tandem with one another. I know that you are familiar with the Buddhist concept of Dukkha, which says that suffering is universal and the only way out of this suffering is Enlightenment. Not Pleasure. Now this concept goes very, very deep, as I'm sure you know, so I won't force you to go all the way down that road with me. But, I will reveal a small part of a contemplation I had on this topic.

I once came to the conclusion that there can be no joy. Joy is the word I used instead of pleasure, but I think they can be interchangeable. You see, all joy I can think of and all joy we perceive is actually the relief of some kind of pain. A massage relieves back pain. Food relieves the pain of hunger. Even though we can get joy from better tasting food, this is just a delusion. We simply try to find ways to increase the joy we feel in order to savor our relief from pain.

Think of everything you get joy from and I'll bet you will find that it actually relieves some sort of pain . . . think about it, sex, alcohol, water. We even create pain for ourselves so we can relish in its relief, i.e., cigarettes. Cigarettes are a perfect example of this whole concept. Cigarettes do nothing other than relieve the need for them. The entire concept of being a smoker is so philosophically flawed that it needs no explanation. Ultimately, I had to come to the conclusion that there can be NO JOY, ONLY RELIEF THAT WE PERCEIVE AS JOY.

I must say, though, as true as this concept will reveal itself upon intense contemplation, there are a couple of flaws. Find them and they will lead you to pure joy—not merely the relief of pain. Within the constructs of this idea, though, there is only ONE PATH to joy. This is true, pure, and profound enlightenment. I have experienced it, so I am sure it is true.

Although there is one fundamental flaw with enlightenment that I see. It is fleeting. It goes away and although it can be remembered, this is not the same as being encompassed by it. The achievement of it required for me, a level of extreme external suffering accompanied by constant and deep meditative contemplation. I have only cracked the surface of this concept, so I hope you will contemplate this yourself. If you want.

FORMULA TO CHANGE THE WORLD

$$U = ET^2$$

Utopia = Enlightenment x Truth Squared

In May 2009, David was required to provide a "show cause" letter to the D.C. court. I received an email from David with his draft attached. He asked me to review and comment on his draft and wrote, "I am fighting for my life!!"

I reviewed the letter and emailed a redline version back to him with my comments. When he posted the letter on his blog, he added commentary to explain the purpose of the letter, its validity, and why he didn't use any of my edits. The letter is long and details his life as a drug addict for the past year.

THE FINAL REFUGE OF A SCOUNDREL

This is a letter I wrote in May 2009, to a judge for a show cause hearing. A show cause hearing is what they call a probation violation. The judge is a very large, very cold, and very "by-the-book" black lady, who presides over The Superior Court of Washington, D.C. I say this because it is very important to understand why I wrote this letter the way. I did. It's also important to note that this letter is in no way sincere. It is the final refuge of a well-spoken manipulative person who doesn't want to go to jail.

Of course there are many truths in it and it is by no means all lies, but much of it truly is exactly that, a lie. The reason I have put it with my writings is to study my manipulation, to try to understand what I believe my drug-addled mind was trying to do to affect this woman's mind. It is also important to note that the judge never received this letter. On the day I went to court, my lawyer informed me that I had a warrant and if I went into the courtroom, I was for sure going to jail. So I left. When I finally went before the judge, I did not have this letter. So, of course, there was no sympathy for me, and I went to prison.

I want readers to go through it and really try to point out the subtle manipulations in it and how they contribute to the ultimate design, which is to solicit a desired response from the judge. I think this is a major point to the argument that people are bound by their perspectives. They put their perspectives out for display and a smart person can identify weaknesses in them and exploit them for their own benefit. It is not about the art of exploitation, though. *Actually, my point would be the value of freeing ourselves from these perspectives and experiencing the world from an objective point of view.*

This is the major point to "Constructs of a Feeble Human Intellect."

This letter is put here to help support the overall argument that if we free our minds, we can free ourselves.

I also think it is important to note that this letter had little to no chance of actually influencing this judge. I don't post this because I believe it would have worked. Rather, I want the reader to concentrate on the way the language is designed to solicit a certain outcome. I had my mother review the letter for editing before I was to present it to the judge in court, but her version greatly took away from my intention. The original version of my show cause letter follows:

Judge,

It will be my intention to show cause why I should not have my probation revoked and pay my debt to the court in the form of the remaining seven month prison term still available, thereby ending probation and all other stipulations, which were agreed to in lieu of jail time. It is my belief that jail time has no benefit to me recovering from my affliction, which is the disease of addiction; although, I am aware that it is not intended to rehabilitate a criminal, but rather, to remove a criminal from society so the deviant cannot cause harm to society.

To this I would respectfully argue that I am not a deviant, as the crime I continue to commit is the possession of the drug that I am addicted to. I would like to note that I do not steal or hurt people in order to support this habit. I have a good job, so I primarily hurt myself and my family. Although I do take into consideration the broader sociological implications of my actions. I am aware that I am contributing to the marginalization of an impoverished class caught in a vicious cycle. They are attempting to come out of their plight and seeing few opportunities and soon believing that they have no choice but to seize the opportunity of an available market right outside their door, so they decide to sell drugs. Simply, I am the market.

Without me, and those like me, there would be no mistaken belief that prosperity can be achieved through selling drugs. So many otherwise fine men and women are caught up in this cycle, and I understand my contribution to this and thereby accept that my actions are inherently criminal. For this I am truly regretful. This, as I will demonstrate later, further shows how my values have been stifled by this terrible affliction.

Simply stated, if I stop using drugs then I will no longer be a criminal. Not only will I no longer be a criminal, but I will be a productive and helpful member of my community. I care a great deal about the community I live in, and I am entirely regretful that I have contributed by facilitating a system that destroys lives. For this I am very ashamed and hope that one day I can be completely honest with society as a whole and will have contributed enough positively that I can be forgiven. I cannot explain with the limitations of language to the degree that I had become dependent on heroin. I sacrificed everything I am, stand for, believe in and, most of all, the relationships that mean so much to me.

I would now like to offer evidence that my attempts at arresting my affliction have been genuine and not just an attempt to look good for the court. At first glance, the violation report appears flagrant and shows a person with no intention of doing the right thing. But if we investigate deeper we can see that there are patterns that are not so apparent. This is no justification for the failed urine tests, but rather, it will illustrate the insidious grip addiction had on me and the lengths to which I went to try and arrest it.

On September 2, 2008, I gave a positive urine. Immediately following that I went down to Richmond, Virginia to get what is called a "Naltrexone implant" at the Coleman Institute. Under local anesthetic, a pill of sorts was inserted into my abdomen. A one-inch incision is made to the abdomen where a drug called Naltrexone is placed and then stitched up. This drug, Naltrexone, is an opiate blocker. It knocks all of the opiates off the receptors of the brain and does not allow them in at all. This is particularly important because it is very dangerous to have an implant put in if one is addicted to opiates.

Within 20 minutes of receiving the implant, I was sent into acute opiate withdrawal. I will spare details, but essentially this was the most painful, horrible experience of my life. The real point is that I knew this would happen but I could not come up with another solution. Addiction had such a grip on me. This was the only way I could come up with to stop.

After about a week of pain I eventually came around and felt better. The implant kept me clean for two months until the end of October. The problem was, although I was unable to use heroin during those two months, I did nothing to change my way of thinking. I thought that if I could break the cycle, I would not start up again. Unfortunately, that was not to be. As the obsession once again took over my mind, I soon gave in to it, hence, the positive urines given in the month of November.

Now, faced with the same problem again and completely immersed in the grips of addiction, on December 2, 2008, I went back to Richmond for another implant. I lied to the doctor again about being clean. I risked my life again, and I once again faced the worst pain any one man could experience. (I had an accident when I was 15 that crushed all of my toes, and I had two amputated. This pain cannot compare.) This time though, I paid extra and got the three-month implant. Again, I was clean for the time the implant was in, but the obsession to use just went underground. This did earn me approximately five months of clean time in the past year, which signifies effort.

At the end of April the implant wore off, and it didn't take long before I was back in full-blown addiction. At this time, I came to the realization that I needed to get help of a different sort, specifically, drug treatment. On March 26, I signed up to start the CATS Program at INOVA Fairfax Hospital. I got assessed by CATS and was scheduled to begin treatment the following Tuesday. I was to discontinue using heroin and begin getting weaned off opiates while using Suboxone under the supervision of a doctor. I was going to get clean, try to address my obsession, and find a new way to live.

On Saturday, March 28, 2009, I decided to do heroin one last time before I got clean. I went to Southeast D.C. and bought it. On the way out, I was swarmed by a large number of police officers. They searched my car and found the heroin. When I asked them what so many cops were doing there, they simply said, "To catch White Boys buyin' drugs in black neighborhoods." I am not sure if there are coincidences or fate, but it seems that this event, although very uncomfortable, was necessary. It seems my path could be no other than to go to Minnesota. This was where I would find my way. There were only these strangely positioned, extremely aggressive and ill-tempered cops to make it so.

I sat in jail all weekend, feeling as if all was lost. When I finally saw the judge on Monday evening, I could only hope for a miracle. The judge did not want to let me out. She said that I was a menace to society. My lawyer, wife, and mother told the judge that if she let me out, they would take me straight to a detox, and then straight to a 28-day treatment facility. We did exactly that. We didn't even go home first. We went straight to detox at Fairfax Hospital.

I was weaned off of opiates using Suboxone, and they helped me find a long-term treatment facility. The facility—Hazelden, which is located near Minneapolis, Minnesota—they recommended is largely considered to be the best in the world. Hazelden came highly acclaimed, and I was fortunate enough that my wife's health insurance was willing to cover the nearly $30,000 price tag. After I left detox, I visited my probation officer and received written permission to go to Minnesota for treatment.

Hazelden turned out to be everything it claimed to be and more. Aside from the beautiful Minnesota setting, the place was simply and completely effective. What makes it the best is the caliber of the staff. Most everyone there is a recovering addict, and the vast majority of the staff have at least a Master's Degree. Plus, the resources made available to the patients were well-thought-out and all-encompassing. Hazelden has been there for some 70 years, its system setting the precedent for other treatment facilities.

After I left Hazelden, I was set up with Hazelden Alumni. I also have gone to AA and NA meetings almost every day, and I am doing everything I can to ensure that I don't fall back into my obsession. If I start to think about using, I call my Sponsor. I am also re-enrolled in the Intensive Outpatient Program: INOVA CATS that I was originally signed up to do. I go three days a week and have to attend at least five AA/NA meetings a week. My treatment is ongoing and weaved into my life.

I called my boss and was completely honest with him about what has happened to me. I had thought that I would probably lose my job since I pretty much disappeared for over a month. He is being completely supportive. He said that he had known that there was something wrong with me, and had hoped for a long time that I would get better. I guess I didn't hide my addiction as well as I thought I did. Now everyone knows that I have a problem, and I am ok with that. No one seems to look down on me. It seems that people just don't want me to die. They seem to think that I could do some good things if I could just stay clean. I am not saying it will be easy, but if you will give me the opportunity to make right all I have wronged, then I will be the productive, thoughtful, and helpful person I was designed to be. Allow me, Judge C, to continue my probation and continue down the path I am on. Given the knowledge I attained at Hazelden, and the positive, specifically treatment-oriented lifestyle I am living, I am confident that I will succeed.

Thank You.

CATS TREATMENT WORKSHEET

Name:

David

Date:

September 2013

Define People Pleasing:

For me, I try to tell my loved ones what they want to hear. I also try to give them what I think they want to compensate for my shortcomings.

TASK TO ANSWER QUESTIONS:

Why have you come to treatment?

Because of my horrible heroin addiction.

What specific event led up to coming to treatment?

I gave my PO several dirty urines.

Write a "harmful consequences" list.

Multiple arrests and jail times, messing up my job, destroying cars, blowing money, lying to friends and family.

Changes in family relationships.

My wife left me and, although we are still best friends, she is scared to live with me again.

Changes in relationships with friends.

I stopped associating with my friends.

School.

I cannot stay in school because of my addiction.

Jobs / Career.

My job is very much in jeopardy.

Accidents / Injuries.

I have wrecked several cars and ruined them going back and forth to D.C.

Legal Problems.

I have several arrests / been in jail way too many times and I'm always on probation.

Money / Financial.

I am flat broke and I have been working for years and I have nothing to show for it.

Have you ever substituted one addiction or compulsive behavior for another?

Yes, heroin for women.

The early warning signs that I may be about to relapse to alcohol or drugs are:

Stop going to AA; hanging out with old friends; and more and more longer lasting cravings.

Feelings I experience when I want to start using are:

I'm indestructible, guilt, and shame.

TASK TO FINISH A SENTENCE:

One thing I like about myself is:

The way I think.

One thing others like about me is:

My sense of humor.

One thing I do well is:

Cut hair.

A recent problem I handled very well is:

My procrastinating.

When I'm at my best I:

Can do anything I set my mind to.

I'm glad that I:

Still have a place to live and my wife still talks to me.

A compliment that has been paid to me recently is:

I look much younger than my age.

Those who know me are glad that I:

Am in treatment and trying to get my shit together.

A value that I try hard to practice is:

Not lying.

People can count on me to:

Do what I say I will do.

They say I did a good job when I:

Work hard.

Something I'm handling better this year than last is:

I am following through with treatment.

One thing that I've overcome is:

Anger and resentment.

A good example of my ability to manage my life:

I have had the same job 10 years.

I'm best with people when:

I am confident.

One goal I'm presently working toward is:

Complete treatment.

A recent temptation that I managed to overcome was:

I was tempted to use my sickness as an excuse to not continue treatment.

I think that I have the guts to:

Stand up and deal with all of the problems I have.

If I have to say one good thing about myself, I'd say:

I am funny.

One way I successfully control my emotions is:

Denial.

One way that I am very dependable is:

At work.

One important thing I intend to do within two months is:

Get healthy, start working again, and do it while staying clean.

My biggest problem is:

My addiction.

I'm quite concerned about:

My legal issues / jail.

One of my other problems is:

My health / infection in my back.

Something I do that gives me trouble is:

Procrastinating.

Something I fail to do that gets me into trouble is:

Deal with problems as they come.

The social setting of life I find most troublesome is:

I am living alone.

The most frequent negative feelings in my life are:

About my legal problems.

They take place when:

I use drugs.

The person I have the most trouble with is:

My wife.

What I find most troublesome in this relationship is:

She is constantly on me.

Life would be better if:

I wasn't a drug addict.

I tend to do myself in when I:

Use drugs and lie about it.

What sets me most on edge is:

Talking about my legal problems.

I don't cope very well with:

My many issues.

I get anxious when:

I think about these issues.

A value I fail to put into practice is:

Being assertive.

I'm afraid to:

Go to D.C. to deal with my charge there.

I wish I:

Was stronger.

I wish I didn't:

Procrastinate so much.

What others dislike most about me is:

My drug use.

What I don't seem to handle well is:

Stress.

I don't seem to have the skills I need in order to:

Deal with these problems day in and day out.

A problem that keeps coming back is:

My probation.

If I could change just one thing in myself, it would be:

My drug problem.

FEELINGS GRAPH:

My mood was enhanced when I first started using heroin. I had money, a great home, and my wife and I had a great connection. It lessened as I became more addicted and consequences started coming in. My mood continued to deteriorate until my incarceration in 2002. After I went to treatment and my mood became very good again, I felt very strong and believed my future to be wide open. Eventually I relapsed. Deterioration of mood returned. These cycles continued a few more times.

POWERLESSNESS:

How have chemicals placed your life or the lives of others in jeopardy?

> I have gotten Hep C, a terrible infection in my spine, and my veins are all messed up.

How have you lost your self-respect due to your chemical usage?

> Because of my drug use, I didn't finish college; I have failed in several things I've tried because of it; and my multiple relapses have made me feel weak.

What is it about your behavior that your spouse, family or friends object to the most?

> Using heroin itself, they just hate it; they hate that I am such a convincing liar; and the fact that I do not take care of myself when I am using, my place is filthy, don't pay bills, etc.

How have you tried to control your consumption of drugs and/or alcohol?

> Saying I will stop tomorrow; trying to be an occasional user; and saying I will only use "extra" money after bills are paid.

Five examples of how powerlessness (loss of control) has revealed itself in your own personal experiences:

> 1) I make plans to control my use but don't stick to them.
>
> 2) I know that if I use more than 3 days in a row, then I will have withdrawal, so I try to avoid that.
>
> 3) Once I have gone past the 3 days, I just stop trying to control it and give in to full-on addiction.
>
> 4) I go through withdrawal, go through all of that pain and get myself together and start feeling good, then after all of that pain and suffering, I foolishly start using again.
>
> 5) Just once, maybe twice, then the cycle just repeats itself.

What types of physical abuse has happened to you or others as a result of your chemical usage?

> Not sure about physical abuse; I guess I could say the physical damage such as liver damage; extensive damage to my spine; and my veins are all messed up.

What is your current physical condition?

> My spine is in very bad shape. My infection has subsided, but I am still in a great deal of pain.

What is the difference between compliance and acceptance?

> When someone complies, they follow the rules and do what is necessary to get through the program. Someone who is acceptant, that person is using the program to actually get better.

Are you complying or accepting?

> I am accepting. I fully want to get better. I struggle with it. Good days and bad. It isn't easy but that shows that I am not just complying. If I was, it would be much less difficult. I think I am accepting because of the struggle I continue to have.

Are you an alcoholic or chemically dependent person?

> Yes.

What does unmanageability mean to you?

> When I cannot control my drug use.

What could you identify as "social unmanageability"?

> Unable to manage relationships; weaving webs of lies; and can't be trusted.

Give 5 examples of emotional unmanageability when you are abstinent:

> 1) Depression
>
> 2) Wanting to "just give up"
>
> 3) Wishing things were different

4) Enormous guilt

5) Terrible shame

What goals do you have for your life that you haven't met due to your chemical dependency?

Didn't finish college, have kids, and don't own a home.

Prior to treatment, how did you try to achieve these goals?

I was barely hanging on. These goals were the furthest things from my mind.

Give 3 examples of feelings you have tried to alter with the use of chemicals:

1) depression, 2) guilt, and 3) shame.

Have you ever tried to change your image prior to treatment?

Yes, I have tried to appear that I have it together when I do not.

What crisis, besides the one that got you into treatment, would have eventually happened?

Jail, sickness, Hep C going untreated.

How are you different as a chemically dependent person from other people?

I lead a double life; I have an obsession in my head that I have to hide; and I have no time for most leisure activities cuz all my time goes to dope.

Give 8 reasons why you should continue with a recovery program:

1) So I have someone to call when I have a crisis.

2) To deal with cravings.

3) So I can build a clean / sober social network.

4) Obligations give me no free time to start sneaking around.

5) So I can have someone to help me deal with PAWS[35] (Post-Acute Withdrawal Symptoms) cuz they are persisting and I think they will continue.

6) Get answers to questions about myself from outside sources instead of myself.

7) Start having some clean fun.

8) Have as much cushion around me until I can really put together some clean time and I am safe to drive a car again and live a normal life.

ENDNOTES

1   Addiction is a complex condition, a brain disease that is manifested by compulsive substance use despite harmful consequence. People with addiction (severe substance use disorder) have an intense focus on using a certain substance(s), such as alcohol or drugs, to the point that it takes over their life. (www.psychiatry.org/patients-families/addiction/what-is-addiction)

2   *Opioid* is a broad term used to describe any type of substance, either natural or man-made (synthetic) that binds to opioid receptors in the brain (these control pain, pleasurable, and addictive behaviors). Opioids include natural substances, such as codeine, morphine, and heroin; synthetic substances such as fentanyl and methadone; and semi-synthetic substances such as hydrocodone (Vicodin) and oxycodone (Oxycontin). *Opiate* refers to natural substances that can be extracted from the flowering opium poppy plant, such as heroin, morphine, and codeine. All opiates are opioids, but not all opioids are opiates. It is also important to note that because opiates are natural does not mean that they are less harmful. Opiates are also highly addictive and are frequently misused. (www.drugs.com)

3   Beth Macy is a journalist who writes about outsiders and underdogs. Her writing has won more than a dozen national journalism awards, including a Nieman Fellowship for Journalism at Harvard and the 2013 J. Anthony Lukas Word-in-Progress award. Macy was a reporter for The Roanoke Times from 1989 to 2014. She writes essays and op-eds for "The New York Times" as well as magazines, radio and online journals. (Wikipedia)

4   Beth Macy, *Dopesick: Dealers, Doctors, and the Drug Company that Addicted America,* 2018, Author's Note.

5   Beverly Conyers is the mother of three grown children. She began writing about addiction when she discovered that her youngest daughter was addicted to heroin. She knows first-hand the anxiety and heartache that families endure, and she has gained deep insight into the process of recovery from addicts who share their experiences in her books. Above all, she knows that there is no such thing as a hopeless case. Everything can change even when we least expect it, and the miracle of recovery happens every day. Beverly Conyers has worked as a teacher and freelance writer for the past ten years. An avid gardener, she lives with her dog and two cats in the Northeast. She continues to be active in Twelve Step recovery programs. (Conyers, *Addict in the Family,* 2003, About the Author)

6   A continuance is a request to postpone a hearing, trial, or other scheduled court proceeding.

7   I am not sure what David meant with the abbreviation, N.W.A. Wikipedia says that it is an abbreviation for Niggaz Wit Attitudes, an American hip hop group from Compton, California.

8   An arrest warrant is issued once sufficient evidence of criminal activity has been gathered and probable cause has been established.

9   For people who become addicted to heroin, dope sickness typically occurs when the active heroin user's body has become dependent on the regular use (a "fix") of heroin and the addict isn't able to get a fix for a period of six to 12 hours. Symptoms of dope sickness and their intensity varies by person, drug of choice, and the amount of drugs used on a regular basis. With the onset of dope sickness, an addict's body begins to experience the physical effects of withdrawal from the drug and may include similar symptoms to the flu: nausea, vomiting, diarrhea and/or constipation; loss of appetite/return to appetite; hot and cold flashes; muscle aches and spasms; sensations of bugs crawling on or under skin; hyper-awareness; dry mouth; headache; insomnia; and sweating. Physical symptoms often are accompanied by mental and emotional symptoms including: agitation, anxiety, paranoia, frustration, depression, and despondency. The period of purging the body of drugs is called "detox" and should be done within a professional treatment center for detoxing because dope sickness can cause serious effects on the mind and body. Physical symptoms usually peak within three or four days. (www.drugabuse.com)

10   Detox is the first step to treat addiction and substance abuse problems.

11   A bench warrant is commonly issued when an individual fails to follow the rules of the court or fails to comply with a court order.

12   Bobby Newman is an Internationally Certified Drug and Alcohol Counselor, Certified Prevention Specialist and Certified Intervention Professional. (www.newmaninterventions.com) Since the beginning of 2001 Robert "Bobby" Newman has been helping addicts recover from drug or alcohol addiction after having completed his own program in December of 2000. He immediately knew he wanted to help others, specifically educating kids about the dangers of substance abuse and was instrumental in starting a drug education program that reached over ⅓ million children. (Newman, *Secrets to Successful Recovery Solutions,* 2020, About the Author)

13   I don't know what E-doggies are and could not find a reference.

14   *Detachment, The Key to Survival,* Nar-Anon.org (https://nar-anon-webstore.myshopify.com/products/detachment-key-to-survival?_pos=1&_sid=4584e5e25&_ss=r&variant=309269405).

15 "He needs to reach his bottom" is a phrase often used as a way to say that the addict has reached their lowest point in life and has no choice but to stop using and to seek treatment or die. Some addicts may reach bottom when they become homeless, when they are sent to jail, when they lose their job, or when their spouse leaves them. "Rock bottom" means something different for everyone. Article: "7 'Rock-Bottom' Myths and the Truth Behind Them," American Addiction Center Editorial Staff (https://drugabuse.com/7-rock-bottom-myths-and-the-truths-behind-them/).

16 *Queen of the Damned* is a 2002 vampire horror film, and a loose adaptation of the third novel of Anne Rice's The Vampire Chronicles series.

17 Second Genesis Inc. is a private, non-profit organization providing rehabilitation treatment for individuals exhibiting irresponsible, self-destructive and anti-social lifestyles expressed primarily through drug abuse and criminal activity. The treatment modality consists of a highly structured, thoroughly supervised, 24-hour per day, residential drug abstinence program which generally takes adults six months to complete. (Second Genesis Orientation Manual)

18 "Fade to Black" is a song by Metallica released on the album, "Ride the Lightening" in 1984. Metallica is an American heavy metal band. The band was formed in 1981 in Los Angeles by vocalist/guitarist James Hetfield and drummer Lars Ulrich, and has been based in San Francisco for most of its career. The band's fast tempos, instrumentals and aggressive musicianship made them one of the founding "big four" bands of thrash metal, alongside Megadeth, Anthrax and Slayer. (Wikipedia)

19 Naltrexone is a non-addictive opioid blocker that reduces cravings for alcohol, opiates, and opioids.

20 https://thecolemaninstitute.com.

21 https://www.narconon.org/drug-abuse/rules/.

22 Prozac (fluoxetine) is a selective serotonin reuptake inhibitor (SSRI) antidepressant. Fluoxetine affects chemicals in the brain that may be unbalanced in people with depression, panic, anxiety, or obsessive-compulsive symptoms. (drugs.com).

23 CATS treatment materials, October 13, 2013.

24 https://www.drugs.com/suboxone.html.

25 A white, sleeveless, ribbed undershirt; commonly known as a "wife-beater" T-shirt.

26 www.encyclopedia.com.

27 The Merck Manual of Medical Information, Home Edition, 1997, Chapter 67, Movement Disorders, Tourette's Syndrome, p. 312. For additional information, search Tourette's syndrome | definition of Tourette's syndrome by Medical dictionary (thefreedictionary.com).

28 The Merck Manual of Medical Information, Home Edition, 1997, Chapter 53, Bone and Joint Infections, Osteomyelitis, p. 246.

29 www.ndcrc.org.

30 Osteomyelitis is a bone infection usually caused by bacteria but sometimes by a fungus. Causes: Bones, which usually are well protected from infection, can become infected through three routes: the bloodstream, direct invasion, and adjacent soft tissue infections. The bloodstream may carry an infection from another part of the body to the bones . . . People who undergo kidney dialysis and those who inject illegal drugs are particularly susceptible to an infection of the vertebrae (vertebral osteomyelitis) . . . Symptoms: Infections of the vertebrae usually develop gradually, producing persistent back pain and tenderness when touched. Pain worsens with movement and isn't relieved by resting, applying heat, or taking analgesics. Fever, the usual sign of an infection, is often absent . . . If a bone infection isn't treated successfully, chronic osteomyelitis may develop. Sometimes, this type of infection is undetectable for a long time, producing no symptoms for months or years. More commonly, chronic osteomyelitis causes bone pain, recurring infections in the soft tissue over the bone, and constant or intermittent drainage of pus through the skin . . . Diagnosis: Symptoms and findings during a physical examination may suggest osteomyelitis. The infected area almost always appears abnormal on bone scans (radionuclide scans using technetium) . . . Computed tomography (CT) and magnetic resonance imaging (MRI) also can identify the infected area. However, these tests can't always distinguish infections from other bone disorders. To diagnose a bone infection and identify the bacteria causing it, doctors may take samples of blood, pus, joint fluid, or the bone itself . . . Treatment . . . For adults who have infections of the vertebrae, the usual treatment is appropriate antibiotics for 6 to 8 weeks, sometimes with bed rest . . . When a bone infection results from an adjacent soft tissue infection, treatment is more complex. Usually, all the dead tissue and bone are removed surgically, and the empty space is packed with healthy bone, muscle, or skin. Then the infection is treated with antibiotics. *The Merck Manual of Medical Information, Home Edition, Copyright 1997, Chapter 53, Bone and Joint Infections, p. 246-247.*

31 *Psychology Today*, February 8, 2021; https://www.psychologytoday.com/us/blog/minority-report/202102/the-contradiction-addiction.

32 www.naranon.org/forum.

33 Ketamine (K) is a dissociative anesthetic developed in 1963 to replace PCP; also known as a date rape drug. K is used in human and veterinary medicine, primarily for the induction and maintenance of general anesthesia, usually in combination with a sedative; also used as a recreational drug and associated with ecstasy. K can be effective in treating depression and bipolar disorder in patients who have not responded to antidepressants; it produces a rapid antidepressant effect, acting within two hours as opposed to the several weeks taken by typical antidepressants. (Wikipedia; drugfree.org)

34 Works Cited (as listed in David's essay):

West, Thomas G., "Four Texts on Socrates," Plato, Aristophanes (1998) Ed. Cornell University Press.

Cornford, Francis Macdonald, "The Republic." Plato, (1941) Ed. Oxford University Press.

Sartre, Jean-Paul, "Nausea" (1964) NY New Directions, 2.

Sartre, Jean-Paul, "Being and Nothingness" (1956) NY Washington Square Press.

Sartre, Jean-Paul. "Existentialism in Voices of Wisdom: A Multicultural Philosophy Reader, 5th Ed." (2004) Gary E Kessler, Ca. Thomas Wadsworth Learning.

Locke, John, "An Essay Concerning Human Understanding," (1990) Ed. P.H. Nidditch Oxford: Clarendon.

35 There are two stages of opiate withdrawal. The first stage is the acute stage, which usually lasts at most a few weeks. During this stage, physical withdrawal symptoms may be experienced. PAWS is the second stage of withdrawal, during which there are fewer physical symptoms of withdrawal, but more emotional and psychological withdrawal symptoms. Post-acute withdrawal occurs because brain chemistry is gradually returning to normal. As the brain improves, the levels of brain chemicals fluctuate as they approach the new equilibrium causing post-acute withdrawal symptoms. (CATS Brochure)

Very good Book Tells the story of adiction. I lived this with my daughter Tessa as she used Heroin. Her outcome was the same as David. She did not overdose but destroyed her body with the drug use ended up in Hospital The Hospital drugs were Keeping her alive We as a family decided to let her go. She passed on June 3, 2018 Tessa Danielle Picton

Made in the USA
Columbia, SC
14 November 2023

26287717R00240